Jerry:

To a fellow sojourner who still
is in the trenches with our fellow
& sister vets. I salute your
dedication, caring & tireless
efforts all these many years,
and all the Vet Center staffs.

Thank you for being there,
from the beginning in Venice ...
        Peace & Blessings,

            Ray

A VIETNAM TRILOGY

A VIETNAM TRILOGY

Veterans and Post Traumatic Stress:
1968, 1989, 2000

Raymond Monsour Scurfield

Algora Publishing
New York

ISBN: 0-87586-322-1 (softcover)
ISBN: 0-87586-323-X (hardcover)
ISBN: 0-87586-324-8 (ebook)

Library of Congress Cataloging-in-Publication Data —

Scurfield, Raymond M.

A Vietnam trilogy : veterans and post traumatic stress, 1968, 1989, 2000 / by
Raymond M. Scurfield.

    p. cm.

Includes bibliographical references and index.

ISBN 0-87586-322-1 (soft : alk. paper) — ISBN 0-87586-323-X (hard : alk.
paper) — ISBN 0-87586-324-8 (ebook)

1. Post-traumatic stress disorder—Treatment. 2. Veterans—Mental health. 3.
Vietnamese Conflict, 1961-1975—Veterans—Mental health. I. Title.

RC552.P67S375 2004

616.85'21206—dc22

                    2004020045

Printed in the United States

SOME TERMS AND DEFINITIONS

Character disorder: term used for persons with long-standing negative personality or psychological traits or characteristics and attitudinal and behavioral problems. While such are considered to be pathological, the person is fully responsible for one's actions because he can tell right from wrong. More recently, such characterological problems are called "personality disorders."

Combat medic: medically trained personnel who are attached to combat units and accompany the units into the battlefield.

Disposition through administrative channels: a military person who has problems of attitude and behavior will receive some kind of punishment if he is determined to be able to tell right from wrong and is fully responsible for his actions.

Disposition through medical channels: a military person is considered to have a legitimate medical (physical) or mental problem that impairs the ability to perform his or her duty to such an extent that the duty must be limited or the person may have to be given a medical discharge from active duty.

Flashbacks: a perception that one is reliving a prior traumatic event; in more severe flashbacks, the person fully experiences and believes he is in the actual event and has no consciousness of current reality.

General Medical Officer (GMO): a military physician who is a general practitioner

Mental Hygiene Clinic: outpatient psychiatric and counseling center. If fully staffed, it would have a psychiatrist, social worker, psychologist, psych or social work technicians.

Million dollar wound: a wound that is serious enough to merit being medically evacuated out of the war zone but not serious enough to leave the patient with chronic serious medical problems.

NVA (North Vietnam Army): the uniformed, regular forces of the Hanoi-based communist regime.

Psychiatric casualty rate: what the DOD released as official figures regarding how many troops had to miss three or more duty days due to a psychiatric problem or illness.

Social Work Officer (SWO): military person in the Medical Service Corps with an MSW degree.

Unit consultation: medical officer visit to a field unit to conduct an evaluation on a soldier.

VC (Viet Cong): the irregular enemy forces indigenous to southern Vietnam who were opposed to the Saigon-based Vietnamese government.

VC sympathizers: Vietnamese civilians who felt more allegiance to the VC than to the Saigon-based regime, although oftentimes their support was coerced by threat or violence from the VC.

TABLE OF CONTENTS

CHAPTER 1. TROUBLED WAR VETERANS — OVERBLOWN MYTH, OR REALITY?

Just how harmful is it to be involved in war — any war? How many US war veterans continue to be sorely troubled for months, years and decades by their war trauma experiences? Our understanding of this issue fundamentally impacts our emotions, values, perceptions, beliefs and judgments concerning the true and full impact and cost of war: on its combatants, their families and friends, and on the nation. Ultimately, our views on these topics fundamentally influence our convictions concerning the nation's policies regarding defense and war, and the extent to which we hold the government and society responsible for their commitments to the millions of military veterans and their families. Finally, our understanding of the issue will influence whether we think that books like this one are merely hyping an already overblown myth, or are an accurate reflection of reality for many more veterans — past, present and future — than we could ever wish or fear to be true.

Over the decades, negative stereotyping of Vietnam veterans has been dramatized in popular movies, in books and on television, and has been reported in a number of research studies and mental health reports about Vietnam veterans. Yet, the issue is not of historical interest and relevance alone; recently, the same issue has been raised concerning US troops in Iraq, Kuwait and Afghanistan. Concern is mounting, in the context of:

1. The four highly publicized murder-suicides at Ft. Bragg, involving highly trained and seasoned combat veterans and their partners soon after the soldiers had returned from Iraq and Afghanistan. An Army investigation

concluded that these tragedies had "absolutely nothing" to do with the fact that the soldiers had very recently returned from a war zone.

2. The suicides of 23 soldiers in Iraq and Kuwait from April through December, 2003. It has been debated whether this rate of suicides is alarming or to be expected. [1]

3. The significant and still-growing numbers of dead and wounded Coalition Forces in Iraq, substantially beyond what political and military experts had predicted.

Information is, of course, still coming in concerning psychiatric casualties among our troops stationed in and returning from Middle East deployments. The full nature and extent of such casualties will not be known for several years.

On the other hand, the psychiatric casualty rate among hundreds of thousands Vietnam veterans has been heavily documented and debated over some three decades. Their suffering and the results of therapeutic efforts should provide lessons to help us in easing the pain for the next generation of American veterans.

My purpose in writing this book is threefold: to provide some hint at a realistic picture of what the psychiatric, psychological and social impact of war is on many of its participants; to help those involved with military and veteran affairs, the families, and the veterans themselves, to learn what we can from the post-Vietnam experience and extend the benefit of successful therapies to more veterans; and to avoid or minimize the creation of substantial numbers of psychiatric casualties among veterans of more recent conflicts.

The media-reported stereotypes of troubled Vietnam veterans can give the impression that suicide, depression, rage, being haunted by horrid flashbacks to the war, inability to keep a marriage or job and even homicidal acts are characteristic of perhaps even a majority of veterans since the Vietnam War. Conversely, there are illustrious military, political and mental health professionals who denounce such generalizations as gross exaggerations, and who assert that, indeed, the vast majority of Vietnam veterans are not only doing quite fine, but that many are living extraordinarily fulfilling and contributing lives.[2]

A *USA Today* cover story typifies this controversy. Over 80% the article, "Dispelling myths about Vietnam veterans," was devoted to the viewpoints of

---

1. Robert Burns, Associated Press. Report acknowledges shortfalls in addressing troop morale, stress. *Army Times*, March 26, 2004.

2. David Moritz, "Dispelling myths about Vietnam veterans," *USA Today* (November 16, 2000), 1A-2A.

those want to "reverse the stereotypes that have followed Vietnam veterans into middle age," that is, to assert that the problems of Vietnam veterans have been dramatically overblown. [3] The article does mention the findings of the National Vietnam Veterans Readjustment Study (NVVRS), which are startling: 15.2% of all Vietnam-theater veterans had full-blown PTSD at the time of the study's data collection in 1986-88, and another 11% had "partial" PTSD related to the war.[4] In real numbers, that statistic means that over 700,000 veterans were affected! And sub-groups of Vietnam veterans (African-American, Hispanic, heavy combat and those wounded during the war) reported even higher rates. [5]

The article presented nothing that seriously questioned or in any way invalidated the scientific rigor and methodology of the NVVRS, which was conducted by the highly reputable Research Triangle Institute in North Carolina. Indeed, the mental health and scientific research community consider the NVVRS to be by far the most definitive and sophisticated national psychiatric epidemiological study ever conducted on any era of veterans.

In addition, there is still a view that Vietnam veterans who remain "troubled" long after the war must have had pre-existing problems or a genetic predisposition and that such predisposition explains why they continue to have problems — rather than having been in a war. This notion is authoritatively dismissed by a second and completely separate study, with a very different sampling strategy and methodology (that was not mentioned in the *USA Today* article). Conducted on 2,042 pairs of male twins who were veterans, it found a PTSD prevalence rate (16.8%) among the twins who had served in Vietnam (almost identical to that found by the NVVRS) in contrast to 5% of the co-twins who had not served in the war zone. Furthermore, when exposure to heavy combat was factored in, there was a nine-fold increase in PTSD compared to the twin who had not served in Vietnam. [6] Taken together, the NVVRS and twin study offer compelling scientific evidence that about one in every six Vietnam war veterans suffers substantial war-related psychological pain and impairment, and that exposure to combat significantly increased the risk of subsequently developing PTSD.

---

3. *Ibid.*
4. R.A. Kulka, W.E. Schlenger, J.A. Fairbank, B.K. Jordan, R.L. Hough, C.R. Marmar & D.S. Weiss, *Trauma and the Vietnam War Generation: Report of Findings From The National Vietnam Veteran Readjustment Study* (New York: Brunner/Mazel, 1990).
5. *Ibid.*

Unfortunately, this startling, conclusion was obscured in the article, over-taken by pictures and quotes[7]from well-known public figures who offered opinions dissenting to the facts reported by the NVVRS (and by the twin study). For example, Secretary of State Colin Powell is quoted as saying that he believes that most Vietnam veterans "have done just fine." And, he agrees that some suffered psychological trauma but says, "most were able to return home and get on with their lives." Similar quotes are highlighted as captions under the photographs of other public figures.[8] No matter that such quotes are markedly unsubstantiated by systematic and reputable scientific or clinical data. The article played down the NVVRS findings as a counter to the subjective and highlighted testimonials of the public figures.

It may well be that "most" Vietnam vets appear to have been doing okay, but it is hardly insignificant that over 477,000 veterans have full-blown war-related PTSD, still, some 15 to 20 years after the Vietnam War, and another 345,000 veterans still have partial war-related PTSD. Downplaying the syndrome, or saying that "only" 15% were traumatized — as reported in a Center for Disease Control Study, [9] allows for three very disturbing implications: that the number of veterans who have suffered from their war experiences is quite minimal and indeed inconsequential, that perhaps many so-called troubled veterans aren't really that troubled because of their experiences in war, and that, hence, we really do not need to devote a significant amount of resources to help troubled veterans and their families. In reality, the problem is quite significant and does merit a substantive and on-going response by the government — at

---

6. J. Goldberg, W.R. True, S.A. & W.G. Henderson, "A twin study of the effects of the Vietnam war on post-traumatic stress disorder," *Journal of the American Medical Association,* 263 (9), 1991, pp. 1227-1231. Note that this twin study was able to control for pre-morbid conditions to a much greater extent than is possible in other studies that are conducted retrospectively (in which respondents are asked to remember factors about their earlier lives). Identical twin brothers, of course, have been raised in substantially the same environment and typically have very similar personalities. Thus, this study's finding that the twins who went to Vietnam had a 16.2% PTSD prevalence rate that was significantly higher than the PTSD rate among their twins who did *not* go to Vietnam is an extremely strong scientific point, reinforcing the NVVRS findings that factors inherent in the experience of war itself better explain the war-veteran's continuing problems than do pre-war factors.

7. David Moritz, "Dispelling myths about Vietnam veterans," 2-A.

8. *Ibid.*

9. *Ibid.*

least at the same level as the commitment to active-duty military and Department of Defense matters.

There is a continuing collusion of silence and sanitization masking how much war harms those who participate in it. [10] It appears that the government and society cannot admit the full reality and validity of both facts: that "most" war veterans are doing fine, and that there is a significant minority who are not. Instead, efforts are still make to minimize and discredit the war-related problems of those who have been troubled or conflicted during and/or after the war.

THREE KINDS OF VETERANS: SUCCESSFUL; TROUBLED; SUCCESSFUL AND CONFLICTED

Without a doubt, most Vietnam veterans have made successful, and sometimes outstanding, post-war adjustments. Highly successful Vietnam War veterans in the national public arena include such luminaries of personal courage and achievement and patriotism as Secretary of State, Colin Powell; US Senator John McCain; presidential candidate John Kerry; former Georgia senator Max Cleland and former Secretary of the Navy and author James Webb. Countless numbers of unsung Vietnam veterans are now solid, every-day citizens in every walk of life and among every ethnic and racial group, in every socio-economic stratum, in big cities and small towns and rural areas throughout the country.

On the other hand, a significant minority, on the order of one of out of every six war veterans, were or remain deeply troubled, in large part due to their war and post-war experiences. This quite substantial number is validated by health care utilization statistics of the Department of Veterans Affairs, by numerous clinical studies, and decades of clinical experiences of thousands of mental health therapists and counselors, both within and outside the Department of Veterans Affairs. And, last but certainly not least, hundreds of thousands of families and friends of such veterans have personally witnessed and been life-long companions in the post-war readjustment struggles of this group of Vietnam veterans. [11]

---

10. This tendency of our nation's leaders and the country was vividly illustrated following the Persian Gulf War. See Scurfield, R.M. "The Collusion of Sanitization and Silence About the Impact of War: An Aftermath of Operation Desert Storm." *Journal of Traumatic Stress, Vol.* 5 (3), 1992, pp. 505-512.

And, there is a third sub-group of veterans who are seldom recognized — and who are mistakenly lumped in with the "successful" majority group. This sub-group is comprised of veterans who have made a successful post-war recovery and yet still are troubled to some degree or a considerable degree. They have felt a profound and indelible impact, both negative and positive, from their war and post-war experiences; they lead relatively or substantially satisfying lives; and they continue to experience war-related demons and hauntings that remain "unfinished" or unresolved. These can include sporadically felt and sharply painful war- and post-war memories and nightmares from time to time, or fairly regularly, and/or vague or pervasive and chronic under-currents of pain and malaise.

Does this mean that veterans in this third group necessarily have psychiatric problems? No. Have they been unable to "move on" and do they not have reasonably or very satisfying lives? No. Does it mean there is nothing more they can or should consider doing, to perhaps bring more resolution and peace within themselves and in their lives? Again — no.

FORMER SENATOR BOB KERREY: A CONTROVERSIAL REVELATION

The relatively recent revelations by former US Senator Bob Kerrey, decorated war hero who has a post-war record of high achievements, are a case in point. Kerrey revealed that he still is haunted by a salient event during the war in which he believes that "innocent Vietnamese civilians were killed by him and his unit."

> Hell is not an imaginary thing. It's a real place and you experience it on Earth and I experienced it that night (during the Vietnam War). [12]

Kerrey's revelation was surrounded by considerable controversy, with varying accounts by different veterans as to what exactly might have happened that night three decades ago. Kerrey and his unit were there that night, and whatever transpired in fact, and/or what lives on in the memories of those who were there, continues to be deeply troubling to at least him and some members of his unit. What can they and hundreds of thousands of veterans of all wars do

11. See: Shad Meshad, *Captain For Dark Mornings. A True Story* (Playa del Rey, CA: Creative Image Associates, 1982).
12. C. David Kotok & Jake Thomson (Omaha World Herald), "Kerrey in firestorm," *The Sun Herald* (Biloxi, MS, April 27, 2001), A1-A2.

in order to come to a more peaceful co-existence with the indelible and searing memories that still haunt them?

A Vietnam Trilogy charts the continuing journeys of recovery and healing of hundreds of veterans. It offers a description of national and international dynamics and developments, and very personal accounts from numerous war veterans and myself both during and following the war. National policies and community attitudes intrinsically converge with the personal destinies illustrated by the experiences and lessons learned over three decades of care-giving and personal experiences of trauma. By following these veterans' journey along their paths of pathos and healing, it is hoped that readers will come to a fuller understanding of the issues and, at the same time, experience some healing of their own.

This book is written for all Vietnam veterans, and all veterans of other wars. It is written to provide windows to allow the family members and friends to witness the different ways that veterans have proceeded along their war and post-war journeys. Finally, much of the book speaks as well to those who have experienced non-war trauma in their lives, such as physical or sexual assault, traumatic physical injury or the traumatic loss of significant others. Above all, readers will be able to intimately witness the pathos, and the courage and strength, that are part of the healing journey for all of us who have been directly or indirectly impacted by war and other trauma. These are journeys that, for the most part, move from survival to at least partial redemption and enhanced recovery — and in some cases, to transcendence.

CHAPTER 2. PREPARING FOR WAR

Like many Americans, I did not consciously identity myself as being from a family with a strong military history. My family was proud of its participation in the military, but there was little talk about specific military experiences. Still, I had certainly picked up the notion that the United States of America was "the home of the free and the land of the brave," and that the country had an obligation as a world power and defender of democracy to be active militarily in other lands; and, of course, I believed we were the champions of the oppressed, in a world threatened by Communism, I also assumed that I would be drafted one day and would serve my active duty obligation. We trusted our leaders.

I identified closely with my mother's extended family who were of Christian Syrian heritage. I was proud of my Arab-American identity; but we didn't make a big deal about it. Growing up in the Pittsburgh area, my concept of "ethnic" meant Syrian and Lebanese Americans, Polish, Italian and other European, Mediterranean, and Black ethnic and racial heritages. Most of all, we were blue-collar western Pennsylvanians who enjoyed sports, taverns, bowling leagues, roller skating rink, church, rock 'n' roll, dances and family and friends.

My family upbringing, like so many other veterans', also involved an important religious component that became both a strength and source of conflict during the war and afterwards. I converted to Catholicism in middle school and was a devout Catholic throughout college. I took the church's teachings very seriously, to include "thou shalt not kill."

I entered Dickinson College in 1961, and found my way into Army ROTC. It was better than two years of gym, and offered me a chance to serve as an officer, with deferment of active duty until after graduation. And, since I applied and was accepted to receive my commission as a second lieutenant, social work officer, Medical Service Corps, I was granted a further deferment to attend the University of Southern California to obtain my master's degree in social work. Thus, I got the opportunity to obtain the master's degree of my choice, and to fulfill my military obligation as an officer and in my chosen professional field — social work.

Our ROTC military history classes were very convincing in presenting the "falling domino theory": if the US lets Vietnam fall to the Communists, then Cambodia, Laos, Thailand will surely follow...and then, what? My colleagues and I truly believed that there was a strong military, anti-communist justification behind the US involvement in Vietnam. I clearly remember our ROTC instructor telling us, in May, 1965, "Look around. Within one year, over half of the cadets you see sitting in this room will be in Vietnam."

We graduated the next month. I was the #2 ranking cadet in our class. I was very proud to be commissioned a second lieutenant in the US Army Medical Service Corps.

In the summer of 1965, I went to the University of Southern California, in central Los Angeles, just north of Watts — an area that was racked by violent race riots just before my arrival. How ironic, I thought — I get a deferment from active duty and possibly being sent to the Vietnam war zone, and I end up in a war zone in Los Angeles.

At this time I did not make a connection to the race-related hypocrisy and anguish that the country was facing from within. On the one hand, the US was escalating its military commitment in Southeast Asia "to protect the freedom of the South Vietnamese from the communists." Simultaneously, the country was being racked from within by race riots, and we had so many people in the United States who were not truly free due to the twin burdens of racism and inter-generational poverty. (Maybe our own economic system was due for some re-thinking?) My awareness of the influence and relevance of racism and how deeply it was interconnected with the Vietnam War started at this point. There would be many more lessons ahead.

I got my first big lesson in military psychiatry during my second-year internship, when I was a psychiatric social worker at the Sepulveda VA Hospital in the San Fernando Valley. I was assigned to be the caseworker with a young combat marine Vietnam veteran on the locked psychiatric ward. One young

Marine had a diagnosis of schizophrenia. Psychiatric wards were "locked" facilities, in the days before the dramatic advances in anti-psychotic medications to control psychotic symptoms.

This young man had suffered a serious psychiatric breakdown while in Vietnam and had to be evacuated back to the United States. Even with his schizophrenia, he at times had periods of lucidity in which he was in touch with reality. During one such period, when he was aware of his surroundings and knew who I was, he looked me in the eyes and revealed to me a profound obsession, one that he would never be able to fulfill. His own eyes swimming in tears of anguish, he pleaded:

> I have got to get back to Vietnam; I let my fellow Marines down terribly. I deserted them in battle [e.g., broke down and had to be medically evacuated]. I have to go back to Vietnam — and prove that I am a man.... Can you help me, Ray, to get back to Vietnam?

His anguished plea pierced my heart and was seared into my memory. Of course, with his psychotic condition, he was never going to be able to go back on active duty, let alone return to Vietnam. He could never make right what, as I later came to understand, is perhaps the most unforgivable and egregious shame that can befall any combat soldier — "deserting" or otherwise letting down one's buddies in the heat of battle. The image of this tormented soldier stays with me still.

As my experience grew and I came to understand military combat psychiatry a bit better, this searing episode grew in my mind. Realizing that this young Marine would never be able to return to the war zone to "rectify" what had gone wrong, I was struck with a lasting impression: "prematurely" removing a soldier from the war zone condemns him to never "work out" his psychiatric reactions. Just like this tortured young Marine, the psychiatric casualty would be haunted for life about having "failed" in combat.

I received my M.S.W. degree in June, 1967, and was immediately called to active duty for a two-year stint. I completed the Army's basic training course at Ft. Sam Houston, San Antonio, Texas, in a program designed for medically-related officers, that is, physicians, nurses, dentists, social workers, and psychologists. Among this group, I found that my ROTC experience made me much more "regular Army" than many of my medical cohorts.

One of the primary drill instructors had a severe speech impediment. The new men could hardly understand a word he said. This seems to have been a sign of how inadequate our training for Vietnam would be. Among the new skills and knowledge being transmitted, rampant racism was a significant part. The enemy was continually referred to as "gooks," "chinks," "slopes," "slant eyes," "Charley."[13]

My first duty assignment was at the Social Work Outpatient Clinic, William Beaumont General Hospital, El Paso, Texas. Many of my colleagues considered this to be a plum assignment; it meant one would, in all likelihood, be able to spend the entire two-year active duty commitment in El Paso.

However, it was both a boring and a bizarre assignment, coming after so much preparation. I felt dead-ended and isolated. My clinical supervisor was a well-meaning, middle-aged Department of Defense (DOD) non-veteran female civilian, and most incongruously, as an unmarried and inexperienced young man, I spent much of my time doing family counseling and leading pre-natal educational classes for pregnant young wives.

I went to see my commanding officer and noted that this position could be filled by any social worker, without military training. The officer generously suggested that I consider carefully before asking to be re-assigned, but I persisted; two weeks later I received orders — for Vietnam. (Even officers can be "rewarded" for complaining.) I was excited — and scared...

My specific military training before going to Vietnam consisted of three days of weapons familiarization. As fate would have it, a cold front had moved in for just those three days. Despite the snow storm and freezing cold, I qualified, somehow, as an expert marksman. However, as far as climate-readiness, I was now ready for Siberia more than Vietnam — just a taste of the bizarre nature of all that was to come.

There was no specific training about functioning as a social work officer in a war zone, or the history, strategies, principles, or techniques specific to military psychiatry in a war zone. One had to learn on the job, in Vietnam. However, I was issued the Army Social Work Handbook, and I thought that might have something helpful. The manual had less than one relevant page, devoted to "Transient Personality Disorders Due To Acute or Special Stress" and a few sentences about Combat Exhaustion and Acute Situational Maladjustment. [14] Apparently, it was appropriate and expected that social work officers were to

---

13. For a geographically descriptive account of the conditioning inflicted on our troops in basic training, see R. Eisenhart (1975), "You can't hack it, little girl: A discussion of the covert psychological agenda of modern combat training." *Journal of Social Issues, 31* (4), 13-23.

simply apply, as best they could, civilian social work training when treating psy-chiatric casualties in the war zone.

A current slogan suggested we should "win the hearts and minds of the Vietnamese people," underscoring the necessity of combating a guerilla war by gaining the support of the civilian population. I therefore requested to go to Vietnamese language school prior to arriving in Vietnam. I agreed to extend my tour of active duty to compensate for the several months in language training. However, the Army decided that as a social work officer, I would not need to learn Vietnamese. Perhaps the commitment to winning the hearts and minds of the Vietnamese people was not what I'd thought.

---

14. TM 8-246, Department of the Army Technical Manual (Headquarters, Department of the Army, January, 1962), 146. My entire "military reference" to diagnosing and treating psychiatric casualties in the war-zone was distilled into the three paragraphs on page 146 under Section VII, Transient Personality Disorders Due to Acute or Special Stress:

"232. General. Transient personality reactions to stress are primarily superficial maladjustment or reversible reactions brought on by the individual's struggle to adjust to trying and difficult situations. They may be manifested by anxiety, low morale, weakness, poor efficiency, and unconventional behavior. In general, they disappear when the stress is removed or when adequate treatment has been given. In some instances, if not relieved, these reactions may progress into more chronic types of mental illness or more severe disruption of the personality.

233. Combat Exhaustion. This category includes those transient personality reac-tions which are due to stress of combat. When treated promptly and adequately, combat exhaustion may clear rapidly, but it may also progress into one of the neurotic reactions. It is justified as a diagnosis only in situations in which the indi-vidual has been exposed to severe physical demands or extreme emotional stress in combat.

234. Acute Situational Maladjustment. The clinical picture of this type of reaction is chiefly one of superficial maladjustment to newly experienced environmental factors or to specifically trying and difficult situations, with no evidence, however, of any serious long-standing or underlying personality defects or chronic neurotic patterns. It may be manifested by anxiety, alcoholism, asthenia, poor efficiency, low morale, unconventional behavior, etc. If untreated or not relieved, such reactions may progress in some instances into typical psycho-neurotic or psychopathic reac-tions."

CHAPTER 3. GETTING THERE

MARCH, 1968

I board the plane, dressed in my uniform, on travel orders for Vietnam. I am to fly from my hometown of Pittsburgh to Philadelphia, in order to catch a flight to the West Coast and then onward to Vietnam. The plane seems to be entirely filled, except for the empty seat right next to me. Just as I dare hope for some peace and quiet to go over my thoughts, I see, entering through the doorway at the front of the plane, a uniformed young man being assisted onto the plane. He is wearing a black patch over his eye, and he is struggling with forearm crutches; both legs are gone. And, now, he's coming down the aisle, so very slowly, on two prostheses, and I find myself mesmerized, trying not to stare. And then I realization that he is moving inexorably toward the seat right next to me!

I am caught up in my own roiling thoughts and emotions, the wounded man having triggered my own worst catastrophic fantasies about Vietnam. After take off, I find myself extremely awkward in my silence. Suddenly, he starts talking to me. And he tells me how rough it was for him the first time he went home on convalescent leave from the hospital, especially when one of his high-school buddies had told him, "It's such a shame that you lost your legs and eye — for nothing."

I am struck silent, not knowing how to — or if — I can respond. And then, after a further pause, he turns to me and says, "But you know, sir, I'm the lucky one — no one else in the foxhole survived."

15

This comment, before I ever made it to the war zone, stuck with me over the years.

The trans-Pacific flight was on a regular commercial airline, served by airline stewardesses; but all of the passengers were in military uniforms. All of the rows of seats, except for a few in the front, were filled with enlisted personnel. My ROTC and active duty experiences to date had been in places where there were large numbers of officers. For the first time, I am struck by how few officers there are in the Army compared with the number of enlisted personnel. I also am keenly aware that I am what many enlisted personnel consider the lowliest of the low — a second lieutenant, a "butter bar" (the insignia for the rank of a 2nd It is a single bar, gold/yellow in color). Thankfully, the insignias on our fatigues in Vietnam are black.

It is a very, very long flight. Finally, as we start our approach and descent to Saigon, my excitement starts to surge: and mix with fear. My adrenalin is pumping. We are going to land in an airport in a war zone. Will we be greeted with enemy fire? I am acutely aware that we do not have any loaded weapons! Ironically, this is for our own protection and that of our fellow soldiers. The military does not want a bunch of nervous newbie arrivals with trigger-happy fingers and loaded weapons disembarking.

Stepping off the plane at Long Binh, in the Saigon area, we all were immediately struck by the heat and humidity — generating instant and profuse sweating. I became more preoccupied with the fact we did not have any loaded weapons. We boarded buses — the windows covered with wire screens to prevent explosives from being thrown inside by guerillas. Now, I felt trapped in a cage, and defenseless.

It took me a few days to get orders as to my specific assignment in-country. I knew I was lucky when I was assigned to be a social work officer on one of the Army's two psychiatric teams in Vietnam and attached to a field hospital (versus being directly attached to an operational unit in the field). And I got a second bonus: I was assigned to the psychiatric team in Nha Trang, a relatively safe and beautiful area on the seacoast.

Vietnam, here I am.

THE HEADSHRINKERS: OUR PSYCH TEAM

Nha Trang, a major city on the east coast of Vietnam, was north of the huge military base at Cam Ranh Bay and south of Quin Nhon. I reported to the 98th Medical Detachment or "KO Team." The unit was commonly referred as the "KO Team"; note that "KO" is simply a military alpha designation of the unit and the letters do not have any meaning per se. Still, "knock out" did strike me as ironically apt for a psychiatric team. Of course, the various combat, combat support and rear echelon units used another quite descriptive phrase when talking about sending someone to the 98th Medical Detachment: we were "the headshrinkers."

Theoretically, both of the Army's KO Teams in Vietnam were fully mobile units, capable of picking up and relocating to the most appropriate location per operational requirements. The two KO Teams were the most extensive and final psychiatric treatment facilities to serve all of the Army's units in South Vietnam. The 98th Medical Detachment was located in the lower part of II Corps, in the city of Nha Trang, and was responsible to serve psychiatric casualties throughout I and II Corps, e.g., the northern half of South Vietnam. The other KO Team was in Long Binh and served III and IV Corps, e.g., the southern half of South Vietnam.

The KO Team was attached to the 8th Field Hospital, the most fully-equipped level of medical facilities in the war zone and adjacent to the large US Air Force Base in Nha Trang, and an Army base. The KO Team was organized into two operational sub-units, a 12-bed psychiatric ward at the 8th Field Hospital, and an Outpatient Clinic, reflecting our two distinct missions.

A mental-health outpatient clinic served all Army personnel for whom Nha Trang was the closest mental health resource. (Units that are further away were served by a Social Work Officer and a Psychiatrist who each served a number of units at various locations in I and II Corps.) Thus, ten months after graduating with a Master's Degree in Social Work, I found myself in Vietnam as the only social work officer on a psychiatric team, and I also was the administrative officer for all functions of the psychiatric team. I was assigned primarily to the outpatient clinic, along with a psychiatrist and a Ph.D psychologist and about five social work specialists.

Second, the psych team operated the only inpatient psychiatric ward for any Army personnel in I or II Corps who required more than several days of psychiatric hospitalization. At the KO Team, we could keep psychiatric casualties hospitalized for up to 30 days. Within those 30 days, we had to make one of three medical dispositions: RTD (return to duty), reassignment in-country, or medical evacuation out of Vietnam. A psychiatrist and about 8 corpsmen were assigned to the psychiatric ward.

PICKING UP THE PIECES

> I had been doing body-bagging duty for quite awhile, landing in choppers, often-times in hot LZs, picking up body parts while exposed to incoming fire, and tossing the bags onto the chopper. One day, again, I found myself scurrying around on the ground, tossing as many body parts into body bags as fast as I could, the chopper crew yelling for me to get back on the chopper due to the heavy incoming fire. But I had to get those last remains. I finally do get on the chopper, and am able to sit back, still shaking; the heavy incoming fire still ringing in my ears and breathless from the rush to get back onto the chopper.
>
> As the chopper takes off and clears the LZ [Landing Zone], I reach into my vest pocket to pull out a cigarette. But, instead of pulling out my cigarettes — I *pull out a bone*...which I apparently had stuffed into my pocket in the last few crazy moments. That's the last thing I remembered, for 28 days.

He found out later that he had an immediate full-blown psychotic break. And ever since, he was haunted by the fear that if he dwelled too much on that experience again, or even talked about it, he would go completely psychotic again — and never come back out of it.

An indescribable terror haunts this man. Even the seemingly simple thera-peutic task of "talking about" such an experience was terror-filled and threat-ening to his very sanity. How did so many combat men survive, both physically and psychologically? I was about to find out.

EIGHT WAYS TO SURVIVE IN THE NAM

During the course of one year in Vietnam (and clinical experiences with hundreds of war veterans in 30 years after leaving the war zone), one hears of various strategies used by combatants, combat support and rear echelon per-sonnel to survive, both physically and psychologically. And all the strategies had enormous import regarding both acute psychiatric casualties in the war zone and ultimately the longer-term post-war psychiatric problems among literally hundreds of thousands of veterans.

> I had been in-country about two months and hadn't killed anyone yet. The guys in my unit told me that tomorrow was going to be my day; that they would make sure

that I got my first kill. I had been a hunter back home, and an excellent shot with the rifle. However, I didn't want to take another person's life and was dreading the moment when I would have to do it.

In the morning, we went out on patrol, in an area known for enemy activity. We spotted a figure in the distance, a profile carrying a rifle on his shoulder. We get down real quick, so as not be seen. Everyone tells me that this is my time, my target, my kill. And so I am pushed by the entire patrol to line up this figure in my rifle sights and squeeze off a round, long-distance.

I carefully line the target up in my rifle sight, trembling and almost nauseous, but knowing that there is no way to avoid this. I aim, and slowly squeeze the trigger, firing a round; the figure is hit and immediately falls...All the guys are cheering me, and we get up and carefully move forward to the body. But it is a farmer, with a rake, not a rifle. Even so, the guys tell me that "this is my kill," and that I need to search the body. I pull a wallet out of his pocket and it contains only a picture — apparently of his wife and children.

I can't forget my first kill; it haunts me. He wasn't an enemy soldier, he was   an innocent farmer. The guys said that he probably was a VC sympathizer if not a VC who just happened to be farming today. And so I "got credit" for a kill, my first kill. And he was a farmer. A husband. A father.

It is a wonder that so many armed forces personnel survive the insanity of repeated exposures to the horrors of war.

It is a wonder that so many armed forces personnel survive the insanity of repeated exposures to the horrors of war — and not go crazy, or break down or get killed. Of course, the vast majority of the soldiers who were successful at surviving were not treated as psych casualties. However, for soldiers in psychological trouble it was essential that we were able to help them cope with the endurable — or they would be a serious danger to themselves as well as to others.

While serving my tour of duty, I was unaware of quite a number of survival strategies that were conducive to getting through Vietnam. They came to my attention during extensive clinical contacts with well over 800 Vietnam and other war veterans during my 25-year career with the VA (Department of Veterans Affairs). They can be grouped into some eight categories, and are not mutually exclusive. Tunnel vision, for example, can be considered one means to achieve detachment.

Fight or Flight: The Classic Survival Techniques

For a front-line combatant in a war zone, the obvious and foremost survival strategy is to kill, eliminate, disable, or repel the enemy. This, of course, is the natural survival technique for combat personnel who carry weapons — when there is a reasonable possibility that the threat can be eliminated, neutralized or rebuffed. Ironically, if one persists in fighting in the face of insurmountable odds, in some circumstances that is considered to be heroic; and yet, in other circumstances, it is considered a waste of lives and is not a viable survival technique. There is an alternative when the odds are overwhelming: "Di Di Mau" (a GI version of the Vietnamese, meaning "let's get out of here!").

In the face of overwhelming environmental threat, to flee from or otherwise to escape is a very functional survival technique. However, there are two major limitations, especially in a war zone. First, flight may not be possible because there are no escape routes available, e.g., one's unit is surrounded and entirely cut off. Second, there are extraordinarily powerful "ethical" or "peer pressure" influences that counter any consideration of flight or escape as a viable alternative. The shame at being "cowardly" or fearing that one's peers will see you as cowardly, that you are "deserting" your comrades, may be the most powerful force in a war zone; it can supercede one's willingness or ability to flee or escape — even when fleeing may be the only rational or realistic survival technique available.

Detachment, Numbing and Denial

In a universe that pounds the senses with overwhelming shocks, one after the other (and all at once), many combat troops strike back at the world with the foulest language they can come up with, and obscenities become the only terms that can convey their anger and frustration.

At the same time, they do whatever they can to mentally and emotionally detach themselves from events around them. Elaborate strings of curse words can be part of that effort, as well as a short mantra that insists, "It don't mean nothin'."

That was the reaction to anything negative that happened to anyone. It was a way of protecting yourself, taking care of yourself, taking care of number one, not letting things get to you. It won't mean nothin' after you leave this place, anyway.

- A dead Vietnamese woman or child alongside the road? "*@! It don't mean nothin'."

- Someone in your unit gets wasted? "*@! Don't mean nothin'."

- You accidentally kill a Vietnamese civilian? "*@! Don't mean nothin'."

You learn to say, "*@! Don't mean nothin,' " over and over and over; you've got to, you've got to let nothin' mean anything anymore — or you won't be able to survive, day after day after day...This is how many vets can survive repeated exposure to the traumas of war.

When the trauma is unavoidable and inescapable, detachment, numbing and denial mechanisms are by far the most common survival technique. You learn to detach yourself from what you are doing, to deny the reality of the horror of what you are doing and seeing. You learn to "be somewhere else" while you are in the middle of unspeakable horror.

One Vietnam vet says:

> I learned to "escape" to the past and to the future as much as I possibly could — to have my mind be *anywhere* but there. I'd think about my life back in the world, how it used to be; and I'd think about how it would be when I got on that Freedom Bird and got back home.

> As a combat medic, there was the constant fear and rage. It was like, "it's open season on medics." There also was the constant grief, with all the guys that were constantly dying, that was never expressed. All of the emotions were buried, deep.

Fear and death must become your companions — or they will consume you.

Nothing but a feeling-less or robot-like state of detachment will get you through:

> I was part of a detail to clean out the charred remains of an American flight crew on a downed chopper. It was really nasty, having to pick up the charred body parts inside the chopper. And then, finally, I thought that we were finished. I stepped out of the chopper — and I saw one more body of a crew member lying on the ground, a little bit away from the chopper; he must have gotten out, even as he was being burned alive...And there were three dogs there, chomping on the remains! I became incensed, grabbed my M-16 and shot the m-f dogs. Later, after my anger had died down, I came to the realization: human bodies are just another piece of meat, dog meat yet.

And that's how I looked at it through the rest of my time in-country.

Even the enemy:

> The bodies lay scattered all around. Then some people emerged, running mindlessly, falling into more debris. Kien began stepping through the bodies as though it were an everyday event for him. This was his new-found strength, to stay cool under fire...Scores of bodies lay in all imaginable twisted positions; there was nothing to scream or take fright about. To him, in his hardened state, it seemed perfectly normal.[15]

> In later years (of the war) Kien experienced several identical moments, long periods of withdrawal. Like the dead, one felt no fear, no enthusiasm, no joy, no sadness, no feelings for anything. No concerns and no hopes. One was totally devoid of feeling, and had no regard for the clever or the stupid, the brave or the cowardly, commanders or privates, friend or foe, life or death, happiness or sadness. It was all the same. It amounted to nothing.[16]

---

15. Bao Ninh, *The Sorrow of War* (London: Secker & Warburg, 1993). P. 196.
16. *Ibid.*, p. 196.

And I, Ray, the social work care-giver, found myself detaching from the very combat veterans I was there to help. I saw a number of them as racist, as cold-stone killers, as perpetrators as much or more than as victims. Was this an attempt not to get too close to the war, by not getting too close to these combat vets, by deflecting the overwhelming horrors of the war that they were immersed in — and that seems to corrupt or make monsters out of so many of us?

Be Numb — Or Enraged

In all the purposeful numbness, only one emotion remained. Especially for personnel who carried weapons, one emotion could be very conducive to survival in the war zone: Rage. Rage could get you through the day. Rage could make you forget your hurt, your fear, your pain. Rage could propel you to get back at the enemy — and in some cases to go kill-crazy. Rage could get others to fear and possibly respect you. Rage could make you feel powerful and that you could do something.

And, rage could make you feel good, alive, energized.

Yes, rage was a very powerful motivator for a number of combat troops. Of course, one could become consumed with rage to the point that he became a danger to himself and to others as well. (And that rage went on burning, in many vets, long after the war was over, eating away at their insides — unless they could learn to let it go somehow.)

Social workers and other care-givers, such as medics, nurses, doctors, psychologists and chaplains, are in no position to get in touch with their rage at all, during their time in the war zone. Toward what target could they possibly discharge that rage? I, Ray-the-care-giver, do not generally allow myself to be aware of my feelings of rage; but at the time, I did feel anger and bewilderment — and projected it towards the hard-core combat vets who were displacing their rage onto the Vietnamese people. And the rage builds: at the government, at the military leaders, at war protesters, at the horrors of war and the victims it spawns everywhere, at how society sits back and lets soldiers be confronted day after day with the horrors that others have gotten them into.

Dehumanizing the Enemy

Training for war always includes training to and being conditioned to dehumanize the enemy — the classic detachment strategy.

> As soon as I hit boot camp in Fort Jackson, South Carolina, they tried to change your total personality. Transform you out of that civilian mentality to a military mind.
>
> Right away they told us not to call them Vietnamese. Call everybody gooks, dinks.
>
> Then they told us when you go over in Vietnam, you gonna be face to face with Charlie, the Viet Cong. They were like animals, or something other than human. They ain't have no regard for life. They'd blow up little babies just to kill one GI.
>
> They wouldn't allow you to talk about them as if they were people. They told us they're not to be treated with any type of mercy or apprehension. That's what they engraved into you. That killer instinct. Just go way and do destruction. [17]

Soldiers cannot consider the other side to be human beings, like you and me. It's a way to make the killing and death a more manageable task to perform, repeatedly and efficiently. In effect, you engage in "cognitive reframing" — changing the definition or perception of reality in order to make it more tolerable or understandable.

> You get to the point where "the only good Vietnamese is a dead one."
>
> They're just Vietnamese; they don't care about life and death the way Americans do. They believe they are reincarnated if they die, so dying is not that big a deal to them.
>
> If, every time you saw a dead Vietnamese (enemy soldier or civilian), you would think, "That is somebody's brother, or somebody's father, or somebody's uncle, or somebody's wife or sister or somebody's child" — you would go crazy or get killed.

Tunnel Vision

Most everybody learned to perfect the art of tunnel vision: to maintain an intense, focused, full engagement if not rigid and obsessive attention to completing a particular task, be that task one of killing, treating medical casualties, or graves registration. Having tunnel vision permits one to function in the midst of what would otherwise be overwhelming trauma. The DEROS, and R&R, as described later, were two "built-in strategies" that were used to enhance the ability of armed forces personnel to engage in tunnel vision. Many vets had a "short-timer's calendar" on which they would mark down each day closer to their DEROS; "Hey, I can survive anything for another __ months or __ days."

With tunnel vision, you focus all of your energies and attention on completing the tasks or objectives — to the exclusion of everything else.

An Army evacuation hospital nurse described how she coped with mass casualties. One of her duties was to make split-second decisions when large

---

17. Haywood T. Kirkland, in W. Terry, *Bloods. An Oral History of the Vietnam War by Black Veterans.* New York: Ballantine Books, 1984, p. 90.

numbers of casualties arrived by helicopter at the emergency room: which men would go directly to surgery, which men would wait, and which men would not receive any medical intervention because they most likely were going to die anyway.

> I never looked around when we started getting a lot of incoming (casualties). That was the first thing I learned. Never look around.
>
> Don't look ahead, don't look back, just keep moving from one to the next. Because it was overwhelming, if you looked around. [18]

Medics and corpsmen starts out treating "wounded soldiers or marines." Over time, as the casualties start to become overwhelming in number and time, they begin to treat "a sucking chest wound" or "a traumatic amputation."

And I, Ray, the social work care-giver, keep my blinders on about the larger war effort raging around us, at a distance. I don't delve too deeply into the absurdity of trying to help young men and women survive the horrors psychiatrically, and what effect it might be having on me. I choose to focus on my little world, day-to-day life here in Nha Trang.

Bizarre or "Gallows" Humor

Another strategy to achieve detachment is the use of bizarre or "gallows" humor. Make sick jokes, laugh at times of horror, do stupid things to get a laugh or reaction from yourself or from others: anything to detach yourself from the insanity that you are in the midst of.

> Sometimes, we would be sorting through the various body parts, trying to figure out which limb went with what body. And if we couldn't really tell, sometimes we would get creative and try to out-do each other. Hey, doesn't this [obviously mismatched] arm look good on this body?
>
> Hey, did you hear about the VC with no arms or legs? He really lost weight!

Isolation

Isolating oneself from others, not letting anyone get close to you, is another common way to promote detachment. Oftentimes, a soldier might start off in Vietnam by getting close to one, two or several buddies. Indeed, the bonds forged during war can be so powerful that men become closer than brothers. Unfortunately, this is a two-edged sword. Brothers-in-arms protect each other, look out for each other, help to get each other through the war. On the other

---

18. Stevan M. Smith, *Two Decades and a Wake-Up*. Television documentary aired nationally by the Public Broadcasting System, November 11, 1990.

hand, if something happens to your close buddy, it can be devastating. Many vets talk about how, at some point in their war tour, they suffered the tragic loss of someone whom they had let themselves get close to; the impact is profound.

> I had been warned by some of the seasoned vets not to let other people get close to you — "because it hurts too much if something happens to them." In spite of my better judgment, I did get close, real close, to someone. Jack and I got closer than I have been with anyone before or since; we became as close as any two people could possibly be. And, after Jack got killed, I hurt so bad...And I knew, right then and there, that I was never going to let *anyone* get close to me again. And I didn't. I looked out for number one. Period.

And I, Ray, the social work care-giver, keep myself apart from many of my hospital peers. Oh, I was friendly and I interacted, but deep inside I was my own little island. Yes, I was friendly on the surface, but I let hardly any Americans get very close — and I immersed myself in much of my off-duty time with the city and Vietnamese people of Nha Trang.

Drinking and Drugging

Substance use is one of the most common tactics fighting men and women can use to achieve detachment and relief. For some soldiers, abusing substances is an effective way to promote emotional numbing and mask the hurt and the pain. Indeed, in the latter years of the Vietnam War, substance abuse became epidemic in a number of units. The military, of course, keeps plentiful and cheap (and sometimes free) supplies of alcohol available to armed forces personnel, especially in a war zone.

Vietnam was no exception. You could get totally wasted, time and again, as long as you were able to report to your duty station and do your job the next day. Or even most days — because they could cut you some slack if you were usually good at what you did.

There were some soldiers who would always stay high. Many vets became addicted or heavily habituated while still in the war zone.

> As a helicopter door gunner, it got to the point where I had to get wasted on grass, just to get myself back in that chopper to face another day of killing and being shot at.

> I was on graves' registration duty for over six months. We received remains of US military. We would have to un-bag them, inventory the body parts, inspect and sort out the body parts to try and insure that the right parts were with the right bodies, tag them, and re-bag them. Body after body, day after day...I started shooting heroin, to get high and escape when I was off-duty. But, gradually, I couldn't stand the thought of returning to the morgue the next day, the endless bodies, unless I was strung-out when I got there. That's how I was able to survive, to make it through my tour, and not go crazy or go AWOL. Of course, I was then an addict by the time I left country...

25

Even the enemy:

> After just a few puffs they felt themselves lifted, quietly floating like a wisp of smoke itself floating on the wind. The tasty *canina* had many wondrous attributed. They could decide what they'd like to dream about, or even blend the dreams, like preparing a wonderful cocktail. With *rosa* one smoked to forget the daily hell of the soldier's life, smoked to forget hunger and suffering. Also, to forget death. And totally, but totally, to forget tomorrow. [19]

Many armed forces personnel in-country would get totally wasted. This was a common component of what is an almost universal war zone motto: "Work hard and play hard." And most people did; you had to let your hair down, sometimes, or it would get to you. Also, it was quite permissible and accepted to get totally wasted, and even miss a day or two of duty, when you suffered a tragic personal loss.

However, there were a number of personnel in-country who never got high or used substances. This may have been for religious or personal ethical reasons. More commonly, they were people who had come to the conclusion that the only way that they were going to survive in-country was to always be hyper-vigilant, to always be totally in control of their senses and maintain the most heightened state of awareness and ready-responsiveness — at all times, everywhere.

I, Ray, the social work care-giver, was a very religious Catholic. I had never taken an illicit substance in my life. And somehow I had blinders on, avoiding noticing the substance abuse that was going on around me at the hospital — other than alcohol, of course, which, after all, was accepted and encouraged by the military and one's peers — as a way to counter the traumas of life in the war zone.

Risk/Thrill Addiction

Another effective survival technique is to become immersed in and "addicted" physiologically, psychologically and behaviorally to the thrill, the risk, the danger, and the adrenaline rush. For some, this is literally an intoxicating high. Once, I got into a conversation about the thrills of combat with a vet who was working as a car mechanic:

> I will never forget my first air assault into a hot LZ... We were in the chopper, coming in to land, and we started to yell, pumping ourselves up, bouncing up and down...Man, I was *so alive*. I've never felt so high and alive in my life.

> And, you know, war is the ultimate thrill: that's why here will *always* be wars. When your ass is on the line, *that's really living* life to the max, man.

---

19. Bao Ninh, *The Sorrow of War*, 9.

To attain and maintain this risk/thrill addiction requires satiation through repeated exposure to and/or engagement in high-risk behaviors and situations. This risk/thrill addiction also has a secondary reward. It facilitates denial or avoidance of unwanted and painful memories and feelings that are masked by the high. Some take this to the extreme, by constantly seeking out high risk situations and/or becoming a kill-crazy perpetrator. As one vet put it, when you're in a war zone with a weapon:

You're the congressman: you make the laws.
You're the lawyer: you interpret the laws
You're the sheriff: you enforce the laws
You're the jailer: you take away their liberty
You're the jury: you decide innocence or guilt
You're the judge: you decide the punishment
And you're the executioner: you waste them.

And for me, Ray, the social work care-giver, my thrills came from going into town to be with Vietnam and the Vietnamese people, and my Vietnamese girlfriend, in off-limits areas, at night — the only American, and sneak back into base early in the morning at a gate where I had befriended the Vietnamese-Chinese sentry. (The 8th Field Hospital used Vietnamese-Chinese as security guards to supplement the security of our hospital compound as we did not have enough of our own security forces available — and Vietnamese of Chinese descent were considered much less likely to be VC sympathizers.)

External Discharging of Emotions

There is an inevitable build up or accumulation of trauma-related feelings such as grief, guilt, rage, helplessness, fear and anxiety. These pent-up emotions are associated with the constant exposure to death and dying and the threat of such, coupled with exhaustion from the one's job and/or the unrelenting pressures and threat. The build up demands an outlet — unless one has developed detachment mechanisms so profound as to be able to disconnect from the inner turmoil. Or else, the build up is manifested inwardly, psychologically and physiologically, in the form of depression, panic, chronic anxiety, and, if it is severe enough, dysfunction.

Typical emotional discharge tactics include immersion in, and expression of, rage — especially when directed outwardly towards others. This is a viable outlet when there is a ready and appropriate target, for an infantryman, for example, who can kill the enemy. However, when there is no ready outlet — for example, when the enemy is very elusive and does not present himself as an available target — it is a problem. Besides, it is impossible to maintain a constant state of active rage for a long period of time. Therefore, an individual may alternate back and forth between rage and detachment/numbing, or between terror or grief and detachment.

For those whose duty in medical care, graves registration, or other function does not involve engaging with the enemy, typically no viable target is presented towards which they can discharge their emotions outwardly. Restricted targets, or the absence of targets, towards which to direct one's emotional expression can result in internalizing, and then the pent-up emotions will be damaging to oneself. An alternative is to immerse oneself in "binge discharge behavior," such as acting crazy, playing very hard, binge drinking or sexual activity.

And I, Ray, the social work care-giver, discharge my emotions occasionally by binge-drinking and sex. I help to organize social activities at the hospital, and sing and play in the officer's club. But, more often, I maintain focus on my job, and initiate an expansion of my activities to organize and conduct community-service components with the Vietnamese people: running medical aid clinics in a Hamlet, visiting orphanages and teaching English.

Belief in Fate/Randomness/Higher Power

> I come from a very religious family. So I'm carrying my sister's Bible, too. All my letters that I saved. And a little bottle of olive oil that my pastor gave me. Blessed olive oil. But I found out it was a lot guys in basic (training) with me that were atheist.

> [But] when we got to Vietnam there were no atheists. There was not one atheist in my unit. When we got hit, everybody hollered, "Oh, God, please help, please." And everybody want to wear a cross. Put a cross on their helmet. Something to psych you up. [20]

Words from James Taylors *Fire and Rain* resonated in the jungles of Vietnam: "Won't you look down upon me, Jesus, You've got to help me make a stand. You've just got to see me through another day."

Of course, belief in God goes beyond wearing or carrying a talisman — although many soldiers were extremely superstitious and had their own personal good-luck charms. Beyond that, some people are able to cope with the repetitive and extensive tragedies that are characteristic in a war zone by having a strong belief in a higher power.

Of course, some soldiers lose their faith during war, through being exposed to the horrors that people, or they themselves, inflict on each other. Others find solace or acceptance, and still others find fear or anger, coming to the conclusion

---

20. Richard J. Ford, "Specialist 4 Richard J. Ford III, Washington, DC, in Terry, *Bloods*, 35.

that one's fate is entirely or significantly determined by randomness or chance. "Well, I guess his number just came due; my number hasn't been called yet."

For me, Ray, the social work care-giver, somehow my strong Catholic faith was a blur during the war. Oh, I loathed the killing, and the carnage, and the denigration of Vietnamese by so many Americans. And I tried to practice being a good neighbor to my fellow and sister peers and to the Vietnamese, and to be kind and generous to my Vietnamese girlfriend and her family. But where was God and Jesus in all of this?

THE COLLISION OF MORALITY WITH WAR-ZONE REALITY

Many, perhaps most, American military personnel, including myself, had been raised with certain moral principles that were unquestioned guides as to how one should live and treat others. Among these were:

Thou shalt not kill; [especially, Thou shalt not kill women and children;]
Thou shalt not commit adultery;
What you do to the least of my brethren, you do to me.

However, all of these heretofore absolutely sacred moral principles were suddenly and violently confronted, if not grossly violated, by the realities of the war.

To many of us, military chaplains were in what seemed to be a profoundly incongruent role. It seemed particularly absurd that chaplains appeared to be in the position of "invoking God's blessing for Americans and for our safety."

Even the chaplains would turn the thing around in the Ten Commandments. They'd say, "Thou shalt not murder," instead of "Thou shall not kill." Basically, you had a right to kill, to take and seize territory, or to protect lives of each other.

Our conscience was not to bother us once we engaged in that kind of killing. As long as we didn't murder, it was like the chaplain would give you his blessings. But you knew all that was murder anyway. [21]

---

21. Haywood T. Kirkland, "Specialist 4 Haywood T., "The Kid" Kirkland (Ari Sesu Merretazon), Washington, DC.", in W. Terry, *Bloods. An Oral History of the Vietnam War by Black Veterans* (New York: Ballantine Books, 1984), 91. For an eloquent description of war and chaplains and God, see Vietnam veteran Bill Mahedy's superb book, *Out of the Night: The Spiritual Journey of Vietnam Vets* (New York: Ballantine, 1986). Also, there is the excellent book by Walter Capps, a professor who taught extremely popular Vietnam courses at the University of Santa Barbara and was a pioneer in inviting Vietnam veteran guest speakers: *The Unfinished War: Vietnam and the American Conscience* (Boston: Beacon, 1982).

It was as if God was on our side and the enemy was godless. Was this not the ultimate dehumanization of the enemy? They were not God's children — and we were!

It is hard to imagine anything more stressful and conflictual than to be a man of the cloth in a war zone. Chaplains were to provide moral and ethical and spiritual guidance and support — while in the middle of a world replete with immoral and unethical and apparently god-less acts against humanity.

> An Army chaplain has gathered a group of soldiers in the bunker. He has become increasingly upset that they are having sex with Vietnamese girls in town. He starts lecturing them about going into town and "taking advantage of economically deprived Vietnamese women." Suddenly, from the back of the bunker one soldier yells out to the chaplain:
>
> "You mean we can *shoot* them, but not *have sex* with them, Chaplain?"

Needless to say, many chaplains never were able to reconcile the catch-22 roles that they found themselves in. In 1982, having just moved to Washington, DC, I walked into a real estate office to get some information about buying a house. The man behind the desk looked at me and did a double take. He asked, "Weren't you at the 8th Field Hospital in Nha Trang?" Amazingly, sitting there was a man who used to be a military chaplain in Vietnam. I am stuck by the change of occupation, from what I sometimes felt was selling religion in Vietnam to selling homes in the nation's capital. I had wondered about him, from time to time — wondered how he had coped in Vietnam, and afterwards. I thought, sadly, that he appeared to be another unsung casualty of the war.

And my own defenses become activated: my instinct to avoid, to keep the pain of the war at a distance, and to not get too close. And so I choose not to get his telephone number or to ever contact him again.

Thou Shalt Not Kill Women, Children or Old People — Except in A Guerilla War

Another factor that contributed heavily to the tendency of a number of bush vets to dehumanize not only the enemy but almost all Vietnamese, and that was the guerilla nature of the war. Vietnam, of course, was not a conventional war fought entirely by uniformed forces, with clearly demarcated front lines and secure rear echelon areas, adult male against adult male. No, the Viet Cong, the major fighting force of the enemy, consisted mostly of rural villagers, men and women, throughout South Vietnam, who oftentimes would appear to be simply farmers and supporters of the Saigon-based and American military effort. But, in fact they were supporters of the Hanoi communist military effort to overthrow the Saigon regime

The VC operated clandestinely. They used terror very effectively, with public executions to coerce or intimidate other Vietnamese villagers into compliance. It became extremely difficult for US forces to tell who was the enemy and who was not. Indeed, there are many stories about American troops finding out that Vietnamese who they had befriended turned out to be VC.

> The Vietnamese barber at the base was really friendly. I used to get my haircut from him regularly. Then, one night there was a major sapper attack at the perimeter. We were able to repel the VC and drive them off. The next morning, we went out to recon the perimeter. One of several dead VC sappers, tangled and maimed, was lying by the barbed wire in his black pajamas, where he had been shot by our troops. And, as I looked a little closer, I recognized him: *he* was our goddamn barber! Our barber, the one who cut my hair all the time!
>
> I couldn't believe it. I was shocked...I decided, right then and there, you couldn't trust *any* Vietnamese. They were all gooks. And after that, that's how I treated them, all of them.

The VC also used women and children to wage war against Americans. Many American soldiers say they arrived there pretty well prepared to fight against enemy soldiers: adult men.

> They were going to try to kill me, and I was going to try to kill them. That's the way it was. But the VC used women and kids, and many Americans had a hard time with that.

One favorite ploy of the VC was to strap explosives to or otherwise booby-trap a child and then send him over to an unsuspecting American. One soldier who had been traumatized by such an incident said,

> I hadn't been in country too long, maybe a month. We knew that there were VC in the area; the villages around were suspected to be VC or VC sympathizers. I was on patrol, and we were in position, waiting. Then, we saw a little boy, maybe six or eight years old, come slowly out of the tree line a distance away, heading towards us. He looks really frightened, and then he starts running in our direction. The Sergeant yells at me, as I'm the closest to the direction the kid is running from, "Shoot that kid!" I reply, "But, Sergeant, why shoot him? He's just a kid." My sergeant screams, "Shoot him, now, that's an order!"
>
> I reluctantly sight my rifle on the kid, and the Sergeant continues yelling at me, "Shoot him, now!" I'm fighting back crying, as I squeeze the trigger — and then the kid explodes. He literally explodes. I see him, in my sights, as I pull the trigger, his body flying apart. The VC had strapped explosives to him.
>
> And, I can't stop seeing that incident; I keep seeing that poor, little, frightened kid, in my sights, running right towards me and exploding, as I carry out the order and squeeze the trigger; I keep seeing his body, splitting apart, again and again...

What You Do To The Least of My Brethren, You Do To Me

Unfortunately, some of the people at the 8th Field Hospital had little interest in doing anything for the Vietnamese and were not supportive of the role my colleagues and I played in MEDCAPS. This resistance and at times antagonism against providing services to the Vietnamese people was mirrored in the attitudes of many of the combat teams who served mainly out in the bush, in the field. Their major or only contact with the Vietnamese was in fighting either VC (Viet Cong — the guerillas in the South, who supported the communists) or NVA (regular North Vietnamese, that is, communist, Army) enemy military forces, or Vietnamese villagers who may have been sympathetic to or supporters of the VC or NVA (or were terrorized into supporting them).

And so, in the midst of a guerilla war, where it could be extremely difficult to discern who was friend and who was enemy, a number of such "bush vets" (and a number of rear-echelon vets, as well) became extremely prejudiced against anyone who was Vietnamese. They were cruel and denigrating towards them all, constantly calling them "Gooks," "Chinks" and "Slopes," or worse, and saying "the only good Gook is a dead one."

At the time, and for several years afterwards, I just could not understand; I was appalled at how any Americans could have such a prejudiced attitude towards the Vietnamese. To generalize the "dehumanization" to all Vietnamese obviously was diametrically opposed to the official military slogan, "to win the hearts and minds of the Vietnamese people." Also, of course, it meant blatantly racist stereotyping and scapegoating of the entire population that we were supposedly there to protect and support.

But I was lucky: I did not to have to search out and kill the enemy as part of my role in Vietnam, nor were the people alongside whom I served constantly being wounded and killed, nor did I have to constantly wonder how many of the Vietnamese I saw daily were VC. In other words, I wasn't in a position where it would be easy to view the Vietnamese negatively and treat them in a dehumanized way.

MILITARY PSYCHIATRY IN THE WAR ZONE

The attitude of the commanding officers in Vietnam determined whether the psychiatric team would ever see a soldier from the various military units. If a soldier had any emotional or psychiatric problems, the critical first step was whether the soldier's unit command considered him a behavioral problem. If so, he would be handled, e.g., disciplined and/or punished, through administrative channels. On the other hand, if he was deemed to have or probably have a mental health or psychiatric problem, he would be assessed and treated through medical channels.

Many unit commands viewed most of their "troubled" soldiers as behavior problems, and handled them through discipline and punishment, without referring them to medical channels. And so, untold numbers of soldiers with problems never ended up seeing a psychiatrist or social worker; they were never assessed by professional mental health personnel. On occasion, as a social worker I was asked travel to a unit to do a "unit consultation visit" — to provide mental health consultation to the command and to the identified problematic soldier, and to help determine if he was to be dealt with administratively or medically. (To the best of my memory, I was told that the typical sequence of treatment for persons in the field with emotional or psychiatric problems in Vietnam was as follows. First, treatment is by a medic or chaplain's assistant at the local unit level. Second, if he is still having problems, the psych casualty might be sent to a battalion aid station or wherever the closest General Medical Officer (i.e., physician) was located. Third, assessment and/or brief treatment could be provided by a visiting Social Work Officer. Fourth, the casualty might be sent to the nearest medical hospital where there was a psychiatrist; typically, a couple of beds were designated for psychiatric purposes. Finally, if the person's psychiatric condition improved satisfactorily within 7-10 days, our KO Team's inpatient ward had up to 30 days to assess, treat and make a disposition — return to duty, reassignment in country, or medical evacuation out-of-country.)

If the commanding officer "did not believe in psychiatric casualties," and felt that troubled soldiers were "willfully misbehaving" or were "incompetent" or were "sniveling cowards" — they would be treated as a disciplinary problem deserving punishment.

He's a psycho, a wacko; probably couldn't take it, anyway.

He'a a coward, a wimp, a weakling, not a real man. Real men (and women) do not break down in battle, nor do they have problems after the battle. They just suck it up and move on.

He's a bad apple, a malingerer, a malcontent. He needs to be whipped into the right attitude and behavior — and punished. We'll make him or break him. And if he can't hack it, that means he's unfit for duty — and I'll drum him out of the service.

This was the prevailing mindset among many unit commands about psych casualties in the war zone, and this mentality prevails today among many career military personnel.

The reality in many units was to consider almost all soldiers with emotional and psychiatric symptoms to be behavioral problems. This was a prime contributing factor to the extraordinary number of less-than-honorable discharges that were meted out during the Vietnam era. The true psychiatric casualty rate in Vietnam may have been significantly under reported, with large numbers of military personnel given "character disorder" or personality disorder diagnoses, punished through administrative channels, and/or given less than honorable military discharges — rather than a disposition through medical channels. [22]

Acute Psychiatric Interventions Near The Soldier's Duty Station

An abnormal reaction in an abnormal situation is normal behavior.

— Viktor Frankl [23]

When we received psychiatric casualties, their problems typically occurred in response to a series of factors: extended sleep deprivation, continued and imminent threat of harm, and/or witnessing or participating in particularly gruesome or terrifying incidents. The "abnormal" psychiatric reaction to such extraordinary events oftentimes would involve an acute and florid temporary breakdown in the soldier's normal defenses and in the soldier's normal ability to cope.

The vast majority of soldiers who suffered extraordinary reactions to extraordinary events were not hospitalized psychiatrically, nor evacuated out of

---

22. C. Kubey, D. Addlestone, R. O'Dell, K. Snyder, B. Stichman & Vietnam Veterans of America (Eds.). *The Viet Vet Survival Guide: How to Cut Through the Bureaucracy And Get What you Need And Are Entitled To* (New York: Ballantine Books, 1985).
23. Viktor Frankl, *Man's Search For Meaning: An Introduction to Logotherapy* (Boston: Beacon Press, 1959), 38.

their duty stations. They received minimal or no psychiatric treatment, and were sent back to duty within several hours.

> The night before, this 20-year-old black male infantryman returned to base camp from a 19-day operation during which he averaged four hours of sleep per night; at base camp he became intoxicated, violent, assaultive, and threatening; he was subdued with injections of thorazine [a powerful anti-psychotic drug].

> Patient admitted for anxiety...on river patrol duty since he arrived in-country four months ago. Two weeks ago, his boat was attacked by the VC. The craft ran aground, one of the 7-man crew was killed; the others hid out on shore until after dark, after which they swam for three hours to safety. Patient had been then hospitalized for one week at Vung Tau for jellyfish stings.

> This sergeant has just completed his tour (he is now past his DEROS) and was at the Replacement Company awaiting a plane flight to the US when he became markedly agitated, stated that numerous people were trying to kill him here, and ran in and out of various offices. Patient states he has not slept or eaten since he came down from Cam Ranh Bay three days ago. On admission he slept for 22 hours and subsequently was completely clear and non-anxious.

> Patient is an 18-year-old PFC referred by battalion surgeon for ulcer symptoms. He developed anxiety, burning pain, and loss of appetite 8 days ago when he was in a 6 ½ hour firefight near Lai Khe; 400 VC were killed. A close friend of his was shot and killed by machine gun fire while standing about 10 feet from the patient. Patient went on to help pile up VC bodies; he estimates about 100. That night the bivouac area was mortared; patient slept through the attack, whereas his buddies made for the bunkers. His sergeant woke him up afterwards. Since that time he has been afraid to go to sleep.

> Patient is a 22-year-old in RVN 7 months; brought in by chaplain because of anxiety and depression. Is preoccupied with combat experiences, especially deaths of buddies, and one recent incident in a fire fight when he froze when be came face-to-face with a VC. He shot him reflexively only after the VC fired at him. The image of the Vietnamese soldier's face and eyes stand out in his mind with particular intensity. Patient has considered going AWOL and hiding out until the war is over.

> Patient was admitted because of crying and depression. He said that he had seen the body of a dead Vietnamese woman a few weeks ago; she had been cold, he touched her foot. He wanted to bury her but wasn't allowed to by his C.O. Since then he has been seeing religious visions, is hypersensitive to noise, cries, is suicidal.

> Patient is a 22-year-old E-3 admitted after he shot himself in the upper chest with his M-16. Patient shot himself in an effort to get transferred out of this theater and is being seen for psychiatric screening before being sent back to duty. [24] (Many vets would dream of getting "the million dollar wound" — a wound that was severe enough to be evacuated back to the States — but not so severe as to be permanently disabling. And we saw several, like this one, with a self-inflicted injury — or one

---

24. These case vignettes are from the notebook of then Captain Arthur S. Blank, Jr., who was a psychiatrist on one of the two Army psychiatric KO teams (located in Long Binh), as written down in Vietnam in 1965-66. Transcribed and presented in The First Training Conference Papers, Vietnam Veterans — Operation Outreach (St. Louis, MO, September 24-28, 1979), 2-4. Unpublished manuscript. As described by Dr. Blank at this training: "Most of these men were not hospitalized, not evacuated, not treated, and were sent back to duty within a few hours." p. 2.

that happened under very suspicious circumstances. And it was our job to determine if the soldier was a "psychiatric casualty" — or a "malingerer".)

Psychiatric Casualties Among Combat versus Rear-Echelon Soldiers

The above case descriptions might lead to the conclusion that it was the
combat troops who were the psychiatric casualties. Indeed, when I arrived in
Vietnam, I assumed that the vast majority of psychiatric casualties we would be
treating would be personnel serving in front-line combat units. In other words,
that front-line troops with the highest participation and exposure to armed hos-
tilities and death would be highly over-represented among psychiatric casualties. However, that was not the case. (There is an important parallel, here, to
US military forces in Iraq. Psychiatric casualties are not confined to "front-line
combat troops"; terrorists can strike anywhere, at anytime.)

It is important to note that there were some 8 to 10 personnel serving in
rear or combat-support roles for every man who carried a weapon at the front
line. As it turned out, the 8 or 10-to-1 ratio of non-combat to combat troops is
very much what I saw among psychiatric casualties in the Mental Hygiene
Clinic as a social work officer. [25]

In other words, direct combatants were only a small portion of the total
psychiatric casualties. Indeed, there was a great a risk of becoming a psychiatric
casualty in Vietnam regardless of one's military role.

OFFICIAL PRINCIPLES OF MILITARY PSYCHIATRY IN VIETNAM

For medical personnel, the overall mission in Vietnam was the same as the
military medicine mission everywhere else — to conserve the fighting strength.
This is extremely important, in that our mission was not to do what was necessarily in the best interests of the longer-term mental health of the individual
soldier.

Also, it is critical to note that the military defined a psychiatric casualty as
someone who had "lost duty days" due to psychiatric/emotional problems — not

---

25. My impression and experience is corroborated by a survey completed on 85 Vietnam
veteran psychiatrists. The mean percentage of clinical caseload devoted to "combat
reactions" was only 12.6%; in contrast, over half of their clinical efforts were devoted
to personality disorders, adjustment reactions or substance abuse syndromes. N.H.
Camp & C.H. Carney, "US Army psychiatry in Vietnam: From confidence to dismay,"
California Biofeedback, 7 (3), (Summer, 1991), 10-12, 15-17.

due to the fact that someone was having psychiatric or emotional problems, per se. Thus, if a soldier was having serious psychiatric difficulties but was still able to perform his/her duty, then by military definition that person was not a psychiatric casualty. And many soldiers in Vietnam were indeed suffering significant psychiatric problems and still performing their military roles.

I quickly learned, on the job, the official principles of military psychiatry for operating in a war zone. I do not remember ever receiving any actual training regarding these five principles, the history of military psychiatry in previous wars, any objective data about the outcome of treating acute (or longer-term) psychiatric casualties, or the military rationale and empirical data behind these principles. [26] Indeed, I received no such training during my entire four years on active duty — before, during and/or following my tour in Vietnam. Nor do I remember ever seeing these principles anywhere in writing while I was on active duty. However, I do recall that there was at least some discussion about some of the principles. A few of them made good sense.

Principle #1: Proximity

The first principle was to treat the psychiatric casualties as close to their duty station as is possible. The rationale was quite logical — the further away from the soldier's duty station you remove him, the more you "reinforce him to stay in a sick role" and not return to duty. In other words, if he had any desire whatsoever not to return to duty, the further away you took him for assessment and treatment, the more likely he would resist being returned to duty. This idea conformed with civilian social work training, where one learns that the longer psychiatric patients are removed from their communities and remain hospitalized and isolated, the more likely they will become "institutionalized" and find it difficult to want or be able to leave the hospital environment.

---

26. For a description of the classic principles of acute military psychiatric strategies and interventions implemented during World War II and which still serve as the basis rationale for modern day military psychiatry, see T. Grinker & J. Spiegel, *Men Under Stress* (Philadelphia: Blakiston 1945) and for a historical perspective of military psychiatry up through the Vietnam War, see: A. Wiest, L. Root & R. Scurfield, "Post-traumatic stress disorder. The legacy of war," in G. Jensen & A. Wiest, *War in the Age of Technology. Myriad Faces of Modern Armed Conflict* (New York & London: New York University Press, 2001), 295-332.

Principle #2: Immediacy

A second military psychiatric principle was "immediacy," to treat the psychiatric casualty as soon as possible after he begins to manifest psychiatric symptoms. Again, the logic seems quite sound: the longer you wait to treat a psychiatric casualty, the more difficult it is to have a positive impact — in this case, to be able to return him to duty as soon as possible. Again, this principle agrees with general psychiatric practice. Chronic psychiatric conditions are much harder to treat and mitigate than are acute psychiatric conditions. Thus, the objective is to treat the person during the acute stage of symptoms, when the symptoms may not yet have become entrenched, and to treat the symptoms before they become "fixated and chronic." The principles of proximity and immediacy parallel an important mental health intervention strategy (critical incident debriefings) that have been endorsed by modern-day mental health strategies to intervene at the site of natural disasters (i.e., hurricanes) and human-induced disasters (i.e., hostage situations). The immediate hours and days following such trauma exposure offer unique opportunities to accomplish mediating support to people soon after their exposure to trauma and prior to problems becoming fixated or entrenched s chronic symptoms. [27]

---

27. Some descriptions of modern-day critical stress debriefings that incorporate the classic military psychiatry intervention principles in the war zone include: A. Busuttil, "Psychological debriefing," *British Journal of Psychiatry*, 166 (1995), 676-681; A. Dyregrov, "The process in psychological debriefing," *Journal of Traumatic Stress*, 10 (1997), 589-605; J. Mitchell, "When disaster strikes: The critical incident stress debriefing process," *Journal of Emergency Medical Services*, 8 (1983), 36-39; F. Parkinson, *Critical Incident Debriefing: Understanding and Dealing with Trauma* (London: Souvenir Press, 1997); and S. Rose & J. Bisson, "Brief early psychological interventions following trauma: A systematic review of the literature, " *Journal of Traumatic Stress*, 11 (1998), 697-710.
Also, there is considerable controversy concerning the effectiveness of one-shot CISD interventions and whether they have any or even a negative impact. See, for example, R.J. McNally, R.A. Bryant & A Ehlers, "Does early psychological intervention promote recovery from posttraumatic stress?" *Psychological Science in the Public Interest*, 4 (2), November, 2003, pp. 45-79; and R. Scurfield, J. Viola, K. Platoni & J. Colon, "Continuing psychological aftermath of 9/11: A POPPA experience and critical incident stress debriefing revisited." *Traumatology: The International Journal of Innovations*, 9 (1), March, 2003, pp. 31-58.

Principle #3: Centralization

The principle of centralization meant restricting medical authority (to evacuate psychiatric casualties out of Vietnam) to the two psychiatric teams in country. We were that centralized authority for the upper half of South Vietnam. The decision whether to medically evacuate a patient was removed from the discretion of many individual physicians in many locations, and restricted such to one or two physicians at each of the two KO Teams.

This was apparently done in order to reduce the "inappropriately high" psychiatric evacuation rate of previous wars. And it worked (the rate of psychiatric medical evacuations from Vietnam was half that of the Korean war, which was half that of World War II). [28] However, the overall medical evacuation rate is misleading in that it obscures the fact that there was a dramatic increase in the psychiatric casualty rate in Vietnam in the last years of the war — a fact that has received almost no public acknowledgment by the military or mental health officials. While the psychiatric hospitalization rate was around 12/1000 per year in 1965, it peaked at 40/1000 per year by 1971 and remained high thereafter. Also, the psychiatric out-of-country evacuation proportion rose to 30% in 1971 and by late 1972 had reached 61%. This meant that one out of every eight soldiers in Vietnam was being medically evacuated for psychiatric reasons! Also, rates rose rapidly for behavioral problems, especially heroin use, racial incidents, judicial and nonjudicial disciplinary actions and convictions for the specific crime of "fragging," e.g, the use of explosives in assaults on superior non-commissioned and commissioned officers.

In addition, military psychiatrists in this latter phase of the war had been described as being very embittered and feeling clearly troubled by the demands of their psychiatric role in Vietnam. Therefore, someone writing this chapter who served in a military psychiatry role in the latter years of the war would undoubtedly have a quite different experience to report.[29]

Experience shows that individual physicians, working alone at many different sites, are more likely to be responsive to the medical needs and individual well-being of their patients than to military-dictated policies designed to con-

---

28. P.G. Bourne, Men, *Stress and Vietnam* (Boston: Little, Brown, 1970).

29. See: N.M. Camp &Y C.H. Carney, "US Army psychiatry in Vietnam: From confidence to dismay," *California Biofeedback*, 7 (3), (Summer, 1991), 10-12, 15-17; and H.N. Camp, R.H. Stretch & W.C. Marshall, *Stress, Strain and Vietnam: An Annotated Bibliography of Two Decades of Psychiatric and Social Sciences Literature Reflecting the Effect of the War on the American Soldier* (Westport, CT: Greenwood Press, 1988).

serve the fighting strength, which may well be at odds with the welfare of the individual soldier. In other words, the "centralization" principle was a way of dehumanizing our own fellow soldiers, by placing their fate in the impersonal hands of a high-volume, high turn-over centralized facility.

Years later, I was told that a clear message was sent from military authorities to the commanding officers of each of the two KO Teams. Their individual performances were in large part based on maintaining a low evacuation rate out-of-country.

> I never told the staff on our KO Team that my individual performance rating was based on the unit maintaining a very low medical evacuation rate out-of-country. Therefore, oftentimes I found myself in medical situations where I felt the pressure from above to be very conservative about making the decision to evacuate out-of-country. And I have felt quite guilty that I sent many young men back to duty who I might otherwise have evacuated out-of-country...

— Former psychiatrist on a KO Team in Vietnam

Principle #4: Expectancy

The principle of "expectancy" meant we were to communicate to the psychiatric casualty that his difficulties were "only a temporary and natural reaction" to a severe event, and that he certainly would recovery very quickly and return to his duty station. In a briefing about psychiatric casualties in the war zone, I was told that it was essential that the psychiatric casualty be told, firmly and unequivocally: "This is only a temporary reaction. You are having an acute and understandable response to a stressful situation. It will soon pass. You can rest, get off your chest what is bothering you, and you will then be going back to duty in a few days...You may not think that you can handle it, but believe me, you can and you will."

To a fresh 2nd lieutenant, this principle seemed to be benign and indeed the epitome of the "power of positive thinking." It implants in the mind of the psychiatric casualty the message that his problem is normal, understandable, will be very short-lived, and that there is no question that he will be returning to his duty station. Ironically, while this principle serves the purpose of the military command, it also ignores the fact that the soldier was very likely functioning at a very poor or dangerous psychiatric condition level for a considerable period of time prior to coming to the attention of medical personnel. Hence, even if the current psychiatric symptoms were reduced, the soldier might still be operating at a level of serious psychiatric impairment. Our team did not take that into account.

Principle #5: Simplicity

The final principle, "simplicity," seemed firmly grounded in the realities of the war zone: provide the casualty a brief sanctuary and provide basic services. We had neither the time nor the resources to do any fancy or elegant psychotherapy. Keeping it simple meant three hots (meals) and a cot, some emotional ventilating, perhaps some medication, and lots of sleep and rest.

At the time, this seemed reasonable to me: a kind of analogy to the common saying that suggests a horseback rider who suffers a fall should get up and ride again as soon as possible. Of course, it is one thing to choose to go riding and another to be stuck in a situation of mortal danger beyond your own control.

All these principles were geared to "conserving the fighting strength"; they had nothing to do with what was in the best longer-term mental health interests of the individual soldier. Returning a soldier to duty ASAP, he would be immediately exposed to further trauma The motto could just as well been, "What doesn't break you makes you stronger — and if it does break you, too bad."

THE PSYCHIATRIC MANTRA: "DON'T EVACUATE THEM PREMATURELY"

Before I picked up the five principles of military psychiatry outlined above, one military psychiatric mantra was preached to us and repeated by us throughout our tour: do not prematurely evacuate anyone out-of-country. In the very brief orientation about psychiatric interventions in the war zone, we were told:

> Don't forget the problems of secondary gain and fixation of neurosis. If you keep a soldier away from his duty station too long, it will become increasingly difficult to get him to go back to duty. And, if you prematurely evacuate him out of country, his symptoms may well become fixated and permanent. Therefore, return the psychiatric casualty to duty ASAP. And *only* med-evac out of country as a last resort.

This was the overriding operational principle in working with psychiatric casualties in Vietnam. We were constantly reminded of the "fixation of neurosis" that would likely befall any soldier prematurely evacuated out of the war zone, e.g., his acute psychiatric symptoms could become fixated or entrenched into chronic symptoms. It was strongly implied that going back to duty was markedly better for longer-term adjustment than medical evacuation.

Tragically, we were never given the corollary caution: that to send soldiers back to duty "prematurely" (or at all) could also be damaging to their longer-term mental health. One message only was inculcated into the medical teams: It is both in the best interests of the mission to conserve the fighting strength and it is in the best interests of the individual psychiatric casualty to help him to return quickly to duty.

Belief in this dangerous notion was buttressed by constant reminders and by two other factors. First, as combat troops will tell you, the most dangerous person by far in any combat unit is a new guy: whether an enlisted man, a non-commissioned officer or an officer. The new guy is considered to be much more dangerous, for example, than someone who has been in-country for several months, may have gone kill-crazy or got caught up in killing, or perhaps was strung out emotionally. If any soldier was evacuated out of Vietnam, the unit would be short a person, or would suffer the risks of breaking in a new guy.

Second, those who were evacuated risked following the pattern of that young Marine whom I had worked with at the Sepulveda VA Hospital in 1966-67, believing he had "let his buddies down" by being psychiatrically evacuated out of combat and "had to go back to Vietnam" so that he could prove that he was a man. That man's words were always with me, and I was anxious to avoid prematurely evacuating anyone out-of-country and thereby creating more chronic psychiatric casualties.

The internal conflicts this policy raised in the medical, psychiatric and social work personnel fed an anger, indeed a rage, that we suppressed: rage at the government, at the country, at being in a catch-22 situation. Freudian-based psychiatric theory was at best being unwittingly used by well-intentioned military mental health officers and at worst was being perversely misused to justify a military policy that was far more concerned about "the mission" than about the men and women who carried out the mission.

The Profound Psychiatric Paradox

The mantra about premature evacuation clashed daily with the painful evidence of the horrendous impact the war was having on so many soldiers. The clash placed us in an awful and paradoxical position: deciding whether someone was too crazy to be sent back to killing, or was crazy enough to be evacuated out of the war zone — or was in "danger" of "premature evacuation."

We quickly found out that, if there was any "easy exit" from Vietnam, plenty of armed forces personnel would quickly find and exploit it. A favorite song was, "We Gotta Get Outta This Place (If it's the last thing we ever do)," by Eric Burdon and The Animals.

Some soldiers, convinced that they were going to die or be maimed or go crazy if they stayed any longer in the war zone, would do and say anything to try to build a case that they were "crazy" and had to be evacuated out of Vietnam. It was our responsibility as psychiatric gate-keepers to keep that gateway from blowing open.

The military instituted a simple but exquisitely designed rule to help keep people from getting an early ticket home. If anyone committed a crime in Vietnam and was incarcerated at LBJ (the Long Binh Jail) or at the brig in Da Nang, the amount of time spent in jail was added to the Vietnam tour of duty. Otherwise, the brig would have been full of soldiers keeping safely out of harm's way. The incarceration facilities in Vietnam were purposely rendered unlivable, besides, to further discourage this kind of "malingering." One vet whom I treated years later said his most traumatic Vietnam experiences were unrelated to his considerable combat experiences. Rather, they had to do with violent sexual assault by other inmates while imprisoned in the Da Nang brig.

However, if you could convince your unit chain-of-command, your buddies, and a military psychiatrist that you, indeed, were crazy, then you could get your early (medical) ticket back home. In contrast, if you were judged to be a "behavioral problem," you would get administrative punishment and possibly receive a less than honorable military discharge. The psychiatric team was responsible for helping to make that determination.

One soldier had been dumping and peeing in his pants for three weeks, not shaving or changing his clothes, not washing, not talking to anyone, not responding to any orders. He was given disciplinary details (repeated latrine duty) and yet his behavior hadn't gotten any better. His unit initially suspected that he was "faking" it, so he could get evacuated out... However, they — and we — started to wonder: if anyone could "fake it" to that extent, was he not perhaps "crazy" after all?! And wouldn't it make anyone crazy to feel himself to be in such a quandary? On the one hand, you have to serve with your buddies and not let them (or your country) down in a war. On the other hand, you believe that you are going off the deep end and that your very sanity and physical survival depend on escaping by any means possible from the craziness of the war.

And there was yet another deterrent to medically evacuating soldiers out of Vietnam. There was the possibility that they would be sent right back! A number of soldiers who were medically evacuated to Japan ended up being re-evaluated there and were sent back, not to the psychiatric unit but directly to their original unit. As described by my former VA colleague, friend and Nam vet social worker, Shad Meshad:

> It was worse than if he'd never left. I learned quickly to think twice before sending anyone off to Japan. It was a real Catch 22. The problem was that people were not crazy. They were in a crazy, maddening situation. After three weeks in Da Nang in a relatively stressless environment, with medication, their symptoms disappeared. They'd get on that plane for Japan, figure they were on Easy Street, headed for home. They would hit Japan acting just fine. "You can withstand active duty. We're flying you back," they'd be told. That served as another trauma in itself. They'd be sent back. Only to flip out again. [30]

THE DEROS AND R&RS: BLESSING OR BANE?

Military psychiatrists learned two lessons in World War II and the Korean War, two strategies to prevent psychiatric casualties. First, military forces were given a limited (12- or 13-month) tour of duty. Second, "rest and recreation" trips (aka R&R) were offered to give soldiers, in effect, a 5-day vacation during their tour of duty in the war zone. Along with the refinement of military psychiatry assessment and treatment procedures described earlier, military authorities were confident that the limited tour of duty and R&Rs would be very helpful in reducing the acute psychiatric casualty rate in the war zone. Unfortunately, experience revealed dramatic limitations and trade-offs stemming from these two innovative strategies.

DEROS

Military psychiatry had made a profound discovery. Soldiers who were in sustained combat conditions over an unbroken period of time were at extremely high risk to become a psychiatric casualty. And in World War II, the results were devastating; almost one-fourth of all medical casualties were psychiatric! [31]

---

30. Shad Meshad, *Captain for Dark Mornings*, 22-23.
31. Bourne, 1970.

This was perhaps the primary rationale for instituting the limited tour of duty in Vietnam.

With some exceptions, each soldier had his/her own personal date of exit from Vietnam one year after arrival (thirteen months, in the case of Marines). After all, if they were not kept in Vietnam long enough to be "over-exposed" to sustained and unremitting combat, then they should not become psychiatric casualties. There also were complementary in-country military strategies, for example, having a secure base camp out to operate from and return to. This, it was thought, would alleviate some of the stress for the vast majority of combat troops in high-combat exposure.

The personal DEROS (Date of Expected Return from Overseas) did facilitator one's tunnel vision. The DEROS gave each soldier his/her own personal date to aim for, and it was a marvelous strategy to reduce the acute psychiatric casualty rate. People are far more likely to believe they can survive something for a time-limited period, versus being exposed to trauma for an indefinite period that might be prolonged for two, three, four or who knows how many years. The DEROS helped the military personnel focus on their personal survival and do whatever they had to do to make it through until their individual DEROS.

The Downside of the DEROS

Unfortunately, the personal DEROS had quite negative effects, as well. First, it dramatically compromised, if not shattered, the concept of unit cohesion and integrity. Typically a unit would end up with one or two people approaching their DEROS, another one or two with a few months left, some with several months left, and one or two with a DEROS many months in the distance. Under the best of circumstances, this allowed a built-in transition period to integrate new arrivals with more seasoned troops. However, it also meant that the DEROS, in combination with the inevitable combat casualties, resulted in considerable and constant turnover within most units. So much for the cohesive and secure small unit that was supposed to last throughout the war.

Another negative legacy of the personal DEROS is that many soldiers left country only to find out that their unit, or individuals they had served with and left behind were killed or wounded soon after. The shame, guilt and rage at not having been there for their "brothers" can become an unbearable post-war legacy.

One completely unexpected consequence of the DEROS had a marked impact on psychiatric casualties. As individual soldiers got closer to their personal DEROS, they might become extremely preoccupied with the fact that they only had a short time left in country (e.g., "the short-timer" syndrome). The short-timer syndrome meant that some soldiers became flooded with anxiety and a fear of any harm befalling them now that they had survived so long.

There were innumerable stories of short-timers who were "punished" by their unit command. They were arbitrarily sent out on dangerous missions, even if they were extremely short. And this was in conflict with the common understanding in many (but certainly not all) units that, when you reached a certain number of days before the DEROS, you would be kept in "protected" roles as much as was possible. Some short-timers, especially if in the last days or weeks of their tour, would refuse to go on such dangerous missions — even soldiers whose tour of duty had been exemplary up to this point.

Many of the military personnel, as they started getting short, would do almost anything to get out of the field. It might come in their ninth month, the eleventh month or the last week before DEROS. There were guys talking about seeing things, or hearing voices. And they would get themselves sent in for assessment. Of course, for many of them, being a little crazy was the only way to survive.

The heightened preoccupation with fear for one's personal safety was further provoked by the fact that everyone had heard about or knew soldiers who had gone out in the bush, just before their DEROS, and been killed or seriously wounded. Knowledge of such real tragedies intensified the fears of short-timers.

I was requested to go to a unit and provide an assessment and consultation regarding one such situation. The soldier had only two weeks left in-country. He was becoming increasingly agitated and fearful of not making it. His platoon sergeant, with whom he had had several arguments in the past, suddenly ordered him to go out on what has been described as a very dangerous mission — even though soldiers in his unit typically are given "safe" duty in their last two weeks in-country. The soldier refuses to go on the mission as ordered, and becomes irrational, yelling and crying. Disposition: medical (treatment) or administrative (article 15 or court martial)?

In addition, there were short-timers who found themselves unable to perform as they had throughout their entire tour to date. One highly-decorated combat medic had served quite heroically throughout his tour, exposing himself to repeated enemy fire to get to and tend to wounded soldiers, time and time and time again. When he had only two weeks left in country, he found himself unexpectedly being sent out "one last time" with his unit to a hot landing zone.

> I had been totally unprepared for this to happen. I was convinced that although I had somehow survived a very dangerous 11 ½ months of exposure to repeated combat, my luck had run out. *I just knew* that if I went back out "one last time," I would not be coming back. And so here I was, crouched behind a rock for some shelter, with incoming (enemy fire) all around. And then, I heard someone yell, "medic, medic," in an agonized voice.

> But, I just could not move. I felt frozen in place, there, behind that rock.

> I just couldn't do it, I just couldn't risk my life one more time — not here, not now. I was overcome with shame and guilt — but I found myself frozen with fear, unable to move. And I continued to crouch there, behind that rock, unable to move. And then I didn't hear the voice anymore...But, I've heard that voice, yelling out, "medic, medic," over and over and over, all these years. I've been living with this guilt and anguish for over 12 years. [32]

Rest & Relaxation

We got extra R&R in-country if we brought in the enemy alive; they didn't have to be too alive, just breathing.

Another strategy to prevent psychiatric casualties and maximize war zone functioning in the Vietnam War was R&R — Rest and Relaxation. Armed Forces personnel could look forward to having a five-day R&R outside of Vietnam (typically in Thailand, Australia, Hong Kong, Japan — or Hawaii, which was especially popular for married men who would meet their wives there). Some could get an in-country R&R assignment to a resort area, such as Da Lat. [33]

To the best of my knowledge, the systematic provision of R&Rs was extremely unusual in a war zone. On the face of it, R&Rs seemed to be a natural complement to the fixed and limited tour of duty in preventing and minimizing the acute psychiatric casualty rate. (This was, of course, in marked contrast to the NVA and Viet Cong forces, who did not have nearly as extensive an R&R system, and of course had no definite time of rotation to look forward to, and no safe home to return to.)

---

32. Personal communication, Jack Russel Smith, Cleveland, OH, at the Vet Center Training, Los Angeles, 1980.
33. Different units varied in how much R&R was guaranteed, or exactly when such would be granted.

An unexpected consequence of the R&R policy was that it further heightened the surreal character of life in a war zone and therefore was a source of considerable psychological problems.

> Here it is, I'm at the airfield in Nha Trang in 1968. We are standing in line at the airfield, waiting to board a C-130 plane to be flown to Tan Son Nha and from there to fly to Bangkok for five days of alcohol and sex binging.

> All of a sudden, there is incoming fire [rockets] and all of us dive into a ditch next to the runway. As we are receiving incoming, my thoughts are *not* that I might get hit and wounded or killed — but that the incoming might damage the C-130 and our R&R will be cancelled! Even at this moment, there is just a little pat of my awareness that is thinking, "Ray, this is absolutely crazy that this is what you're thinking and worried about, we're in the middle of a war, for God's sake."

> But, as fate would have it, the incoming stopped. We all get up out of the ditch, pick up our gear, hurry on board the C-130, and off we go — magically leaving the horrors of war for five days of non-stop escape into a fantasy land of partying and getting wasted, in Thailand. Trying so very hard to forget that the Nam even existed, or that we would be going back in a few days. And yet, of course, we did go back.

The R&R provided a sort of a "mini-DEROS," another date to focus on, a focal point for tunnel vision, a count-down on the calendar. However, the negative consequences of R&R were substantial. Many men found their units and buddies were killed or wounded while they were off on R&R; this became yet another source of guilt and rage. And, even if that did not happen, there was the jarring incongruity of now going back to war. And that made it harder still for some to do their jobs. Some soldiers were killed almost immediately after returning from R&R, and stories about them freaked out everybody. Their buddies believed that they had not re-adapted quickly enough to the necessary in-country survival mode. There also were numerous cases of soldiers who were deprived of their R&R — as punishment, or to exert the arbitrary authority of the unit command. And this in turn could lead to serious acting out by the soldier, with quite negative impact on one's performance, attitude or fate.

In sum, R&R helped prevent, and it promoted, the craziness that characterized the Vietnam War.

DONUT DOLLIES: THE RED CROSS IN NAM

> How cheering it is to be stuck in Nam at Christmas, dreaming and reminiscing about Christmas back home, when a donut dolly [Red Cross worker] comes along, hands you a bar of soap, and says, "Merry Christmas."

Major holidays are some of the most lonely and poignant times in a war-zone. This veteran's comments are in no way repeated to disparage Red Cross workers ("Delta Deltas"). The reality was that Red Cross workers were not always appreciated or respected, but I have nothing but the utmost admiration and praise for those who were in Vietnam. Several were attached to the 8th Field Hospital. They had a demanding and stressful job, and were not always appreciated by the troops.

The female Red Cross workers were a target of attention, and many were subjected to sexual harassment. As civilian social workers, they had a unique and extremely difficulty mission: to be there to cheer up and console the troops, a friendly feminine ear and support in the insane world of the war zone. They were in the war zone "to cheer up" the troops, a role that could be bizarre and extremely demanding. Their intentions were oftentimes misunderstood by troops who could barely restrain their sexual interest. Partly, this was because female "round eyes" were so rare — and were therefore a poignant and direct reminder of girlfriends and wives from back home. To lonely soldiers, they represented a link and a most powerful connection with the real world.

> There were some guys who would sit back and not talk to us; they just couldn't. Others would come over, and they'd talk about their wives or their girlfriends. It was very depressing and sad, yet so very touching, because it didn't matter who we were but just the simple fact that we were there and were "home" — America and femininity — to them...
>
> I had two younger brothers, and so many of the men reminded me of my brothers — I really felt great compassion for them. That's part of the reason I ran into problems. I got too psychologically involved. I didn't want to leave my young Marines. I wanted to protect them and make all of the pain and anger go away.
>
> In some cases it was very traumatic...I mean, you've seen them two or three hours ago healthy and whole, and then you meet them with everything blown apart. It's hard to take!...You have to go on, just perking along, doing your thing...You would have men who had just lost buddies or wives or girlfriends. They would bring their letters to you and ask you to read them, or they'd sit there with this lost look on their face...you just wanted to go over and put your arm around them and tell them, "It's okay." You know you did it mentally as best you could.
>
> Our job was to be upbeat. It was never to let on, never to have anything wrong. You would go home at night and say Woooh. But during the day, you didn't dare...For some of us who went into the hospitals — where we shouldn't have been — it was a hell of a rude awakening. The guys would show you their wounds with great pride, and you're standing there trying to say, "Isn't that nice" and "Gee, everything will be just fine," even to the guy who just lost two arms and a leg or had half his face blown away. You know you're lying right through your teeth, and it just did you in, but you did it to survive and to help them survive. [34]

Theirs is a largely untold story; as is the story of those who were in Special Services, International Voluntary Services, Catholic Relief Services, American Friends Service Committee, and the civilian airline flight attendants and others. Indeed, these wonderful civilians who served in a war zone have suffered a particularly ignored fate. They were exposed to war stresses and trauma, just like those of us in uniform. And when they left Vietnam, they were not eligible to receive any services from the VA — even if and when they were suffering terribly from their own war-related PTSD.

ARMY SOCIAL WORK IN NAM — AND DEAR JOHN LETTERS

Along with the psychiatric casualties directly or indirectly caused or exacerbated by combat-related trauma, a wide range of problems-in-living confronted many servicemen who were in Vietnam and may have made them at-risk to be psychiatric casualties. As Army social workers, we saw that just being in Vietnam involved many stressful or traumatic situations that triggered psychiatric casualties. Many such situations had little or nothing to do with being in a war zone.

First, things were still going on in the lives soldiers had left behind. For example, it was not unusual for a soldier to be divorced shortly before leaving, or after getting to, Vietnam. Others had very serious disagreements or fights with significant people in their lives — parents, wives, siblings — very troubling last interactions. Others had hastily married before their departure, or their children or spouses or a family member got into serious behavioral, psychiatric or legal trouble just when they were due to leave — or, problems like that developed after they got to Vietnam. Some were fleeing legal or criminal problems, some left their families deeply in debt; some abruptly lost family members to accidents or disease; while others were plucked out of college or a profession — just before they went off to or after they got to Vietnam.

Some soldiers became depressed or enraged when they heard that their spouse was falling apart, unable to cope alone; or that their house had been burglarized or their hometown had been hit by a hurricane or other natural disaster. Now, it was the family at home that needed them, and again they felt guilt and

---

34. K. Walker, *A Piece of My Heart. The Stories of Twenty-Six American Women Who Served in Vietnam* (New York: Ballantine Books, 1985), 77-79.

frustration at not being there where they were needed. Others became suicidal, or went on a series of drunken binges, or defied military authorities, when they received a "Dear John" letter or heard that a spouse was having an affair — and they were stuck in the Nam, alone. That relationship may have been the one anchor that had kept them steady in the craziness of the war, grounding them in a sense of purpose, and hope.

And when an active duty member in Vietnam, dealing with day-to-day survival, was suddenly hit with or gradually is overcome by one or more such events and developments back home, then the social workers had their hands full. Life goes on, even when you're in a war.

Plenty of soldiers were functioning relatively poorly before they ever got to Vietnam, anyway. And, anyone who did not fit the mold — a man who was effeminate in appearance and behavior, who couldn't fire a gun or kill anyone, social misfits, recluses, intellectuals, neurotics, eccentrics, those with borderline intelligence (up or down) or lacking in common sense, those who had poor personal hygiene habits, were physically unattractive, physically clumsy, or physically weak, were in for a hard time. They were treated as outliers from the day they showed up. They might be ridiculed or shunned, ostracized or tormented, threatened, attacked, humiliated, and denigrated. They might be protected or sheltered by someone; they somehow survived sheer hell from their fellow Americans for 12 months, or went crazy, or they got seriously wounded or killed.

And they felt powerless to do anything about it. And they were extremely angry, fearful, anxious about what was happening. They'd come in to see the chaplain, the Red Cross worker, or the social worker. And we'd talk about their spouses, running around with their best friends, or their children getting caught with drugs and kicked out of school, or the letter filing for divorce.

> Hey, what can you really do about it? You're here with a job to do, and they're there. Is it so serious that we could justify you getting a 30-day emergency leave to go home to try and take care of it? What could you do about it in 30 days, anyway?

> If you go back on emergency leave, how do I (and you) know that you are not going to do something foolish — like hurt someone?

> How fair, or dangerous, is it to the other men in your unit if you go home for 30 days?

> I can't imagine how hard it must be to be here, in Vietnam, with this going on here (or, back home), and you're feeling helpless to do anything about it. Yes, you've got this really big problem back home, that you feel responsible to do something about. *And* you have your obligation to the military and to the men in your unit, to do your job here, today and tomorrow.

What do you need to do, here and now, today and tomorrow and the day after that, to take care of yourself, here, so that you are not a danger to yourself or to others, so that you can do your job here and not fall apart?

Are you just going to stay miserable, enraged, depressed, anxious, guilt-ridden that you're here in Nam? Will that solve your problem or get you through the war?

No, life sure doesn't seem very fair, does it? And so what can and are you going to do about it?

It must be really hard, but you can do it, and I'm here to help you as best as I can. Do you want to work with me on this, together?

Yes, social work, in Vietnam. Because life goes on, even when you're in a war.

I lost track of the number of times that I had to counsel a young man, 10,000 miles away from his home, who had received the infamous "Dear John" letter from his girlfriend, or yes, even from his wife. Shock. Dismay. Rage. Disillusionment. Betrayal. Depression. Abandonment. And perhaps worst of all — helplessness.

And I, Ray, the social work care-giver, got one, too. I was shattered. We had agreed not to make any firm commitments to each other since I was going off to the war; but I thought we were going to get married after the war. And while I was away, she decided to marry someone else — and there was not a damned thing I could do about it. I found myself withdrawing even more, feeling less connected to America. Yet one more reason to feel, and be, so alone and alienated. My own Dear John experience was a catalyst that seemed to turn me further away from American women and towards Asian women. I, and perhaps other American soldiers, found *The Who*'s song, "American Woman (get away from me)" to become a very meaningful personal anthem.

Just as Nha Trang seemed unreal to many of the bush vets, much outside of Nha Trang seemed unreal to me. The war "would come to us" via wounded soldiers being med-evacuated to us on helicopters from places that we seldom, if ever, saw. We operated in a total vacuum. We would watch military bombardments taking place on nearby mountains from time to time — but we are absolutely ignorant of what was actually happening, militarily. Similarly, we knew almost nothing about what happened to most of the people we treated; they would go back to their duty stations, and we would never hear of them again. Or, they were medically evacuated out of Vietnam. We were in our own little world, Nha Trang, Vietnam.

Bush vets came to us and bush vets left. We just assumed and hoped that they would be okay. We usually didn't know if the psychological treatments we had provided had proven helpful or not — to their mental health and to their survival — except in those rare instances where someone would show up back on our doorstop. There was no feedback as to what happened to soldiers whom we medically evacuated to the United States, although such information could have been vital to helping us to modify or strengthen our psychiatric strategies and techniques. We kept doing what we were doing, with blinders on, to the best of our abilities.

Those in power know how valuable information is, and they can keep it very close, parceling it out when they decide that you need to know. (Never mind, when you think you need to know.)

WILL THE CASUALTIES NEVER STOP COMING?

Social workers and medical service corps officers had a share of administrative duties around the hospital. I got to know the staff who make a hospital run in a war zone: doctors, and nurses, and medics, and dust-off pilots (who flew into the field to pick up medical casualties), Red Cross workers, the Chaplain, the soldiers who guarded our hospital perimeter, and the Vietnamese mama-sans who cleaned our hooches. Each such person had his or her own story about how they were able to cope or not cope so well while being a care-giver as part of the 8th Field Hospital staff. [35]

If my medical service corps basic training included even rudimentary first aid, it was so negligible that I don't remember it. I certainly didn't know how to do practically anything, medically. Yet, I took my turn pulling Administrative Officer of the Day (AOD) Duty. As AOD, I was the administrative officer-in-charge of hospital operations from 1700 hours to 0500 hours, or "after-hours." It was anguishing to be on duty when acute medical casualties were brought in directly from the battlefields. [36]

Many combat soldiers out in the bush had money in their possession; they didn't have anywhere to spend it or keep it, while out in the field. Wounded men

---

35. For eloquent stories of Vietnam vet nurses and other women Vietnam vets, see Lynda Van Devanter, *Home Before Morning. The True Story of an Army Nurse in Vietnam* (New York: Warner Books, 1983), and Keith Walker, *A Piece of my Heart.* In Chapter 6, I highlight the experiences of an Army nurse; these courageous nurses deserve great credit.

36. See Shad Meshad, *Captain for Dark Mornings*, Chapter 4 (Triage), 33-38, for a vivid description of his experiences as a social work officer pulling AOD in the medical chaos of an emergency room at the 95th Evacuation Hospital.

would be flown in, at times, their pockets literally bulging with money, and with personal valuables such as rings, watches and wallets with family photos. One of my duties as AOD was to go to the ER while acute medical casualties were arriving, inventory their valuables, and safeguard them in a secure area. This involved my carrying around a clipboard with pre-printed inventory receipts on it. I would list the valuables of each patient: watches, rings, wallets, money, etc. Sometimes the casualties, in spite of their wounds, were able to let me know what they had and where; other times, I had to find them, myself.

In the middle of the ER, I would take watches and rings off men who were half-conscious and in acute pain. I would take one item after another, write them down and get the men to sign the inventory — if they were able to; or, I signed for them. And in the meantime, more casualties are hurriedly being taken off the choppers and brought into the emergency room, medical personnel are hurriedly conducting medical triage to determine who would get treated first or last, or not at all because their wounds were too severe.

One night, in the midst of this somewhat controlled medical chaos, while I was going around to various casualties to inventory their valuables, I approached one wounded soldier who was lying in great pain. He was seriously wounded in the lower trunk and legs. I was trying to concentrate on the job at hand and ignoring the cries and hubbub all around.

I introduced myself in a hurried but outwardly calm voice.

"Hello, soldier. I'm Lt. [or, later, Captain] Scurfield. I'm the Administrative Officer of the Day. I'm here to collect any valuables that you have, inventory them and have you sign the inventory to certify that it is full and correct. I'll safeguard your valuables, until you are ready to get them after you receive your immediate medical care."

And the acutely wounded soldier, struggling to be brave and communicative, showed me his wedding ring. I took it, gently, off his finger, as quickly as I could, as I had many more wounded soldiers to see. Then, he told me that he had a wallet and money in his pant's pocket — could I get it for him? I looked down at his blood-soaked pants, and told him that I would be as careful as I could. I slowly inched my hand down into his pocket that is stuck with half-dried blood, slowly extracted the wallet and money. He grimaced, and smiled wanly, shaking from shock and pain, and fear as to what the extent of his wounds might be and what would become of him.

Inside, I was seething with emotions. I was in anguish, cursing myself for choosing to study social work. These young men needed medical attention, now! and all I could do was stand around with a clipboard! Never in my life have I have felt so useless and inconsequential as during those many times as AOD at the 8th Field Hospital ER.

TRYING TO RELIEVE THE STRESS

The strain of continual and multiple interactions with grievously wounded and dying soldiers was intense and unremitting. It took an inevitable toll on the staff of the hospital. Those of us who could would try to cheer people up by playing guitar and singing at the officer's club, where male and female doctors, nurses, Red Cross workers and others could get together. The officer's club was kind of a sanctuary. Some escaped there more often than others, and some drank there a lot more than others.

And I, Ray, the social work care-giver, used my own music to escape, while at the same time offering it as an escape for my fellow care-givers, the hospital staff. And perhaps it also was a way to insure that I played music while I could; I had one obsession of my own about my personal safety — that I would suffer an injury or have a hand or arm amputated in the war, and would lose forever the ability and the pleasure of playing music.

Nha Trang was considered by many to be a refuge from the daily dangers and horrors of the war; and in many ways it was. But that did not mean that we were immune. I have a most poignant memory of hearing about the downing of one of our dust-off helicopters and crew. Finally, we got the "official" word-all crew members had been killed while trying to med evac wounded Americans out of a hot LZ. I remember going to a very emotional memorial service attended by what looked like the entire hospital staff. The dust-off crewmen were particularly brave, and very popular. They would be sorely missed. And James Taylor's words from "Fire and Rain" echoed in my heart: "sweet dreams and flying machines, in pieces on the ground."

"PEACE-CORPS TYPE" ACTIVITIES IN THE WAR

Still, compared to life out in the bush, in direct combat, life in Nha Trang was quite safe. Serving my Vietnam tour mainly in Nha Trang was a sharp contrast to the reality faced by most US armed forces personnel. Nha Trang was an "open" town that American troops could frequent. There had been attacks in Nha Trang during the year before, and during the 1968 Tet Offensive enemy soldiers had infiltrated the city. But, even though that had been just a short few months earlier, I heard that there was an unspoken agreement that the VC would leave Nha Trang alone and that they could spend time there along with

RVN[37] forces (and, of course, us). Curfews and off-limits designations in town were imposed, and lifted, and then imposed and lifted again.

Nha Trang was a large city, in a land mostly of small villages; there were restaurants, including French and French-Vietnamese. There even was a relatively large movie theater in town, whereas most soldiers were restricted to the repeated showings of old American movies on base. I went to the movie theater in town, once; then I became increasingly fearful: sitting alone in the dark, the only American, I would be an easy target for any Viet Cong sitting in the audience. So much for that!

Many Vietnamese Catholics, middle class, educated and genuinely anti-communist, had fled North Vietnam in 1954 after the communist takeover, and settled in and around Nha Trang. They were quite different from the peasant farmers, who might or might be VC or VC sympathizers. I got to know a number of such locals, personally. I made an extra effort to interact with them. Several of us regularly took surplus canned food supplies to the nearby orphanage. I also organized and ran a MEDCAP (Medical Civilian Aid Program) to the nearby fishing Hamlet of Xom Bong. I drove a deuce-and-a-half or a jeep, as part of our entourage of volunteers. I coordinated our MEDCAPs in conjunction with Vietnamese nurses from the Alliance for Freedom program. We drove to Xom Bong Hamlet on a regular basis, and set up a walk-in clinic to immunize the villagers and provide basic medical care.

I also organized and taught an English language class for locals. We held our classes in a small rickety wooden structure on the beach. Our little wooden classroom would be filled with students, young and old, week after week. Their innocence, seriousness about learning English, and laughter are still with me.

One evening, the early winds from an approaching typhoon were kicking up. I thought about whether to cancel the class; a lot of the students would stay home, given the brewing storm. And yet, the students were strikingly reliable in attending class, week after week. No matter what the weather, I thought, probably at least a few students would show up. And so I drove my jeep through the streets, which were eerily deserted as most people had already sought shelter. With increasing trepidation — and also a growing thrill in the face of potential danger (a constant irony, in the war zone) — I made my way to the breach, the one place to avoid with the storm winds increasingly.

---

37. Republic of Vietnam (the non-communist South), as opposed to the DRV, or Democratic Republic of Vietnam, the (communist) North.

We began our English class, trying to ignore the louder and louder howling of the wind as it buffeted against the sides of the building. We all treasured our class time: while class was going on, the war faded away, for a while, for all of us. We were encapsulated together, on a very pleasurable journey of discovery and fun. We all focused as best we could on the lesson, but finally, common sense prevailed; we cut class short so that everyone could get safely home.

JUST WHO IS THE ENEMY, ANYWAY?

The closest I came to being killed was during an encounter with a US Army Special Forces captain. The 5th Special Forces Headquarters Group was near Nha Trang. Special Forces personnel would be out in the field and would rotate through their headquarters group now and then. My Vietnamese girlfriend and another girl she knew shared a two-room hooch in town; the girlfriend had only been there a short while. The town was off-limits most hours of the week, but I still would sneak off the base and spend the night with her whenever I could. My girlfriend's "Americanized" nickname was "Fairy" — she had read it in a children's storybook that she had somehow come across.

One time I was sitting on Fairy's bed (which doubled as a couch). Fairy had stepped out for a little while and I am alone. Fairy had mentioned to me that her girlfriend had moved out suddenly, the day before, and Fairy didn't know where she had gone.

Suddenly, the front door burst open, and a Special Forces Captain and Sergeant came busting in. The Captain has obviously been drinking heavily and is extremely angry. We had never met before. He was upset to find his girlfriend missing, and more upset to find a stranger American man in the room. The air was thick tension and threat. The Special Forces Captain was holding his shotgun, the barrel pointed directly at me and looking very, very big. His finger on the trigger, he proceeded to grill me: who are you, where are you stationed, how long have you known Fairy, do you know the other girl, what are you doing at 8th Field? As he talked, he was alternately angry and depressed. He was very suspicious of me and why I was there. When I explained that I was a psychiatric social worker, he sarcastically commented that I had a cushy job. But then, fueled by his drinking, anger and depression, he started to ventilate about a wide range of topics.

And so we sat for a long, long time. With a gun in your face, the sense of time is distorted; I couldn't say if we sat for 20 minutes or two hours. He had that 1,000-yard stare; he had been through hell and back, and he had done his share of killing. I was convinced that he would have killed his girlfriend that night, if he had found her. But she was nowhere to be found; she was not there — and I was. I was frantically trying to think what to say that might help to help calm him down. We were both in an off-limits area, far from any military base, and it was late at night. He could easily have shot me and walked out the door.

The two attributes that are essential to anyone who is in the psychiatric field dealing with a crisis are patience, and talk. Judicious talk. Somehow, some way, the Captain's anger seemed to dissipate, especially towards me. He became more depressed and appeared to become resigned to the fact that his girlfriend was gone and out of reach. Finally, he stood up, walked over to the door, and turned slightly, giving me a last look. As he turned, his gun swung ever so slightly back towards me. I thought, "here it comes, he's going to shoot me as he walks out the door, just for the hell of it." But he simply walked out.

A PURPLE HEART OFFER

One evening at dusk, as I was just about to slip off to visit Fairy, we were hit with incoming rockets. I started running, fast, down the hospital road. And suddenly, I tripped over a chain that was strung between two posts. I hit it running full speed, flipped over and fell, hard, on my elbow. And then, the enemy fire stopped, so I continued on into town. But after I arrived at Fairy's place, my elbow swelled up and continued to throb; I finally had to go back and get medical attention for what turned out to be a chip fracture.

Someone asked me if the injury had happened during the rocket attack. "You're eligible for a Purple Heart; you were hurt in the middle of a rocket attack. Let's put you in for one." Part of me had an immediate response. "Yeah, I was injured during an enemy attack on our compound. He's right." Thank goodness, I didn't go for it. Later, I had the opportunity of working with many disabled Vietnam veterans (my great colleague and friend, Steve Tice, and so many others like Gary May, Bill VanDenbush, Mike Mohler and LeRoy Pipkin). I learned so much from these men who suffered traumatic losses of body parts and bodily functions, as well as their youth and innocence in the Nam. The Purple Heart is a sacred badge of honor for those who have earned one in war. I hadn't earned one that night at the 8th Field Hospital.

LEAVING

Our daily duties and the continuing barrage of psychiatric casualties forced us to focus on the here-and-now, the shorter-term psychiatric welfare of our troops. However, a largely unasked, and unanswerable, question awaited. What would be the longer-term impact of the trauma of war on so many Vietnam veterans, in spite of — or because of — anything we did or did not do? At the time, we hardly had time to ask ourselves that.

And so, in blissful ignorance, I was ready to leave Vietnam, fairly satisfied with my efforts and those of the entire 98th Medical Detachment in treating psychiatric casualties. Little did I know.

I left Vietnam in March, 1969, in what I thought was pretty good shape. Overall, I felt quite fortunate. I had been stationed where I could use some of my professional training, in a relatively secure area, and even had the opportunity to experience possibly the safest city in Vietnam — Nha Trang. I was able to forge a "Peace-Corps" type of experience and have many positive contacts with the Vietnamese people.

And, I fully believed that we had done our best to keep the welfare and the mental health of each individual soldier in mind as an important factor in our decision-making. Whether we had, indeed, protected their individual mental health was never verified, and there was no systematic follow up that would provide any feedback. However, it appeared at the time that our efforts had been reasonably successful — certainly in terms of promoting the short-term or acute psychiatric welfare of casualties.

Some fifteen years later, I found what could have been a very descriptive "psychiatric motto" to describe what we had actually knew (while we were in Vietnam) about the longer-term impact of war on soldiers. During my first return trip to Vietnam, in 1989, I saw it emblazoned on an American baseball cap worn by a Vietnamese youth. "I know Jack S—."

Chapter 4. Trying To Move On

Although I did not realize it at the time, the four years following my return from Vietnam in 1969, my early readjustment from war to civilian life, reflected my altered relationship with my country. I was "not a Vietnam vet."

For several years, I did not think much about the fact that I was a Vietnam veteran. I was not ashamed; I didn't have negative feelings about being identified as a Vietnam veteran; nor was I consciously attempting to deny my status to myself or to anyone else. Overall, I felt good about what I did during my Vietnam tour, and I still was under the belief that we had been doing the right thing in Vietnam. I was just moving along in my life. However, I did have issues regarding my Vietnam tour. When I rotated from Vietnam back Stateside, to the Valley Forge Army General Hospital, I had four months left of my two-year active duty commitment. VFGH had a large amputee ward filled with Vietnam veterans; however, as the chief social worker on the psychiatric ward, I don't think I ever even visited the amputees — a sign of avoiding my Vietnam?

No Place Like Home? I Want To Go Back to Asia

As my time at VFGH was drawing to an end, I came to a startling realization: I felt extremely uncomfortable being back in the United States. The country seemed foreign to me. What had been important to me before the war, and continued to be important to others, seemed inconsequential: sports, politics and current affairs, "settling down" and establishing myself in a community.

On the other hand, Asia seemed to have gotten under my skin, into my blood and spirit. I found myself yearning to return to live and experience Asia again — just not Vietnam. And so, I requested to extend my active duty obligation in return for a duty assignment in Asia. I committed to an 18-month extension, and the Army sent me to Japan.

Thus, for my last 18 months on active duty I was the first Social Work Officer at the Army Community Service Center (ACS) and then the ACS Director, in Okinawa.

AMERASIAN CHILDREN: A LEGACY OF US TROOPS

Army Community Service provided a range of services to active duty Army personnel stationed in Okinawa and to their families. While in Okinawa, as in Vietnam, I found opportunities to create a Peace-Corps-like experience. I taught English as a volunteer tutor. In conjunction with International Social Service, I led a Big Brother program, recruiting active duty military personnel to be mentors to mixed-race children living in Okinawa. Also, I tried to coordinate adoptions by military families of orphans from Vietnam and other Asian countries. At the time, Vietnam refused to have any of their orphans adopted internationally. I then took a private employment position[38] outside of my military role and became the inter-country adoptions social worker on Okinawa for the Holt Korean Adoption Program.

At the time, I didn't make any connections between my inter-country adoption activities and Vietnam, nor do I recall consciously thinking much about Vietnam or my being a Vietnam veteran while in Okinawa. But, in retrospect, the connection was substantial. The Asian-American kids that we had left in Vietnam were a more recent example of the same legacy from America's long-standing military presence in Korea and in Japan. On an individual level, it seemed that most (certainly not all) American military fathers were quite willing to deny their parental responsibility and did not make any serious attempt to support or bring their children back to the US. Indeed, both the military and the US government made it extremely difficult for American soldiers to bring their children back. In Vietnam, these Amerasian children were stark, embarrassing

---

38. Taking over from Army Social Work Officer David Lewis, who started the Holt program.

reminders to everyone of the foreign intervention in Vietnam — and on the "losing" side, at that! One can only imagine the trials and tribulations that such children went through, especially after 1975.

THE MOVIE "M.A.S.H." — NOT AT ALL FUNNY TO ME

The only other experience in my first two years post-Vietnam that suggested that Vietnam had a lingering impact on me came while I was watching the movie, M.A.S.H., which of course was a blockbuster hit. People all around me were laughing and enjoying the farcical and satirical portrayal of military medicine in the Korean War, but I kept hearing and feeling the whomp, whomp, whomp of the med-evac choppers, and flashing back to real emergencies in a very real war. Instead of laughing, I felt sad, angry, upset, with heavy thoughts consuming me. Exaggerated as it was, the movie was an insult to those who withstood the real terrors and horrors of war — or was it my issues with Vietnam?

Seeing the movie ripped off the scabs on wounds in my psyche, wounds that I had not realized were there. If you want gallows humor, here's some real gallow's humor. A vet picked up the body of a dead Vietnamese:

> When I picked up this one body, the arm came off...I laughed and threw it in the hole and said, "now he's not so heavy." But, it wasn't funny. I laughed because I couldn't deal with what I was doing..."[39]

STATESIDE: FEELING DISCONNECTED

After Okinawa, I was discharged from active duty. It was April, 1971. I went to Los Angeles, where my parents and sister had relocated, and within a few weeks I was hired at the Brentwood VA Hospital in West Los Angeles, one of the largest psychiatric hospitals in the United States. So began a 25-year federal government career with the VA.

---

39. Steve Smith, *Two Decades and a Wake-Up*. Video documentary first broadcast on May 28, 1990, by KCTS, Channel 9, Seattle — Public Broadcasting Service (PBS) affiliate. It was accepted by PBS for a national broadcast on Veteran's Day, November 11, 1990, through various PBS affiliates nationwide.

The local characters in Los Angeles in the Seventies were experimenting with diverse life-styles that were only exceeded by the drug use in a universe that was clearly "anti-establishment." Like so many Vietnam vets after discharge, I in effect became a "working hippy" — with long hair and a beard (both for the first time ever), very "casual" dress, and a "briefcase" that I had fabricated out of an Army surplus canvas ammunition bag, and I got myself introduced to the whole counter-culture life style in Venice. And I worked very hard at my first job with the VA.

My first VA job was as a community social worker, where I had my first contact with angry Vietnam veterans. These were vets with serious post-war problems, and they absolutely refused to have anything to do with the federal government — and especially with the VA.

VA DRUG ABUSE TREATMENT. "THE WAR DOESN'T MATTER"

The first drug treatment program at the VA, a methadone maintenance program for hard-core heroin addicts, was in the planning stages and I had the opportunity to co-lead the process. While this program was established in response to the expected heavy need for drug treatment services for returning Vietnam veterans, surprisingly, the majority of our patients were World War II and Korean War vets, and vets who served between the Korean and Vietnam eras, with a smaller number of Vietnam veterans. Several years later I was struck by the fact that I hadn't even stopped to think whether the military histories of these heroin addicts might have anything to do with their substance abuse problems.

Nowhere in the drug abuse treatment program was there any consideration that military service could be a possible cause or stressor that may have contributed to the veteran's drug problems. The blinders were on, but good. Like the vast majority of substance abuse programs, the program philosophy emphasized that any attempt to identify reasons for using drugs was simply a way of looking for excuses. The war experiences were, in effect, assumed to be of no consequence or relevance to the veterans' presenting problems.[40] We, the staff, were ignorant of or denied the importance of the veterans' war experiences, and most veterans themselves also avoided making any possible link between unresolved Vietnam-related issues and their substance usage.[41]

HAWAII CALLS: DROPPING OUT — AND THEN BACK IN

After about 14 months, I received an offer for a social work position on the Big Island of Hawaii, where I had dreamed of going. The idea of working in such a location, on behalf of native Hawaiians, was irresistible. However, the position was with the Queen LCC in a very isolated rural area, which was not a good fit for me. After only 15 months in this position, I stayed on for some six months and immersed myself in an alternate hippie life style. Eventually, after a four-year journey of wandering, experimenting and healing since Vietnam, I went back to Los Angeles to get my doctoral degree in social work. Without knowing it, I had been coming to terms with life and deciding what I wanted to do. I was finally willing to go home.

---

40. For alternative models of treatment that offer a combined and true dual focus both on PTSD and substance abuse, see: L.R. Daniels & R.M. Scurfield, "War-related post-traumatic stress disorder, chemical addictions and habituating behaviors," in M.B. Williams and J.F. Sommer (Eds.), *The Handbook of Post-Traumatic Therapy* (Westport, CN: Greenwood Publishing, 1994), 204-218; A.W. Meisler, "Group treatment of PTSD and comorbid alcohol abuse," in B.H. Young & D.D. Blake (Eds.), *Group Treatments for Post-Traumatic Stress Disorder* (Brunner/Mazel: Philadelphia, 1999), 117-136; and E. Padin-Rivera B.S. Donovan & R.A. McCormick, *Transcend: A treatment program for veterans with post-traumatic stress disorder and substance abuse disorders* (Cleveland, OH: Brecksville VA Medical Center, 1996). Unpublished manuscript.

41. R.M. Scurfield, "The collusion of sanitization and silence about war: One aftermath of Operation Desert Storm." *Journal of Traumatic Stress*, 5 (3), 505-512. See also: R.M. Scurfield & S.N. Tice, "Interventions with medical and psychiatric evacuees and their families: From Vietnam through the Gulf War," *Military Medicine*, 157 (2), (1992), 88-97.

Chapter 5. Two Decades And A Wake-Up

The Vietnam Veteran's Movement and PTSD Treatment Programs

My personal post-Vietnam journey is intertwined with my subsequent leadership positions with the Department of Veterans Affairs regionally and nationally in the treatment of war veterans with post-war psychiatric and social readjustment problems. It was not until several years after my return from Vietnam (around 1974-75) that I gradually started to become aware of the continuing and indelible influence of Vietnam on its veterans — and on myself. Then, I had the good fortune to become involved in a number of regional and national programs for Vietnam veterans at the same time that the concept of PTSD (Post-Traumatic Stress Disorder) began to gain acceptance. Several important experiences over 20 years turned out to be stepping stones that led to my eventual decision to co-facilitate the controversial first return trip to Vietnam in 1989 by a group of veterans from the Northwest with PTSD.

In the late 60s and 70s, many Vietnam Vets were extremely distrustful of the military, of the government, even of Veteran's Administration health care services (which they saw as the military, without the uniforms). However, the sheer number of men and women who had served in the Vietnam theater was immense — some 3.14 million [42] — and large numbers were continuing to have great difficulty adjusting to civilian life. Increasingly larger numbers of Vietnam veterans started coming to the VA for medical and psychiatric services, despite their distrust. They had no place else to go. Many, especially those who were wounded and physically disabled from the war as well as those with mental problems, were extremely angry and distrustful. Their anger was difficult for many of the VA staff to understand or to tolerate. World War II and Korean War veterans, for the most part, were quite compliant and apparently grateful for and satisfied with the treatment they received. But there was a deep bitterness burning inside many Vietnam veterans. Their rage was grounded in a combination of the horrors of war, and their sense that they had been used up and thrown away by their country and government. Instead of "welcome home, glad you made it," they heard insults; they were ignored or treated like pariahs.

> I was 21 years old when I got discharged. I immediately went and got a vasectomy...I had vowed that I would never father a son who would have to go through the hell that I had to suffer.

> I had made a blood oath to myself. When my son gets of age to enter the service, I had made a blood oath. I will do whatever I have to do to keep him from being in the military. I will shoot him in the foot if he is drafted or if he enlists. A blood oath — and I'll shoot him again if need be.

Another vet says,

> When I got home, there was my family sitting in the living room. They were lined up on the couch and chair just like they always sat. And they were lined up just like this Vietnamese family in that hooch that we had busted into looking for VC and had killed them. Killed them as they were sitting there all lined up, just like my family.

---

42. Many different estimates have been published of the number of US personnel who served in Vietnam during the war. The actual number is difficult to pinpoint due to various factors, i.e., (a) a number of persons were on classified operations in Laos and Cambodia, (b) others flew or were inserted into combat missions in Vietnam but their official duty station was elsewhere, such as Thailand, and (3) there is disagreement as to who exactly should be counted as Vietnam veterans — what about persons who served prior to 1964, and those who served in ships in the waters contiguous to Vietnam, etc.? I have most confidence in the figure of 3.14 million persons who served in Vietnam and in the contiguous waters and airspace as defined and calculated in the (previously cited) National Vietnam Veterans Readjustment Study (NVVRS) — the largest and most sophisticated national psychiatric epidemiological study ever conducted on the veterans of any era, a study that required an accurate estimate of the numbers who had served. This source is not a government agency and is less likely to have an ulterior motive for over- or under-reporting the figures. See R.A. Kulka, W.E. Schlenger, J.A. Fairbank, R.L.Hough, B.K. Jorday, C.R. Marmar & D.S. Weiss: (1) *Trauma and the Vietnam war generation: Report of findings from the National Vietnam Veterans Readjustment Study* (New York: Brunner/Mazel, 1990); and (2) *National Vietnam veterans readjustment study (NVVRS): Description, current status and initial PTSD prevalence estimates.* Washington, DC: Veterans Administration.

What a homecoming. I walked in the door after my discharge, and my family says, "Why were you over in Vietnam? (I had volunteered). You should have been here at home, helping us out."

When I got back, I was radically changed. The old friends back home, I wanted to talk with them so bad, and I tried. And they tried. But we just couldn't communicate anymore.

In fact, the only guys who I felt that I could talk to were other Nam vets — and they were the very ones who I didn't want to have any contact with!

And,

I was back a year. I had been strung out on drugs from almost the time I got back home. I am still extremely bitter about what my parents (my parents, yet!) told me: "We wish you had been killed over there, rather than to see you like this."

Even among the enemy:

...he knew it wasn't true that young Vietnamese loved war. Not true at all. If war came they would fight, and fight courageously. But that didn't mean they loved fighting.

No. The ones who loved war were not the young men, but the others like the politicians, middle-aged men with fat bellies and short legs. Not the ordinary people. The recent years of war had brought enough suffering and pain to last them a thousand years. [43]

Many VA staff considered the onslaught of angry Vietnam vets to be "problem children" who were self-centered, demanding, disruptive, complaining, outspoken and uncooperative. They saw them seen as behavior problems, and treated them accordingly. Most mental health programs and clinicians (both in and out of the VA) failed to consider the possible role that the Vietnam war and/ or homecoming experiences may have had regarding veterans' current life problems. I was late, myself, in coming to understand and appreciate the combat vets' reality, and to understand why combat vets would target me and other VA staff with their anger. I began to be able to conceptualize and express the following to combat vets when we would first meet in counseling:

Why should you trust me, as you walk in the door? Right now, you have no good reason to trust me, and plenty of reasons not to. I'm a federal government employee. I'm a professional social worker, a member of the mental health professions that have ignored the impact of the war on you, and indeed that have blamed you for having the problems. I'm a Vietnam veteran. But to you, I'm probably one of the worst kind of veterans. Not only was I an officer, and an ROTC one to boot, I served

---

43. Bao Ninh, *The Sorrow of War* (London: Secker & Warburg Limited, 1993), 68-69. Originally published as *Than Phan Cua Tinh Yeu (Fate of Love)* (Hanoi: Nha Xuat Ban Hoi Nha Van (Writer's Publishing House), 1991.

in the rear, not at the front, in a seaside town, beautiful and relatively safe. And so, I must earn your trust. I don't expect you to trust me completely. That's unrealistic, considering what you've been through and how you've been treated. But, if I can earn some of your trust, a little of your trust, maybe we can start building some bridges between us... Will you help educate me about what it was like for you — then, later, now? If you are willing to meet me half-way, maybe, just maybe, we will be able to work together. Are you willing to give me a chance, to test me out? What do you say?

In March 1981, Vietnam veteran James Hopkins crashed his jeep into the lobby of the Wadsworth VA Medical Center in West Los Angeles. He then sprayed the lobby with automatic rifle fire to protest a disability he contended grew out of his exposure to the toxic herbicide Agent Orange in Vietnam. [44] Hopkins was found dead "of unknown causes" in his home two months later. Shortly thereafter, on May 21, a group of Vietnam veterans stormed the hospital lobby and occupied it, staging a "sit-in." Several of the veterans also went on prolonged hunger strikes, all to protest the VA's handling of the Hopkins case but also because the VA had been engaged in suppressing information about the long-term toxic effects of Agent Orange. They demanded an independent investigation of VA hospitals. The sit-in and protest lasted 18 days. The occupying veterans made several demands of VA national officials. The occupation and the growing demonstrations attracted national media attention; supporters flocked to the hospital to join in. The VA was ambivalent, and the VA Deputy Counsel from Washington DC, Robert Coy, was flown in to negotiate with the protestors. Along with Shad Meshad, I was then asked to act as an intermediary between the protesting veterans and the VA, since both Shad and I had developed a positive reputation among many veterans and veteran groups.

Things were extremely tense. By this time, not only was the lobby filled with protesters, there was a large and ever increasing tent-city of protestors occupying the hospital grounds. The protesters were becoming increasingly frenetic and frustrated, and were getting more and more media coverage. Negotiations were going on around the clock between the VA (Bob Coy, Shad Meshad and me) and leaders of the occupation. The pressure was severe, on both sides: higher ups in the VA were demanding a quick end to the occupation and eviction

---

44. To obtain a comprehensive accounting of this event from the perspective of a number of persons who were involved, besides me, see Gerald Nicosia, *Home to war: A history of the Vietnam veteran's movement* (New York: Crown Publishers), 2001.

of the protestors, and the more militant among the protestors were pushing for dramatic action quickly by the VA, or else.

There were credible rumors that a number of the veterans occupying the lobby and grounds had firearms. At one point when the negotiations appeared to have broken down (which happened more than once), government officials decided to take the offensive. Armed national guardsmen were secretly airlifted from another location in Los Angeles, intending to make a landing at the hospital. With the joint assistance of a large police force, their mission was to arrest and jail the protestors. We found out about this when the guardsmen already in the air. We were in shock. We had been assured that the VA would not violate our guarantee to the protestors — that there would not be a forced eviction and arrest, as long as both sides continued to negotiate in good faith; the VA had concurred with that. Everyone in the negotiations knew that the use of force by armed personnel would almost certainly be met with deadly armed response by a very determined group of combat veterans.

The protesters already distrusted the government profoundly, of course, and they anticipated that there might be a surprise attempt to overwhelm them. They had made it very clear, early in the negotiations, that that would not be a wise thing to do. The whole reason they were there was because they were edgy, and angry, and in several cases their judgment and self-control were extremely questionable.

When we got word of the impending armed assault, Bob Coy immediately got on the phone. He managed to establish communication with someone above the chain-of-command of whoever was in-charge of the airlift. Bob was vehement, yelling that they must cease and desist and turn the airlift around. If the protestors heard the approaching helicopters, he said, they would almost surely react lethally. Somehow, Bob was able to convince someone in authority that we were in a most delicate stage of the negotiations, were hopeful of a successful agreement, and that the assault had to be stopped. We waited, breathlessly, until we heard that the helicopters were, indeed, turning around.

Ultimately, there was a peaceful resolution, and the VA did agree to address some of the demands of the protestors; even so, I do not recall that much progress was made towards the veterans' concerns. For several years afterwards, I found myself reflecting on two quite different aspects of this experience. First, I was very positively impressed that there was a person of such a high caliber as Robert Coy at a high administrative level in the VA; if Bob existed, perhaps there were other high-level officials of similar integrity.

This uplifting thought was countered by an astonishing interaction I had with the then Administrator of the VA, a retired admiral who had flown to Los Angeles around the end of the sit-in. In a brief discussion with him, I advocated for the VA to institute a national policy that mental health assessments routinely include an inquiry into each veteran's military history, in order for us to give fair and systematic attention to the possible role war experiences may have played in their current mental health difficulties. To my dismay, he could not comprehend why this was a valid concern, and rejected the idea out of hand.

Another disturbing thought that stayed with me over the years was that perhaps I had been an unwitting tool, co-opting the protesting veterans and evading the issues they raised. In other words, while I had contributed to bringing a peaceful resolution to the sit-in, at the same time I had contributed to breaking the momentum that had been building to address their concerns. The unprecedented media attention quickly dissipated, once the protestors had left the hospital grounds, and the nation's attention shifted away from these issues. Again.

VIETNAM VET RAP GROUPS

The vast majority of VA (and civilian) mental health programs were so far out of touch with the needs and problems of combat veterans that most vets refused to come to the VA, or came as a last resort. Many of them were disruptive; some began to start their own alternative organizations and programs outside the auspices of the government.[45]

---

45. There were exceptions scattered throughout the VA system that were initiated and funded by local hospital authorities. One that I was intimately familiar with was the Vietnam Veterans Resocialization Unit, started by Vietnam veteran Shad Meshad in 1971 at the Brentwood VA Hospital (since renamed as the West Los Angeles VA Medical Center) in West Los Angeles and made possible by the visionary support of the Chief of Social Work, John Fulton (who later became the National Director of Social Work Service for the VA). I was a consultant to this program in the mid-70s and was the Director from 1979-1981. For a description of one precedent-setting element of this program, the innovative Veterans-In-Prison Program led by Vietnam veteran Bruce Pentland, see B. Pentland & R. Scurfield, "In-reach counseling and advocacy with veteran's-in-prison," *Federal Probation*, XXXXVI (1) March, 1982), 21-29; and B. Pentland & R.M. Scurfield, "Veterans-in-Prison program: Rebuilding individual responsibility, *The Minority Military and Veteran's Observer*, I (3) (August, 1980), 5-6.

As a counterpoint, the rap group movement sprung up at many store-front locations throughout the US, outside of the auspices of any governmental agency. These groups were comprised entirely of combat vets, and led mostly by Vietnam veterans themselves or by the few mental health professionals who were sensitive to their particular plight. In the 1970s, some 2,000 self-help vet rap groups were established at locations throughout the country: in churches, universities and any organization that would host them. [46]

The rap groups offered a peer forum that talked about things traditional group therapy did not consider appropriate to discuss: the political and social implications of the war, and the idea that the traumas of war and related post-war readjustment difficulties were why the veterans were so troubled —not because they had some kind of psychiatric disorder.

"DELAYED STRESS" AND POST-VIETNAM SYNDROME

The Diagnostic and Statistical Manual of Mental Disorders, Volume II, published in 1968, was the nationally-recognized authoritative missive on psychiatric disorders. Ironically, while it was published during the height of US troop mobilization in Vietnam, [47] there was no diagnostic category that recognized that exposure to a gross or extreme stressor could be a possible cause of any psychiatric condition. The absence of any such diagnostic category placed a growing number of clinicians in a diagnostic quandary: what diagnosis should be used for veterans who were continuing to suffer from their war experiences? They did not

---

46. A. Egendorf, "Vietnam veteran rap groups and themes of postwar life," in *Journal of Social Issues*, 31 (4) (1975), 111-124; R.J. Lifton, "Advocacy and corruption in the Healing Profession," in C.R. FIgley (Ed.), *Stress Disorders Among Vietnam Veterans: Theory, Research and Treatment* (New York: Brunner/Mazel, 1978), 202-230; R.M. Scurfield, "Treatment of posttraumatic stress disorder among Vietnam veterans," in J.P. Wilson & B. Raphael (Eds.), *International Handbook of Traumatic Stress Syndromes* (New York: Plenum Press, 1993), 879-888; C.F. Shatan, "The grief of soldiers: Vietnam combat veterans' self-help movement" *American Journal of Orthopsychiatry*, 43 (4) (1974), 640-653; J.R. Smith, "Rap groups and group therapy for Viet Nam veterans," in S.M. Sonnenberg, A.S. Blank & J.A. Talbott (Eds.), *Stress and Recovery in Vietnam Nam Veterans* (Washington, DC: American Psychiatric Press, Inc., 1985), 165-192; and R.J. Lifton, "Rap Groups," in *Home From The War. Vietnam Veterans-Neither Victims nor Executioners* (New York: Basic Books, 1973, 73-96.
47. American Psychiatric Association, *Diagnostic and Statistical Manual of Mental Disorders-- III, Second Edition* (Washington, DC: American Psychiatric Association, 1980).

fit official psychiatric labels such as "psychotic" or "neurotic" or "charactero-logical" (i.e., behavioral problems). Some clinicians began to use such unofficial diagnostic terms as "delayed stress syndrome," "post-Vietnam syndrome" and "combat stress" to describe problems stemming at least partly from traumatic war-experiences and not solely from non-war etiological factors such as troubled early-life histories. [48]

The VA continued to deny the war-related causes of Vietnam veterans' post-war problems. The military history component of a typical mental health assessment consisted of one or two lines. (And if there was a service-connected condition, another line was added.)

> Army, 1964-66, E-4, served one year at Ft. Sill and one year in Vietnam. Honorable Discharge. Service-connected, 30%, Schizophrenia, paranoid, chronic.

The war experience, in effect, was excluded or dismissed as inconse-quential — by national policy of the health care system that existed specifically to serve military veterans. There truly was a collusion of silence about the true impact of war. [49]

---

48. There are a number of excellent descriptions of the etiology of PTSD and general ther-apeutic guideposts and strategies to utilize in assessing war-veterans for possible PTSD, including: Arthur Arnold, "Diagnosis of post-traumatic stress disorder in Vietnam veterans," in Sonnenberg, Blank & Talbott, *Stress Recovery in Vietnam Nam Veterans,* Washington, DC, American Psychiatric Press, 1985, 99-124; J.Goodwin, "The etiology of combat-related post-traumatic stress disorders," in T. Williams (Ed.), *Post-Traumatic Stress Disorders of the Vietnam Veteran* (Cincinnati, OH: Disabled American Veterans, 1980), 1-24; H.R. Kormos, "The nature of combat stress," in C.R. Figley, *Stress Disorders Among Vietnam Veterans,* 3-22; J. Newman, "Differential diagnosis in post-traumatic stress disorder: Implications for treatment," in T. Williams, *Post-Trau-matic Stress Disorders: A Handbook for Clinicians* (Cincinnati, OH: Disabled American Veterans, 1987), 19-34; R.M. Scurfield, "Treatment of posttraumatic stress disorder among Vietnam veterans," in J.P. Wilson & B. Raphael (Eds.), *International Handbook of Traumatic Stress Syndromes,* 879-888; & R.M. Scurfield, Psychosocial Treatment of War Veterans, in J.R. Conte (Ed.), *Handbook of Trauma & Abuse* (in press), Sage Publications.
49. R.M. Scurfield, "The collusion of sanitization and silence about the impact of war." For a further discussion of various sources of bias and resistance to the notion of war-related PTSD (i.e., pre-morbid bias in traditional psychoanalytic thinking, societal reactions, counter-transference reactions among therapist, Department of Defense resistance, etc.), see: R.M. Scurfield, Posttraumatic stress disorder in Vietnam veterans," In J.P. Wilson & B. Raphael (Eds.), *International Handbook of Traumatic Stress Syndromes,* 285-295.

"Combat Had No Impact on Me"

The ignorance or prejudice of many health care providers, who typically ignored how war experiences might be related to the post-war difficulties of many Vietnam veterans, was compounded by a very powerful dynamic among many of the veterans, themselves. Veterans desperately wanted to put the war behind them, and would do everything they could to avoid or deny the lingering after-effects of war on their lives. It seemed as if everyone, to include mental health providers, the military, politicians, the neighbors and communities of veterans, and both veterans and their families, all were anxious to believe that the war had no appreciable longer-term impact on veterans. [50]

The reality of the impact of combat was graphically described by the late Sarah Haley, a Boston VA social worker who was a pioneer in mental health in the VA:

> Combat veterans may play down or embellish their "war stories," but initially their reports should be taken at face value. The only report that should not be accepted at face value, although one may choose not to challenge it initially, is the patient's report that combat in Vietnam had no effect on him. [51]

The reality that war always has an impact came late. Even I had been convinced for several years that it had had no appreciable impact on me. I had yet to understand that the valid question to ask a combat vet was not whether, but how, the war had affected him.

THE VET CENTER PROGRAM

Throughout the middle and latter 1970s, there was a hue and cry from a growing number of veterans, and veterans' advocates: that traditional VA mental health programs were inadequate or were biased against appropriately assessing

---

50. *Ibid.*

51. This is one of the classic early articles, by the late Sarah Haley, a long-time social worker at the Boston VA Hospital, on breaking the silence concerning clinical interventions with Vietnam war veterans not only about the taboo subject of atrocities but of the larger issues concerning killing and reactions by therapists to hearing such testimony in clinical contacts: S.A. Haley, "When the patient reports atrocities. Specific treatment considerations of the Vietnam veteran," *Archives of General Psychiatry*, 30 (February, 1974), 196. Haley was one of a number of sensitive and proactive mental health providers in the VA system who went out their way to relate to, understand and be responsive to Vietnam and other war veterans.

and treating Vietnam veterans and their war-related mental health problems. Finally, in 1979, with considerable advocacy by then VA Administrator Max Cleland (himself a disabled Vietnam veteran) and other supporters, legislation was passed to establish a "Readjustment Counseling Service," to include a system of about 90 Vet Centers throughout the country. [52]

I became the first National Associate Director of Counseling for the Vet Center Program (RCS), and stayed in Washington DC from June 1982 until June 1985. I joined the RCS leadership of Art Blank, M.D., former psychiatrist in Vietnam, and Ed Lord, Vietnam-era veteran and brother of a disabled Vietnam veteran. Ed had been a Vet Center Team Leader in Minnesota.

This was a frenetic time, during which the Vet Center Program was extended for several years, and expanded from 91 to 136 sites nationwide. However, RCS initially was only authorized for three years. The official rationale for this three-year existence was predicated on the assumption that over 90 Vet Centers could be established nationwide, vets with problems would be located and counseled, and the bulk of their "readjustment problems" treated and resolved — and then the Vet Center Program could shut down. (A more reality-based rationale for the three-year cut-off was that conservative political leaders in the White House and Congress wanted to prevent the establishment of another federal program that would become permanent — along with the con-servative bias that the Vietnam vet problem was entirely over-blown. After all, "WW II and Korean War vets didn't have problems like this.")

Obviously, widespread ignorance and prejudice still prevailed as to the extent and long-lasting nature of moderate and chronic war-related problems among veterans. Also, there was the staunch resistance of the VA administrative and medical hierarchy to any specialized program, especially one forced on them by Congress. The Vet Center Program was much more focused on Vietnam veteran counseling staff providing advocacy, outreach, rap groups and family counseling in a non-medical community setting — rather than an emphasis on

---

52. For a discussion of the history of the establishment of the Vet Center Program and key philosophical and structural program elements, see A.S. Blank, "The Veterans Admin-istration's Viet Nam veterans outreach and counseling centers," In Sonnenberg, Blank & Talbott, *Stress and Recovery in Vietnam Nam veterans*, 227-238. Also, Gerald Nicosia has written an extremely comprehensive book about the history of the Vietnam veteran movement that provides considerable details from many of the principals involved. G. Nicosia (2001). *Home to war: A history of the Vietnam Veteran's Movement*. New York: Crown Publishers.

physician-led diagnostic and medication services for individual psychiatric patients.

The Vet Center Program and "Exposure Therapy"

The Vet Center Program adopted many features of the community rap groups and other programs designed to appeal and be responsive to hundreds of thousands of alienated and disaffected Vietnam veterans. These included requiring absolutely minimal paperwork from clients, having Vietnam veterans as a majority of the staff and peer counselors, offering a one-stop service center concept, and choosing community locations easily accessible to veterans. The original Vet Center motto, "help without hassles," exemplified the streamlined approach to access and responsiveness that the larger VA system was not known for. [53]

The record-keeping system was kept strictly apart from the regular VA medical records system, due to pervasive mistrust of so many veterans for the federal government. Vet Centers sponsored or coordinated such innovative forums as Vietnam veteran art shows, and advocacy to fund and build Vietnam veteran memorials, and local, state, regional and national educational and training conferences.

Two additional characteristics were at the heart and soul of the program — and addressed areas that the regular VA almost totally ignored. A full and accurate military history was considered essential as a routine and systematic component of any mental health assessment. And, there was a special emphasis on peer group treatment with participants exclusively consisting of fellow and sister Vietnam war veterans. Special "Vietnam focus groups" emphasized talking through and attempting to help resolve traumatic war and other active-duty experiences. [54] Vietnam focus groups recognized the treatment maxim that therapeutic exposure to an aspect of the original trauma was essential to PTSD treatment. [55]

As the 1980s unfolded, exposure therapy became widely accepted among Vietnam veterans who had PTSD. This meant, in addition to having vets talk

---

53. Indeed, there was considerable resentment among regular VA officials that "help without hassles" implied that the regular VA provided "help with hassles," which, of course, it did. The Vet Center was obliged to stop using the "help without hassles" motto in response to severe pressures from VA officials.

54. R.M. Scurfield, "Treatment of posttraumatic stress disorder among Vietnam veterans" and J.R. Smith, "Rap groups and group therapy for Vietnam veterans."

about their traumatic war experiences, exposing veterans to physical or other "in vivo" stimuli, such as pictures or sounds of war, in an attempt to uncover underlying issues and/or to promote desensitizing the veteran to such stimuli. [56]

The tenets of exposure therapy served as a central underpinning to extending such therapeutic exposure outside of the four walls of the counseling office. That was where I placed my focus when I left Washington, DC, and went to establish the Post-Traumatic Stress Treatment Program at the American Lake VA Medical Center in Tacoma, WA.

FINALLY, AN OFFICIAL DIAGNOSIS

It was not until DSM-III (Diagnostic and Statistical Manual of Mental Disorders, 3rd Edition, 1980) that a Post-traumatic Stress Disorder (PTSD) diagnosis was included that recognized both the acute (e.g., shorter) and chronic (e.g., longer-term) impact of trauma such as war. [57]

In order to fully appreciate the potential benefits of having Vietnam veterans return to Vietnam as part of their post-war healing, it is important to briefly describe the symptoms of PTSD as defined by the American Psychiatric Association, and to note important PTSD symptoms that are missing from the APA definition. [58] A vet may have some or many of the following symptoms; that does not necessarily mean that he or she has PTSD. Indeed, to a large extent, some manifestation of these symptoms is normal and to be expected among the

55. R.A. Nicholson & J.A. Fairbank, "Theoretical and empirical issues in the treatment of post-traumatic stress disorder in Vietnam veterans," *Journal of Clinical Psychology, 43* (1) (1997), 44-66.

56. See, for example: J.A. Fairbank & T.M. Keane, "Flooding for combat-related s tress disorders: Assessment of anxiety reduction across traumatic memories," *Behavior Therapy, 13* (1982), 499-510; T.M. Keane, R.T. Zimering & J.M. Caddell, "A behavioral formulation of post-traumatic stress disorder in combat veterans," *The Behavior Therapist, 8* (1985), 9-12; and T.M. Keane, "The role of exposure therapy in the psychological treatment of PTSD," *National Center for Post-Traumatic Stress Disorder Clinical Quarterly, 5* (4) (Fall, 1995), 1, 3-6.

57. American Psychiatric Association, *Diagnostic and Statistical Manual of Mental Disorders, Third Edition* (Washington, DC: American Psychiatric Association, 1980).

58. The three core symptom clusters of PTSD have remained essentially the same since 1980, as identified in the most recent edition, DSMS-IV-TR in 2000. American Psychiatric Association, *Diagnostic and Statistical Manual of Mental Disorders, Fourth Edition, Text Revision* (Washington, DC: American Psychiatric Association, 2000).

vast majority of trauma survivors. It is the particular frequency, combination, duration and impact of the symptoms that occur after exposure to an identifiable traumatic experience, accompanied by some perceived distress or negative influence, that characterize PTSD.

Ironically, two of these three sets of PTSD symptoms also are successful, functional, coping mechanisms for surviving in a war zone or during a protracted trauma: detachment and arousal. (See my discussion on war zone survival techniques in Chapter 4.) Therefore, in working with war veterans in PTSD treatment, one must be very alert to the fact that many veterans are manifesting both PTSD symptoms and long-standing functional modes of survival. And, they may well be very resistant to changing them. (Many such veterans view this behavior to be very functional and adaptive in a hostile and uncaring world — and have no intention or very ambivalent intentions as to even trying to eliminate such behaviors or symptoms.)[59] The impact of war is quite universal, as the following quotes (first from American Vietnam veterans and then from an NVA veteran) illustrate.

Numbing, Detachment, Denial

In order not to be overwhelmed by the trauma and its initial and subsequent impact, trauma survivors almost universally attempt to numb-out emotions, detach themselves emotionally, and/or deny to themselves how great an impact the trauma has had.

---

59. Many clinicians have observed that it is extremely difficult for some Vietnam veterans to improve in targeted PTSD symptoms such as hyper-arousal and isolation. However, the veterans' perception that the behavior serves a purpose is often not considered. Ignoring this ambivalence is probably a major factor contributing to the inability to extinguish the symptoms. Ronald T Murphy of New Orleans and Dillard University and formerly with the VA National Center for PTSD in Menlo Park, CA, and associates, have made major contributions to our knowledge about such dynamics. See, for example, R.T. Murphy, R.P. Cameron, L. Sharp, G. Ramirez, C. Rosen, K. Dreschler & D.F. Gusman Readiness to change PTSD symptoms and related behaviors among veterans participating in a Motivation Enhancement Group (*The Behavior Therapist, 27* (4), 2004), 33-36; R.T. Murphy, C.S. Rosen, R.P. Cameron & K.E. Thompson, Development of a group treatment for enhancing motivation to change PTSD symptoms. *Cognitive & Behavioral Practice, 9* (4), 2002, 308-316; and Rosen, C.S., R.T. Murphy, H.C. Chow, K.D. Dreschler, G. Ramirez, R. Ruddy & F. Gusman. PTSD patients' readiness to change alcohol and anger problems. *Psychotherapy, 38* (2), 2001, 233-244.

I have never cried since Nam. Not at my father's funeral, not at my sister's funeral. In fact, I have a hard time having any feelings — other than anger or sadness.

Even among the enemy:

They were destined to be forever lonely. They had lost not only the capacity to live happily with others but also the capacity to be in love. The ghosts of the war haunted them and permeated their deteriorating lives. [60]

Re-experiencing

There is a repetitive and intrusive onset of disturbing memories, thoughts and mental images of the original traumatic experience. Typically, these may last for fractions of a second, or for a few or several seconds. In relatively rare instances, there is a full dissociative experience; during such "flashbacks" the trauma survivor becomes re-immersed in re-experiencing aspects of the original trauma to the point where there is a partial or full-blown dissociation from one's here-and-now functioning.

A Vietnam veteran's daughter was badly hurt in an accident at home. The vet rushed her to the ER. While standing in the ER, he started flashing back to Vietnam and a little Vietnamese girl who had been wounded by American fire.

Even among the enemy:

Since returning to Hanoi, I have had to live with this parade of horrific memories, day after day, long night after long night. For how many years? Often in the middle of a busy street, in broad daylight, I have suddenly become lost in a daydream. On smelling the stink of rotten meat I have suddenly imagined I was back, crossing Hamburger Hill in 1972, walking over strewn corpses. The stench of death is often so overpowering I have to stop in the middle of the pavement, holding my nose, while startled, suspicious people step around me, avoiding my mad stare. [61]

Arousal

The trauma survivor becomes hyper-aroused physiologically. This can be manifested through such symptoms as hyper-vigilance, constant scanning of the environment, and startle-responses, i.e., having an immediate physical reaction to being awakened unexpectedly while sleeping. Initial, middle and/or terminal sleep disturbance, and trauma-related nightmares, also are arousal symptoms.

I had to move out of our bedroom. I would be thrashing around at night, and making noises so loud that my wife couldn't sleep. And a few times, when she tried to wake me up, I struck out at her. It wasn't safe for us to sleep together.

---

60. Bao Ninh, *The Sorrow of War*, 214.
61. *Ibid.*, 41-42.

Even among the enemy:

> The dreams focused and refocused until past scenes and the present became a raging reality within him, images of the present and the past merging to double the impact and the smell and atmosphere of the jungle there in the room with him. Wave after wave of agonizing memories washed over his mental shores. [62]

PTSD Symptoms That Are Missing From the DSM-IV

Practically all clinicians expert in counseling trauma survivors would agree that the three core sets of PTSD symptoms in DSM-IV TR are important characteristic of PTSD. However, others (including me) argue that critical PTSD symptoms are missing from the DSM-IV TR.[63]

Pre-Occupation with Fear of Loss of Control

Trauma survivors typically are pre-occupied that if they fully remember, dwell on, talk at all or too much about their original trauma experience(s), that they will loose control of their emotions and may never be able to "come back out" of the trauma. Some fear that they will "go crazy," or start crying and never be able to stop, or lose control of other severe emotions, or become violent.

> I have yet to find the peace of mind that would allow [me] to watch any of the Vietnam War movies, or talk about the war, without threat of loss of control.
>
> — Army psychiatrist [64]

Pre-Occupation with Blame

Survivors of war-trauma oftentimes will fix the blame for the trauma or for what happened onto themselves and/or onto others. This is part of the attempt to make some sense out of the insanity of war in which who lives and who dies seems to be intermingled with fate, random chance, divine intervention and the unexplainable. The process of affixing blame is directed either outwardly (towards others who may not have reacted perfectly during the crisis) and/or towards oneself — in that in the heat of an emergency or crisis, we after all are human and are not always in perfect control of our responses.

---

62. *Ibid.*, 62.
63. R.M. Scurfield, "Posttraumatic stress disorder in Vietnam veterans."
64. N.M. Camp & C.H. Carney, "US Army psychiatry in Vietnam: From confidence to dismay," California *Biofeedback*, 7 (3) (Summer, 1991), 10-12, 15-17.

I have never forgiven me. I have never forgiven me that I could be so heartless. And take a human being and kill them and not think.

— Army combat medic. [65]

Even among the enemy:

A NVA soldier described how he had dropped down into a bomb crater to seek shelter from incoming fire, and a badly wounded ARVN Special Commando jumped into the same bomb crater. He was so pitiful. I pushed his guts back into his belly and tore my shirt off to bandage him, but it was so hard to stop the bleeding...I was horrified and at the same time felt deep pity for him. So when the raid stopped I jumped out of the crater, telling him to stay there for awhile. "I'm going to find some cloth and bandages," I told him. "I'll be back soon." He blinked at me, the rain pouring down his face, mixing water, tears and blood...I searched for a while and found a bag with emergency medical equipment in it, then turned to go back to help him. But I'd been silly...The ground was pock-marked with hundreds of craters. Where was the one I'd been sharing with the Saigonese? I fell into a crater. The water came over my knees. That meant someone sitting inside a crater would now have water up to his chest...I was going a little mad. I began to imagine his death; water slowly rising on him, a barbaric death stuck in the mud, helpless as the water came over his belly, his chest, his shoulders, his chin, his lips, then reached his nostrils...and he started to drown. He'd died, still hoping desperately that I'd come back and save him, as I promised. In which crater had he died? Now, even after many years, whenever I see a flood I feel a sharp pang in my heart and think of my cruel stupidity. No human being deserved the torture I left him to suffer.

(After many years of peace, Phan was still tormented by the memory. Would the drowned man ever stop floating through his mind?) [66]

Alienation and Dis-Connectedness from Others and from Society

Many Vietnam veterans remain bitter toward the US government and the American society in general for the "unwelcome home" given to so many Nam vets, and for society's failure to recognize both the accomplishments of Vietnam veterans and the depth of the emotional pain that followed the war. [67]

I'll never forget that girl's face at the terminal when I got off the plane from Nam in my uniform. All of a sudden, as I am walking through the terminal, this young girl starts throwing things at me, in the middle of the airport. She screams at me, calling me a baby killer, a murderer...I'll never forget her face, so full of hate towards me.

Even among the enemy:

---

65. Smith, *Two Decades*.

66. Boa Ninh, *The Sorrow of War*, 84-86.

67. Leslie Brown, "Euphoria from visit astounds veterans," *Tacoma News Tribune*, February 16, 1989, A-1.

In truth he had been deliriously happy to return home to Hanoi when the war ended...Still, there has been some pain, even then...At the start, there had been a common emotion of bitterness. There had been no trumpets for the victorious soldiers, no drums, no music. That might have been tolerated, but not the disrespect shown them. The general population just didn't care about them. Nor did their own authorities. [68]

Existential Malaise

Oftentimes, a traumatic experience "throws the survivor out of orbit." The survivor feels confused about who he or she is, one's identity, how one fits in the world anymore, what one believes in, and/or has a profound struggle and is in crisis over the classic existential questions, "who am I," "why am I here," "where am I going?"[69]

Do you know what it is like to be disabled and feel totally useless? That's how I have been feeling for several years. I worked so hard to get my VA disability, because I am disabled from the war. But not to be able to work, to have a purpose day-to-day, to be worth something, to give to others — that is terrible.

Even among the enemy:

He was at a stage when he had no idea how he would spend the rest of his life. Study? Career? Business? All those things he had once considered important, and attainable, suddenly seemed meaningless and beyond his reach. He was still alive — just. He had no idea of how he would earn his daily living. It was a time of utter isolation, of spiritual emptiness, of surrender. [70]

Crisis or Loss of Faith

Frequently, traumatic experiences severely test, call into question, confuse, destroy or dramatically enhance one's beliefs about God or a higher power. At one extreme, they may find a strengthened or transcending experience and faith. " At the other extreme, survivors may lose their belief in a higher power. Survivors may blame God or a higher power. "How could god allow such a terrible thing to have happened?" Or, "God is punishing me." Such a crisis or loss may have happened initially while in the war zone and/or sometime post-war, when the dreams of a post-war nirvana that had sustained many through the horrors of war were eradicated when confronted with the struggles of post-war life.

---

68. Bao Ninh, *The Sorrow of War*, 72-73.
69. See R.J. Lifton, The Broken Connection: On Death and the Continuity of Life. New York: Simon & Schuster, 1979.
70. Bao Ninh, *The Sorrow of War*, 67.

And I used to get so angry at God. I felt like he abandoned me there [in Vietnam]. I felt like he put all this friggin' weight on my shoulders.

— Army combat medic[71]

Even among the enemy:

Those who survived continue to live. But that will has gone, that burning will which was once Vietnam's salvation. Where is the reward of enlightenment due to us for attaining our sacred war goals? Our history-making efforts for the great generations have been to no avail. What's so different here and now from the vulgar and cruel life we all experienced during the war? [72]

Rage, Grief and Terror

DSM-IV TR does recognize terror as a core response to trauma in PTSD. However, the critical role that rage and grief also play as an integral aspect of being traumatized is not recognized. This is extremely unfortunate. For example, the rage of many Vietnam veterans has long been labeled as proof of behavioral or personality disorders — rather than recognizing the inherently trauma-linked rage that is characteristic of trauma exposure. It is inherently rage-producing: to have one's friends or oneself threatened, to become physically or mentally disabled due to the trauma; to be unable to prevent the trauma from occurring or the damage that it does; to be blamed by others for what happened or for being in the trauma; to be blamed by oneself for what happened; to carry hate towards the perpetrator, etc. [73]

Even today, I feel like so much of me died in Vietnam, that at times I wished all of me had died over there. For those who came back, the price of living is never easy or cheap. Laughter and happiness are rare...Like so many other Vietnam veterans, I feel so much rage in me that it exhausts me and isolation is my only sanctuary. [74]

BREAKING THE ALIENATION

By this time, I was 37 years old, and like many vets I still had not married. Then, a new social worker appeared at the West Los Angeles VA Hospital — Margaret Niolet. We were married within one year and lived in Topanga

71. Smith, *Two Decades.*

72. Bao Ninh, *The Sorrow of War,* 43.

73. R.M. Scurfield, "Posttraumatic stress disorder in Vietnam veterans."

74. A. Wiest, L. P. Root & R.M. Scurfield, "Post-traumatic stress disorder: The legacy of war," in G. Jensen & A. Wiest, *War in the Age of Technology. Myriad Faces of Modern Armed Conflict* (New York: New York University Press, 2001), 295-332.

Canyon, which was one of those isolated rustic locations in Southern California that had attracted a substantial counter-culture, not to mention a number of isolated Vietnam veterans, and me.

Washington DC and The Vet Centers: Just Who Is The Enemy, Anyway?

As the Vet Center's first National Assistant Director of Counseling, in Washington, one of my first responsibilities was to coordinate the completion of a video, *The Vietnam Veteran Then and Now.* [75] This video had been started under the supervision of a previous Vet Center national official, Lee Crump. It documented several Vietnam veterans talking about their salient traumatic war experiences during the war, and how they were trying to deal with those issues. The video was expected to be a powerful media tool for use in community education and outreach activities. Remarkably, some 13 years after the majority of Vietnam veterans had returned from the Vietnam War, no such audio-visual aid existed to help promote greater understanding of the continuing psychological and social impact of war on veterans.

When I showed a pre-production copy of the video in a private viewing with several higher-ranking VA officials (White House political appointees from the 10th floor of VA Central Office), prior to receiving a final go-ahead on national distribution, a VA official challenged me. Why do a film with "all these problems that Vietnam veterans are having? You should be showing the successes that Vietnam veterans have had, all the veterans who are doing well, because there are so many more 'successful' veterans than troubled ones." I responded that "the veterans without any problems, who are highly successful, they're not the reason that we have the Vet Center Program. It is the vets who are not doing so well, that's who our program is for, that is who this video is targeted for."

---

75. Readjustment Counseling Service, "The Vietnam Veteran Then and Now" (Washington, DC: Readjustment Counseling Service, Veteran's Affairs Central Office, 1983). This film was produced by the Regional Television Production Facility, VA Medical Center Learning Resources Center, St. Louis, MO. It won an Emmy from the St. Louis Chapter, The National Academy of Television Arts and Sciences, for Outstanding Achievement in Industrial Television. Lee Crump, former national official of the Vet Center Program, was instrumental in coordinating the implementation of this film project prior to my arrival at VA HQ, after which I was responsible for the completion of the project.

I finally realized that the very top VA officials didn't want us to get the word out about the extent to which Vietnam vets were having war-related problems! This experience added to my growing realization about the pervasive collusion of sanitization and silence by a number of government officials since two World Wars, the Korean and Vietnam wars to suppress information about the extent of the long-term negative impact of war on many veterans. (This is perhaps most dramatically true of the Persian Gulf War, which I discuss in my forthcoming book).

VA CENTRAL OFFICE

Arriving at VA Central Office in 1982 (since renamed "VA Headquarters"), I discovered that there were two categories of officials there: the career-types, who were civil service employees; and the political appointees, who were appointed to time-limited positions by the reigning President's administration. The differences between these two categories of VA officials were enormous. Career VA officials attempted to oversee the daily business of the entire VA system. Political appointees were there to carry out whatever marching orders the White House sent down for the VA. And so, if fiscal restraint was the order of the day, the political appointees ruled the VA through the prism of fiscal restraint.

I was named National Director of Counseling for the Readjustment Counseling Service (RCS), or the Vet Center Program — a program that only existed because of the US Congress and the intense lobbying efforts of veteran advocacy groups. The intense lobbying resulted in the passage of a bill that forced the VA to begin RCS and to use ear-marked funds strictly and only for RCS. (Congress prohibited the VA from redeploying those funds to other programs.) [76] And as the last straw for many VA officials, RCS was provided with a separate line of authority in the field and at VA Central Office that, in effect, sidestepped the traditional medical and administrative authority structure in VA Central Office and in the VA hospital system. The White House and many traditional VA programs (and officials both in VA Central Office and at VA hospitals) had been arguing all along that no special programs were needed to address the problems of hundreds of thousands of Vietnam veterans with post-war problems, maintaining that the VA's regular programs could provide adequate services to Vietnam veterans, and could do so within existing budgetary constraints. Veteran advocates were extremely critical of the VA's lack of responsiveness and argued that specialized programs had to be developed to address the unique and enormous extent of unique war-related and post-war readjustment needs of this new and very different era of veterans.

This mixed things up pretty well. Many of the VA Central Office political appointees and the White House strongly resented the very existence of RCS. The *coup de grace* was the discovery that a number of the VA Central Office career civil service officials, as well as many chiefs of traditional psychiatry and other service programs in the field, also strongly resented the presence of RCS in the VA system and the fact that RCS operated outside the purview of VA Chiefs of Psychiatry and Psychiatry in VA Central Office. I served my three years as an RCS Central Office official in the midst of a remarkably hostile and complicated milieu.

In seeking support for extending the Vet Center Program beyond its termination date, our efforts were secretly undermined by a number of VA, Congressional and White House officials. Had it not been for the strong Vietnam veteran advocates among staff members of key Congressional Committees, the Vet Center Program would have been finished.

---

76. Thankfully, members of Congress (and VA critics) strongly agreed. Legislation was introduced but did not pass, from 1974 through 1978, to establish and fund with a protected Congressional appropriation that the VA would be prohibited from using for any other purpose. Finally, in 1979, the legislation was passed, authorizing the VA to establish Readjustment Counseling Service or RCS. RCS was given a strict three-year time-limited life to accomplish its mission. This three-year time limit was adopted in order to be able to attract sufficient Congressional support from those who were strongly opposed to seeing the establishment of "yet another federal program that would become a permanent part of an expanding federal government." And so, at the initiative of the US Senate, the legislation was passed, Public Law 96-22. Now the VA was indeed forced to implement RCS and not use the appropriation for any other purposes. For a really comprehensive description of the establishment of RCS in the VA system, see: G. Nicosia, Home to War A history of the Vietnam veterans' Movement, 2001, and A.S. Blank, "The Veterans Administration's Viet Nam Veterans Outreach and Counseling Centers," in S.M. Sonnenberg, A.S. Blank & J.A. Talbott (Eds.), *The Trauma of War: Stress and Recovery in VietNam Veterans* (Washington, DC: American Psychiatric Press, 1985), 227-238.

THE ART OF SAYING NOTHING — POLITELY

The VA Central Office Vet Center officials became symbolically and literally identified as the contact point for any issue, question, complaint or other query about Vietnam veterans and their readjustment. Whether from Congress, the White House, Veterans Service Organizations, disgruntled veterans, family members, the media or anyone else, such queries ended up being funneled to our office.[77] There was a continuous flood of "controlled correspondence" responses to prepare and submit to higher-level officials for their review and "editing" before the correspondence went out over their signatures. Typically, replies were to be couched in the most general terms possible; the letter writer was thanked for his/her concern, and was assured that someone would be looking into the matter. Almost never was anything specific enough mentioned to give the letter writer anything that he/she could follow up on — unless it was from a member of Congress, who knew enough about the workings in VA Central Office to be able to make extremely specific requests for information.

CHALLENGING THE DOMINANT PARADIGM

One time a veteran came to the front door of the VA Central Office, at 810 Vermont Avenue, just a hop, skip and a jump from the White House. A sign outside the building quotes Abraham Lincoln: "For he who has borne the battle, and for his widow and his orphan." The veteran was in crisis, and insisted on talking to someone. However, he was much too uncomfortable to come inside the VA Central Office building. And anyway, there are no counseling services in Central Office. A security guard, not knowing what else to do, picked up the phone and called us at RCS. The Director was hardly inclined to take the time to go down and indulge this disgruntled man's caprice, but Ed Lord went down and sat with him outside the front door. The veteran was angry because his local VA hospital would not replace his worn-out walking cane. To them, apparently, it was a big deal; but it took Ed just ten minutes to get him a new cane.

The vet beamed and said: "Thanks, man. You're the first guy who listened to me." But, was it easy? Even here, to get such a small thing for a vet in need

---

77. My colleague, Ed Lord, was delegated the primary responsibility to draft such responses. In fact, in 1983 alone, Ed personally prepared the written responses for well over 500 inquiries.

required the intervention of two high-level VA national level officials. Ed took the matter to Fred Downs, national Director of Prosthetics, who was willing, on the spur of the moment, to do the opposite of engaging in the art of responding to controlled correspondence. He and Ed actually reached out to a veteran in need and provided a very concrete and useful service to him — putting veterans and their families first, like the sign says.

EMOTIONAL DEDICATION OF THE WALL

The Vietnam Veterans Memorial in Washington and the statue of the three combat soldiers were dedicated, in 1982 and in 1984, respectively. For both of these events, I was in charge of coordinating teams of Vet Center counselors from across the country. We set up command operations and a counseling center in a trailer adjacent to the Wall, to implement a five-day, 24-hour counseling and outreach operation at the Wall. Our teams provided 24-hour support to the thousands of veterans and their family members, vet supporters, Gold Star mothers and other family members of deceased Vietnam veterans who flooded the Washington area for these two dedications.

I quickly came to realize what the Wall represented to others — and to me. One day just prior to the 1982 national dedication of the Wall, I was there assessing the best place to locate our mobile counseling center for the upcoming ceremonies. I became immersed in memories as I stood on the rise, looking down at the Wall and the grounds. And then, quite jarring to my vision, several joggers ran through the grounds next to the Wall as they were crossing the Mall, and ran on the grass right in front of the rows of names of military personnel who had been killed in Vietnam. I could hardly believe it! Though the bodies of the 58,000+ men and women we lost in Vietnam are not literally buried here, the ground is hallowed. Don't they realize? Then another wave of joggers came by...What I was seeing as "disregard and disrespect" was simply the joggers' use of the national monument and park for their daily running routes. Were the joggers insensitive to the Wall and what it stood for, or was I over-reacting?

Unexpectedly, since the first day that onlookers were able to approach and see the Wall, people have been coming to pay their respects, and they leave not only flowers but letters, notes, photographs, stuffed animals, yearbook pictures, wedding rings, and other personal mementos. It was as if the Wall were a magnet, irresistibly attracting an unending procession of people and their expressions: tears, prayers, commiserations, hellos, goodbyes, grief, hurt, tenderness. And perhaps, most of all, acknowledgment. Acknowledgment that the existence on this planet of over 58,000 human beings had been prematurely terminated in the prime of their lives — and vowing that they would never be forgotten. [78]

> Dearest Eddie Lynn,
>
> I'd give anything to have you shell just one more pecan for me on Grandma's porch.
>
> — All my love, your cousin Anne

> Before he left, he taught me how to drive his car. Then he left it to me to take care of it "till he got back." "Dad survived Iwo Jima, Guadalcanal and all that. I'm a Marine. I'll be back. Take care of my car." I've still got the car. I would rather have my big brother back.

> My dearest Ben:
>
> I miss you and think of you so much. Every day in my prayers, I thank God and Jesus for caring for you and pray that will continue. I'm bringing Teddy Bear and a picture of your loved race car. I realize they can't stay there long, but they are yours and I want them to be with you. In time, I hope we can all be together.
>
> Love to you my dear, dear Ben, Mama   Much love, Dad

> To watch you die has been the most painful encounter of my life. I prayed for you, my brother of war. When I turned my head in helplessness your breath of life had stopped. I could no longer hear your breathing then. I knew that you were at peace. Bless you, for you are the hero.

> Even though I never really knew you, you still meant the world to me. Thank you, Daddy, for giving me three years of your life. Remembering you through photos, I can only say I love you, Daddy. Happy Father's Day. Part of me died with you.
>
> Love, your son, Joe

The events surrounding the national dedication were remarkable, emotional, laden with grief — and gratification. Many soul-stirring incidents occurred in and around the memorial and statue, and at many hotels throughout the Washington area where vets and union reunions happened over a several day period.

- Vets finding the nurses who had treated them at evac hospitals in Nam.

---

78. L. Palmer, *Shrapnel in the Heart. Letters and Remembrances from the Vietnam Veterans Memorial* (New York: Vintage Books, 1987), 5, 19, 21, 42, 97.

- Vets finding buddies who they had not seen or talked to since leaving Nam.
- Vets and family members scanning the panels on the Wall to try and find a familiar name, and then standing, in deep silence, their fingers reaching out and tracing the names — or breaking down, sobbing, when they found it.
- Total strangers, vet-to-vet, vet-to-non vet, embracing and crying.
- Vets tearfully and joyfully telling each other, "Welcome home, brother (sister)."

Ed Lord describes two very memorable experiences:

I was outside [the Vet Center mobile counseling trailer] and saw this guy on the ground. I walked over to him to see if he was okay. He looked up at me and said, "Get down, get down." I thought he might be experiencing a flashback. I got down next to him and asked, "Where are you?" He looked at me and said, "We're here, fighting the NVA." I said, "No, we're in Washington, not in Nam." But he still was lying there, and still did not appear to realize where he actually was.

And so I said, "Follow me, I'll get us to a safe place." And we low-crawled, slowly, on our hands and knees, for maybe 10-15 minutes. People all around were looking at us, like we were crazy. No, we weren't crazy, just a Nam vet and his counselor getting to a safe place. [Ed adds, "When I got back home several days later, this very vet's picture was on the cover of *Time*!]

The night before the Wall was dedicated, it rained buckets. As dawn broke, a woman and her daughter approached the west side of the Wall. As I stood near her, I heard her exclaim to her daughter: "Look, honey, at the water dripping off this wall...it's almost as if it is crying."

Finally, I'll never forget seeing the father of a Vietnam veteran who had been killed in action:

An elderly man walked into the hotel where the unit his son had served with in Vietnam was holding their reunion. He had a photograph of his son who had been killed in Vietnam. He went from table to table, from vet to vet, showing the photograph and emotionally asking everyone: "Did you serve with my son? He was with this unit and was killed in combat." The father kept going around, trying to find someone, anyone, who had known his son. He so desperately wanted some information, any information, about his son and the circumstances of his death (who believed the official military dispatches, anyway?). And he was sobbing, as he went from table to table...

I experienced another poignant experience at the end of the official dedication of the Wall. There was a vet, dressed in typical Nam vet clothing and insignia that identify his Vietnam vet status. He had a bugle in hand, and he was standing near the top of the Wall. After the official speeches at the end of the dedication, he began playing an extremely powerful, poignant and stirring rendition of *Taps*. The sounds of the bugle wafted over and through the crowd and me. And I know that never has a human being, and his musical instrument, and the melody he played, been any more soul-stirring to its listeners and to me, as was that bugle, on that day, at that sacred place, at the Wall...

The national dedication of the poignant sculpture of three combat soldiers in 1984 also was quite moving. One vet commented, as he stood looking transfixed at the statue: "You know, the Wall is a wonderful testimony to all those who died in Vietnam. But this statue, it feels more like a monument to us, those who are still living."

My experiences at the Wall in 1982 and at the dedication of the statue in 1984 were further stepping stones towards my decision to return to Vietnam in 1989. These were perhaps pivotal learning experiences for me, demonstrating the remarkable therapeutic power of being with vets, especially groups of vets, in settings outside of the therapist's office; being in settings that provided a therapeutic benefit. Not just sitting down and talking in an office — although that, too, can be extremely powerful in war-focus counseling sessions. But this "in-action" activity was potently therapeutic, a catharsis and a healing step that appeared to dramatically enhance traditional therapeutic "talking-only" interventions.

POLITICS AND SUBTERFUGE — SPECIALIZED PTSD PROGRAMS

Two camps with clear political agendas competed within the Vet Center Program and other VA specialized PTSD treatment programs. And we, the national officials of the Vet Center Program, were smack dab in the crossfire. On the one side were the White House and the Reagan Administration; the Office of Management and Budget (OMB); many VA central office and field officials, both those who were political appointees of the White House administration and VA career bureaucrats; and a number of (but not all) "conservative" congressmen from both the Democratic and Republican parties. This camp was more concerned with keeping the federal budget down, claimed that the "readjustment problems of Vietnam veterans" had been markedly exaggerated, and wanted to leave it to the VA to determine what amount of funding to reallocate from existing programs to support specialized programs for war-related problems rather than to provide new appropriations for such programs.

On the other side were those who believed strongly in the notion that war-related psychological and social problems of Vietnam war veterans were not being adequately addressed by traditional VA services, that such services would not be adequately funded by the VA if the VA were left to its own discretion in how much funding to provide to specialized PTSD programs, and that they required required substantial numbers of specialized PTSD programmatic responses, e.g., Vet Centers, and in-patient and outpatient PTSD programs. This group also included Democratic and Republican Congressmen and their staffers, especially those on the Veterans Affairs Committees: people such as Senator Allen Cranston (California) and staffers Bill Brew and Jonathon Steinberg; Richard Fuller of Congressman Bob Edgar's staff; Jill Cochran, daughter of Congressman Olin "Tiger" Teague; Jim Mayer, a double-amputee vet who was a special assistant to Max Cleland; Ralph Casteel, a key staffer assigned to the House Veterans Affairs Committee; Guy McMichael, a senior Senate Veteran's Affairs staffer; and Congressman Lane Evans (Illinois). Also, there were various veteran advocates including the late Lynda Van Devanter, Charles Figley, John Wilson, and a number of staff from various Vet Centers throughout the country who were strong veteran advocates and effective at political networking. There were a few VA officials, such as VA Administrator Max Cleland (subsequently a senator from Georgia) and, later, Deputy Administrator Chuck Hagel (who went on to become a US senator from Nebraska), Deputy General Counsel Bob Coy, Minneapolis VA Hospital Director Tom Mullon and VA Social Work Director John Fulton. Also, particularly in the early days, there were some very supportive veterans service organizations (i.e., American Legion, Disabled American Veterans, Paralyzed Veterans of America, Vietnam Veterans of America). It wasn't until later that other veterans service organizations became equally supportive.

Guerilla Warfare Tactics in the Bureaucracy

We soon learned it was necessary to engage in covert communications with Congressional allies on the Hill. We secretly provided leading or pointed questions or suggested areas of investigation to help them in querying the VA concerning the Vet Center Program. For example, we would discreetly suggest budgetary questions that would help Congress to pinpoint when (not if) the VA illegally siphoned off Congressionally-appropriated funding from Vet Centers to fund other VA programs, and would drop hints as to how to word "controlled Congressional correspondence requests" to the VA Central Office so that it would be difficult for the VA to avoid giving specific answers.

Before Ed Lord was called to Washington, DC, to join the national RCS staff, he was invited to testify before Senator Cranston's Committee that was scrutinizing the VA. His testimony had to be "reviewed" and approved by the Office of Management and Budget (OMB). OMB actually tried to find out where he was staying in Georgetown so that they could review his testimony; he changed hotels and showed up at the hearing to deliver his unsanitized comments.

Several very similar episodes occurred with various Congressional officials; whenever we were asked to prepare a written response "for the VA" to a Congressional inquiry, we were required to submit the responses first for approval by higher VA authorities and by the Office of Management and Budget (if there were any fiscal or budgetary implications) — and the allegiance of the reviewers was to the party in the White House. This caused us to have clandestine meetings, and to manipulate our prepared testimony for Congressional appearances so that OMB and higher-level VA officials could not curtail the communication of important information to Congress.

These were very exciting — and very dangerous — times. At the very same time that we were extremely busy establishing over 30 new Vet Center sites nationwide to supplement the original 91 sites, the Vet Center Program also was fighting to avoid premature termination. The work had hardly begun. But most high-ranking officials of the agency that paid for the program, both political appointees and many of those who were career VA bureaucrats, by and large did not support the Vet Centers and other specialized PTSD programs. Echoes of the guerilla war in Vietnam: both enemy and friend looked the same.

The complexity of the environment within which the veterans' programs were being launched and the very sensitive political nature of the Vet Centers made life difficult for those within the bureaucracy whose job it was to advocate for those programs. On the one hand, we were there to call for appropriate services to address war-related and other readjustment problems of veterans; on the other hand, as VA Central Office officials we were expected to toe the party line — as dictated by the 10th Floor VA officials, who were appointed by the Administration in the White House.

The late Lynda Van Devanter (a former Army nurse with the 71st Evacuation Hospital in Pleiku Province) came to VA Central Office to meet with high-level VA officials. Lynda was a very outspoken veteran advocate, especially on behalf of women Vietnam veterans. She also was an early leader of Vietnam Veterans of America. Lynda was a vocal and tenacious critic, particularly of the VA's remarkable lack of sensitivity and responsiveness to the special needs of women Vietnam veterans and of other war veterans.

Before her meeting, I spent a little time talking informally with her. (I had known her for years.) Later, my boss informed me that I should not be seen associating with Lynda, as it would damage the credibility of the Vet Center Program if one of its national officials was perceived to be friendly with critics of the VA. Instead of listening, and looking for ways to improve services, instead of attempting to develop productive and trusting working relationships with our critics, the VA, long regarded as insensitive and unresponsiveness to the needs of Vietnam vets, seems to have decided we should all just turn our backs.

PRO-MILITARY AND PRO-VETERAN: NOT NECESSARILY THE SAME

As the new National Associate Director for Counseling for the Vet Center Program, I was operating under the assumption that White House and Congressional forces who were pro-military naturally also were pro-veteran. It would appear that supporting a large, state-of-the art, well-trained and well-equipped military force would go hand in hand with supporting a large and state-of-the-art, well-trained and well-equipped veteran's health care system, to serve the needs of members of the armed forces after they were discharged from active duty. But, appearances can be deceiving. A number of VA and Congressional officials from both parties were very pro-military and anti-big government. However, this did not necessarily translate into being pro-veteran and supportive of a substantial federal budget to support medical, mental health and social programs for veterans.

At least one powerful factor driving opposition to the Vet Center Program was pointed out frankly by a VA (political appointee) official. Talking about PTSD could hurt recruitment! Talking about any of the serious long-term problems veterans were suffering from would scare people off. Thus, the very notion of PTSD was anti-war and anti-military. By letting the public know how injurious the war had been to so many veterans, we risked giving them the idea to think first, rather than rush to sign up. No wonder there was such a widespread tendency toward sanitization and silence about the longer-term impact of war.

THE CONFLUENCE OF POLITICS AND SCIENCE

The National Vietnam Veterans Readjustment Study (NVVRS)

Against the backdrop of the national political currents swirling in, around and through VA Headquarters and on Capitol Hill, there was a major problem that confounded our ability to generate proper support for continuing and expanding the Vet Center Program and other PTSD programs. The data about the nature, extent and severity of post-war problems among Vietnam and Vietnam-era veterans was inadequate. Even the VA health care utilization data was seriously flawed and inadequate.

Through all manner of behind-the-scenes politicking, including the invaluable and ceaseless efforts of such congressional staffers as Bill Brew and Richard Fuller, Congress approved funding for a multimillion dollar national prevalence study of veterans of the Vietnam era. Our office was delegated to oversee the NVVRS. Art Blank gave me the responsibility and authority to organize and facilitate the process to develop the Request for Proposals (or RFP) for this national study. [79]

Given the political implications of this multi-million dollar study, numerous authorities intensely scrutinized both the process for awarding the contract and the research design of the program. The methodology, implementation, and analysis of the findings needed to be reputable and scientifically impervious. On the one hand, there were many powerful persons and institutions, including (1) mental health professionals and researchers (including many within the VA's medical, psychiatric and administrative establishment in VA Headquarters and at VA Medical Centers), and (2) many members of Congress (including the pro-war and pro-defense adherents described in the previous section and in a number of the Veterans Service Organizations). They were skeptical that such a thing as war-related PTSD existed; or, if it did, they believed that it affected a very small number of veterans. Their conclusion beforehand was that there were not nearly enough veterans legitimately hurting from their war experiences to justify continuing, let alone expanding the Vet Center

---

79. For which I received a national VA Special Achievement Award. Although Art Blank and I seriously disagreed on many things, his support and interactions with me throughout this very complex process were invaluable; he deserves much credit for his indispensable contributions to the success of the ultimate awarding of the contract to implement the national study.

Program and the numerous specialized PTSD programs that were springing up at VA Hospitals and Outpatient Clinics nationwide. This large and extremely powerful group of persons and institutions was determined to insure that the study would be attacked and discredited if the results could be shown to have "inflated" in any way the number of veterans with PTSD. [80]

There was also the "pro-veteran" lobby, consisting of vocal and increasingly well-organized groups of Vietnam veterans, and their advocates and supporters, including a number of politicians, mental health professionals and some Veterans Service Organizations. This varied group initially believed that it was a mistake for the Department of Veterans Affairs to sponsor the study, since trust levels with the VA were not very high. Also, the VA did not have the requisite epidemiological research expertise to adequately evaluate research entities who might want to conduct the study, let alone had the expertise to oversee it in all its complexity. If the study had to be conducted under the auspices of the VA, the critics wanted it to be under the wings of our program, Readjustment Counseling Service. Furthermore, such critics believed that many higher-level VA officials had little genuine intent to insure that it came up with a valid measure of the extent of the problems of Vietnam veterans.

Among this group of critics there was a conviction that the true numbers of psychiatric casualties during the war, and the true numbers of Vietnam veterans with war-related PTSD and related post-war problems, were much larger and represented a far more a serious national health crisis than many officials were willing to acknowledge.

Under the microscope of these wildly divergent but equally ardent and vociferous critics on both sides of the issue, I was charged with attempting to insure that a fair and equitable process was structured and implemented, one that would result in a study that would be as impervious as possible from any valid criticisms from researchers, administrators, politicians and veterans on both sides of the issue.

The three major strategies implemented were:

---

80. And rightly so! Our program had no reason to wish to hype or exaggerate the true numbers of Vietnam veterans troubled by their war experiences — any more than critics had any grounds to justify suppressing the true extent of the problem (other than to protect budgets, and keep the word from getting out that people in the military can get hurt). It was long overdue for the country to learn the true extent and nature of the impact of the Vietnam War on its combatants.

1. Identifying and bringing in a team of non-VA epidemiologic researchers with impeccable research credentials to operate as consultants to myself and Readjustment Counseling Service. These included research luminaries such as Bruce Dohrenwend and Richard Hough.
2. Working with this team of expert researchers to craft a very detailed, comprehensive and sophisticated Request for Proposals (RFP) that would attract the best and brightest epidemiological researchers in the country, and
3. Operationalizing a sufficient set of evaluation criteria to insure that the selection process was transparent and objective, and would stand up to hard scrutiny from anyone.

These strategies were essential to insuring that the study would be unassailable on research or scientific grounds. The study was awarded to the Research Triangle Institute from North Carolina, under the leadership of Dick Kulka, Bill Schlenger and John Fairbank.

The NVVRS was the largest and most sophisticated psychiatric epidemiological survey ever conducted on veterans of any era of military service. The national prevalence data about PTSD and readjustment problems among Vietnam-era veterans was startling to many people (though John Wilson had projected similar numbers several years earlier). [81]

1. Fully 15.2% (or 478,000) of the 3.14 million Vietnam theater veterans had current PTSD
2. 20.6% of African-American theater veterans had current PTSD
3. 27.9% of Hispanic theater veterans had current PTSD
4. An additional 11.1% (or 350,000) veterans had "partial" PTSD.
5. The percentages of physically disabled war veterans who had current PTSD were even higher.
6. Finally, the *coup de grace*: only a tiny fraction of such veterans had ever seen a VA mental health professional for their war-related PTSD.

This scientifically reputable national study has never been seriously challenged as to the validity of its methodology and findings. The reported results sent shockwaves throughout the VA and Congress.

---

81. Kulka et al, *Trauma and the Vietnam War Generation.*

Finally, there was strong scientific empirical evidence from a highly reputable source to support the countless testimonials and narrative reports from clinicians and veterans nationwide, and clinical program statistics showing that this post-war problem existed in mind-boggling numbers.

This was what was needed to galvanize congressional support for Vet Centers and other VA specialized PTSD programs.[82]

VET CENTER CASUALTIES AND THE PUSH TO COOPT THE VET CENTER PROGRAM

During the first several waves of hiring, we went out of our way to avoid setting artificial constraints on the basis of certain formal educational degree requirements. We hired Vietnam veterans, men and women, and others who were deeply committed to and believed in our mission. Naturally, in hiring a large number of staff in a short period of time throughout the country, mistakes were made and some of the new hires turned out to be poor choices. But, beyond that, many of the good staff members we did hire (Central Office officials included) had personal unresolved issues about the war, and about the misunderstanding and lack of recognition that Vietnam veterans had to confront since the war — and some had serious issues about the agency administering the program, the VA. We knew this; however, we felt that what was most important was to hire a staff who would be staunch advocates for the veterans and had counseling and/or outreach skills — and who either had first-hand knowledge of what vets had been going through or who were otherwise highly sensitive to and concerned about helping to alleviate the impact of war. We recognized that such staff were particularly vulnerable to job-related burn-out — the job meant much more than a paycheck to them.

"Going beyond the normal VA requirements" was characteristic of our program. Unfortunately, our personal war-related issues and involvement inevitably eroded some of the professional boundaries, as a number of staff tended to become overly involved with clients, speak too bluntly in interactions with the

---

82. In retrospect, my work in managing the process that resulted in awarding the NVVRS, against almost imaginable odds, might be my most important contribution at the national level to Vietnam veterans. A great many other individuals made crucial contributions as well, unfortunately, too many to name, here — although Art Blank, my VACO boss, deserves to be at the top of the list.

"regular" VA hospitals and officials, and more often than not go above and beyond normal work requirements to serve the veterans.

We recognized all of these dynamics, and understood that we had a corollary responsibility to provide guidance and support to help such staff do their jobs effectively and not burn out. Such support was especially essential due to the small size of Vet Center staffs — the typical staffing was three- or four-person teams — who worked in community-based sites, oftentimes isolated from any support services. Many of them faced overwhelming workloads. Finally, our mandate for the staff included doing substantial outreach to veterans, which further exacerbated the inadequate staffing and high workload stressors. There was no doubt — conscientious Vet Center staff, under the best of circumstances, were at high risk.

And many did burn out — they left the Vet Centers. Some went voluntarily and many were "forced" out by higher program officials. Indeed, one of our four national officials became notorious for his site visits to Vet Centers that had been identified as problematic, that is, they were either under-producing or were outspoken critics of national Vet Center or local VA Hospital policies. He was sanctioned by the Director of Readjustment Counseling Service to do whatever necessary to bring such staff under control. In many cases, the bureaucratic choice was made to get rid of them. Our egalitarian, grassroots based program began to shift into an autocratically-run bureaucracy. And, worst of all, the welfare of our individual staff and the quality of services provided seemed not to be the highest priorities. Rather, compliance with central dictums and increasingly, sustaining a high body count of clients took precedence. Once again, there was a remarkable parallel to my Vietnam experience, where the individual mental health welfare of the psychiatric casualty was never the highest priority of the military.

Hundreds of Vet Center staff left or were forced to leave. Some who were fortunate to have the right professional degree were able to obtain positions with the regular VA or in the community. Others went on work-related disabilities. Untold numbers ended up unemployed or in serious emotional straits.

Playing the political game at the national level both within VACO and with Congress, OMB and the White House, was not as rewarding to me as it seemed to be to some others. Also, as may be almost inevitable in bureaucracies, innovative programs with more liberal guidelines are frequently forced, over time, to adhere to the more the rigid and restrictive operational and procedural rules of the larger organization. The Vet Center Program was no exception. Consequently, I found myself in serious conflict with new policies and procedures.

There was a push to hold Vet Centers to "body counts" (the number of new vets and total vets seen), with far less attention paid to the quality of the services provided. Perhaps equally harmful was the "body count mentality" that prevailed over everything else: too close a parallel to Vietnam, for many of us. There was a significant increase in required documentation, and the submission of detailed records. In addition, it was proposed that all Vet Center Team Leaders be required to be mental health professionals as defined by narrow VA guidelines. This policy would preclude outstanding leaders from being considered for any vacant Team Leader position if they did not happen to have a VA-approved mental health degree.[83] Illustrating the absurdity of this requirement, Ed Lord, my Vet Center Central Office colleague would not meet the new qualifications.

I strongly opposed applying a strict mental health professional degree requirement for Team Leader positions, rather than assessing leadership qualities as the primary qualification. Findings from a survey that I had conducted among Regional Managers, who rated the outstanding team leaders, were dismissed as irrelevant. Requiring VA-designated professional mental health degrees for our Team Leaders would have rendered 54% of our outstanding team

---

83. I conducted a national survey with all of the Regional Staff throughout the country in order to gather some empirical data regarding the correlation between having a professional mental health degree and being an outstanding team leader, in hopes of facilitating an evidence-based national policy for team leader qualifications. I asked the Regional Staff two simple questions: *Who are or were the outstanding team leaders in each of your regions?* (A number of outstanding Team Leaders had already left the program.) Factors to consider included leadership abilities, successfully establishing collaborative relationships with community resources and leaders, etc. Sixty-nine former or current Team Leaders were identified as outstanding. Important characteristics of these 69 outstanding team leaders were:

68% were Vietnam theater veterans and 19% were Vietnam Era veterans; 91% had substantial prior community-based human services experience; 91% had substantial prior supervisory experience; and less than half (46%) had a graduate mental health degree per the VA definition — PhD in clinical or counseling psychology or a clinical psychology doctoral degree (19%), or a MSW (27%) or a clinical nurse specialist (0%). On the other hand, over one-half of the outstanding team leaders (54%) had a variety of other graduate degrees (such as an MA in counseling or in psychology) or an undergraduate degree in a variety of fields, or an RN degree—and 3% didn't have a college degree.

leaders ineligible. My opposition was chalked up to "unresolved Vietnam-related issues," and characterized as "resistance to authority."

Regional staff informally called me the Chief of Feelings, in recognition of my efforts to maintain open and interactive national office communications with the Regional Manager staff and Team Leaders. Ed Lord and I valued them highly. However, our particular orientation and priorities were not in step with those of other national Vet Center officials. It was time to move on. And so I did, as did Ed not long afterwards.

GROUNDWORK FOR A RETURN TRIP TO VIETNAM

The faded dream of helping to lead a progressive and innovative Vet Center Program was more than compensated for by a wonderful new opportunity. I was selected to be the first director of the 33-bed specialized Post-Traumatic Stress Treatment Program (PTSTP) at the American Lake VA Medical Center, next to Ft. Madigan, Tacoma, Washington (1985-1992). I had the opportunity to create the staffing pattern, which included a number of veteran peer counselors to complement the excellent nursing staff. I made it a priority to hire as many qualified war veterans for counseling positions as possible, so that almost 60% of the staff in our program were vets — by far the highest percentage of war veterans of any hospital-based PTSD program in the country.

I took advantage of this unique opportunity to join with Ann Gregory (Vietnam vet nurse and the nurse manager for the program) to lead the design and implementation of the program from the ground up. It was a humbling responsibility to serve veterans from an 11-state catchment area in the greater Northwest and Alaska. Central to our ongoing success was the decision of a close friend and fellow Vietnam veteran who was the Team Leader at the Eugene (Oregon) Vet Center at the time, Steve Tice (physically disabled vet of Hamburger Hill), to join me as Assistant Program Director.

Our program developed a national and international reputation, and we were soon flooded with veterans applying for admission; indeed, the waiting list rose to and remained at 150 to 200 veterans — by far the highest waiting list in the country. [84] And there were other specialized in-patient PTSD programs that also had earned very positive reputations through the Vet grape-vine — such as at West Haven, CT (directed by David Reade Johnson), at Augusta, GA (directed by Lee Hyer), at Menlo Park, CA (directed by Fred Gusman) and at

Northampton, MA — and later at Brecksville, OH (directed by Beverly Donovan).

60 Minutes and Our War-Focus Therapy Groups

The national and international reputation of the PTSTP was enhanced by several high-profile events, media coverage and very innovative treatment modalities. 60 Minutes and Dan Rather were doing a major story on the VA and specifically requested to film our program. In particular, they wanted to film our war-focus therapy groups as they were happening, uncensored and unrehearsed. Our war-focus groups were the heart and soul of the program; in them, vets and staff worked together, frankly and emotionally dealing with very highly charged long-standing issues from the war.

Despite some concern that the program could backfire, or turn into an expose of the VA and hurt our program, we took the risk and agreed to be filmed. And in June, 1988, "The War Within," a special CBS segment, was broadcast. The PTSTP received extremely positive coverage in the story — although the overall VA did not. (Of course, that did not win us a lot of friends in high places in the VA.)

Visits to the Washington State Vietnam Veterans Memorial in Olympia

Part of our growing national reputation was based on the extremely positive word being put out through the veteran grapevine: the unprecedented large number of dedicated Vietnam veterans we had hired to staff a hospital-based PTSD program, the overall skill and sensitivity of our staff, and our innovative "in-action" therapies, several of which drew regular media attention.

Visits to veteran memorials were an important part of our treatment program. We found, as did many other treatment programs that grieving and resolution over losses were dramatically enhanced by taking groups of veterans to a state or to the National Vietnam Veterans Memorial. The therapeutic impact of visiting a memorial was quite powerful, and might include partici-

---

84. A fairly detailed description of the American Lake PTSD Program and observations about PTSD, stress recovery and obstacles and positive factors to the establishment and operation of a designated in-patient PTSD unit are provided in my written Congressional Testimony that I submitted along with my oral testimony at the V.A. Oversight Hearings Before the US Senate Committee on Veterans Affairs, July 14, 1988.

pating in rituals as a group of veterans, sometimes with lighted candles, speeches to or on behalf of fallen comrades, prayers and/or moments of silence, or leaving letters or other mementos at the site. This was a powerful experience even for veterans who did not know any of the names at that particular memorial.

American Indian Healing Rituals

A number of American Indian war veterans participated in our program. From them, we came to appreciate the power of traditional American Indian healing rituals, traditional healers and other cultural activities for American Indian war veterans, such as participating in Pow-Wows. Along with admitting a number of individual American Indian veterans over the years, we admitted two cohorts of American Indian war veterans to our program (and our hospital hired a traditional healer from the Kalama Tribe as a consultant, to be available for any of the veterans who might desire his assistance). And George Amiote, a Sioux Vietnam vet medic, contributed substantially to our cultural understandings. The first Indian cohort built a sweat lodge on the VA Hospital grounds that a number of them used regularly during their stay in the program, complementing our regular PTSD treatment. This was a very important addition to the healing process for a number of our veterans, both American Indian and non-Indian. [85]

The interface of culture and trauma as manifested by the historical usage of the sweat lodge and accompanying rituals has been eloquently described by John Wilson. [86] Wilson also consulted with Bruce and Char Webster of Port Angeles, Washington, two of the early non-Indian pioneers who utilized a combination of wilderness and "sweats" as part of the healing process that they offered to Vietnam vets with PTSD. [87]

---

85. R.M. Scurfield, "Healing the warrior: Admission of two American Indian war-veteran cohort groups to a specialized in-patient PTSD unit." *American Indian and Alaska Native Mental Health Research: The Journal of the National Center,* 6 (3) (1995), 1-22.

86. J.P. Wilson, "Culture and trauma: The sacred pipe revisited," in J.P. Wilson (Ed.), *Trauma, Transformation and Healing. An Integrative Approach to Theory, Research and Post-Traumatic Therapy* (New York: Brunner/Mazel, 1989), 38-71. For a discussion of the specific problems and approaches recommended for addressing the readjustment needs of American Indian Vietnam veterans, see: H. Barse, T. Rascon, D. Johnson, S. Flame, E. Hoklotubbee, H. Whipple, R. LaDue, T.Holm & S.Silver, *Report of the Working Group on American Indian Vietnam Era Veterans. Submitted to Readjustment Counseling Service, Department of Veterans Affairs* (Washington, DC, May, 1992).

Several American Indians have objected strenuously to non-healing thera-pists utilizing sweat lodge and other American Indian healing rituals outside of proper cultural and community context — and/or over utilizing such with non-Indians. "The problem with being part of a ceremony done without respect for tradition and the support of the tribal community is that an illusion is created in the participant that the ceremony will cure his pain...Finally, there is a limited range of people who might be reasonably expected to benefit from participation in traditional healing ceremonies. We would find it difficult to imagine that someone who was not born into the tradition and who has not been trained in the sacred ways would apprehend and benefit fully from such participation. This would, on the face of it, severely limit the advisability of a non-Indian offering such ceremonial healing or of a non-Indian beneficiary realizing a curative effect."[88] At the same time, there are prominent American Indian healers who do not agree with reserving American Indian rituals exclusively for American Indian participants. Also, a number of non-Indian clinicians and veterans self-report positive benefits from such participation. Adequate attention cannot be given here to fully discuss the important and varying viewpoints on this important and multi-faceted subject. Perhaps most importantly, the utmost respect for the healing traditions must be paramount if we are not to degrade the American Indian culture any more than the White culture has already done over the centuries.

At one Pow-Wow in the Northwest, there was a warrior recognition cer-emony. I went, with many others, into a large building with arena-like seating. As we settled into our seats, a speaker opened the ceremony and reminded everyone that we were there to pay honor to the military veterans who were present. I was one of a handful of non-Indian persons present. The building was full of families, young and old, children, youth, adults and elders. There was a palpable feeling of community, even to me an outsider. And I sat back to observe and enjoy. And then it happened. The speaker asked that all veterans in the building, of all eras and wars, come down to the center of the arena to join in the recognition walk and ceremony. I watch as the Indian veterans start wending their way down the aisles. A few of my companions then tell me that I should be

---

87. J. Walker & B Webster, "Reconnecting: Stress recovery in the wilderness," in J. P. Wilson, *Trauma, Transformation and Healing*, 159-195.

88. In D. Johnson & R. LaDue, "Traditional healing: A cultural and community process," in H. Barse et al, *Report of the Working Group on American Indian Vietnam Era Veterans*, 39-42.

going down there, too. I am surprised and feel like I would be intruding on "their" ceremony. But no, they are quite insistent; I was a veteran, a warrior, wasn't I? And so I reluctantly agree. I finally make it to the arena, and am feeling rather self-conscious, a white guy among all these Indian veterans, and even more so a white guy standing down here with hundreds of Indian people up in the stands looking down. Surely, they must be wondering who the heck I am and why I'm here. The ceremony begins, and we are led in a procession around the arena, the sounds and throbs of the drums and chanting seeming to pick up in intensity and loudness. As the Indian vets are walking in the procession, they begin moving in an Indian way that I won't even attempt to describe — with this rather stiff-legged and stiff-necked white guy among them.

As my self-consciousness begins to recede, somewhat, I become aware of a feeling — not of self-absorbed embarrassment — but of pride, welling up inside, as I participate in an Indian ceremony to honor their (and all) veterans/warriors. My head comes up a little higher, and I am more aware of my fellow veterans in the procession and how absorbed in the procession they are.

And then I look up and I allow myself to really see, for the first time during the procession, the remarkable energy and spirit of recognition and joy emanating from the sea of people surrounding us in the stands. It is an extraordinary feeling, one that itinerant Ray is a total stranger to: an entire community of four generations who are showering us veterans with warmth, appreciation and yes, love. This is intoxicating in the most positive of ways, almost overwhelming; I don't remember when I have felt so accepted.

And the "high" of this experience lasts long after the ceremony has ended. It is only later that I find myself having a profound bittersweet reaction: the recognition that many non-Indian veterans (and those Indian veterans who may have become permanently alienated from their tribes and Indian heritage) are living with the experience of having been rejected, scapegoated, an un-welcome home — or silence. And they never had, nor will they ever have, this profound depth of mutual and multi-generational bond of community and heritage that is anchored in generations of tribal tradition, identity and support for their warriors. It isn't even possible within the communities that many of us were raised in, is it? And the scab comes off an old wound that so many vets carry with them...And at the same time, I continue to savor an appreciation, a taste of the extraordinary power of community that is anchored in generations of tribal history and still connects intimately with proud warriors in proud Indian country.

Outward Bound Adventure-Based Therapy

Several staff members, like Jim Burke, Shawn Kenderdine, and Tom Olson, were involved in outdoor activities like hiking, kayaking, camping and rappelling — popular pastimes in the spectacular wilderness areas of the Northwest. We consulted with a former Green Beret commanding officer in Vietnam, (Ret.) Col. Robert Rheault (who had become involved in Outward Bound activities with the Northampton PTSD program in Massachusetts) [89] Then, I enlisted the participation of the PTSD Program at Augusta, Georgia, led by psychologist Lee Hyer, and made a successful application for an Outward Bound grant through the Paralyzed Veterans of America.

The vets we took on our Outward Bound course were led by outstanding staff from the Pacific Crest Outward Bound School in Portland, Oregon, and several of our staff went along as co-participants. We pushed the envelope of the typical physical ability requirements of Outward Bound to include a number of physically disabled, even wheelchair-bound, veterans. Our Outward Bound trips, over a two-year period, typically included a combination of river rafting, camping, hiking and rappelling. The OB trips at both our programs, by and large, turned out to be "corrective, positive and inspiring adventure-based experiences" that helped to promote the uncovering and treatment of unresolved war-related issues. The positive bonding while on Outward Bound further promoted vet-to-vet positive relationships; only now it was during Peacetime, and no one was killed or wounded. Last but not least, going on Outward Bound brought many of the veterans experiences of joy and success — something that had been in short supply for all of them ever since Vietnam.

The empirical results of our companion program evaluation of our Outward Bound activity did not indicate a substantial improvement in psychiatric symptoms. However, the personal narrative testimonies of many of the participants were almost universally very positive, and in many cases the impact appeared to be compelling. [90]

---

89. B. Rhealt, "Outward Bound as an adjunct to therapy in treatment of Vietnam veterans," in T. Williams (Ed.), *Post-Traumatic Stress Disorder: A Handbook for Clinicians*, 233-237. See also C.M. Stuhlmiller, "Action-based therapy for PTSD," in M.B. Williams J.F. Sommer (Eds.), *Handbook of Post-Traumatic Therapy* (Westport, CN: Greenwood Press, 1994), 386-400.

I found peace within myself on this trip — the first time since Nam...really enjoyed being around you guys; usually, I go by myself or only with my wife, to get away. I have learned to enjoy myself again!

I felt such joy...One time I looked over at [fellow veteran on the outing] while we were paddling down the river, and he was so full of life, and yelling. He then said to me, "I'm charged; I wouldn't change this for anything..." And, I felt really happy to see that man I love so much finally be so happy. I had a lot of issues come up for me on the trip — trust, confidence, fear, willingness to take responsibility — like when the OB staff made me be the boat captain. I had been hiding from it...than, after doing it, I started trusting myself again, for the first time in a long, long time.

I had to depend on people, and had to trust them, and I have a great fear of drowning...I didn't want to depend on people, having people pushing me around in my wheel chair over some of the rougher terrain. I found that I could depend on others; we were really working as a team by the third day. All in all, I now feel that I can go anywhere if I'm willing to let others help!

I remember with a tremendous mixture of awe, admiration and absolute amazement what I was privy to witness and be a small part of when so many veterans were able to conquer their own particular fears or disabilities. One Korean War Navy veteran who had never been back in a boat since his traumatic war experience and who suffered from a serious chronic pulmonary disorder. We had to have an oxygen tank available on-board as we were rafting through rain-swollen gorges and rapids in Oregon. And the sense of accomplishment for that veteran after almost 40 years of traumatic memories associated with being on the water was one of the most liberating I have had the honor of witnessing.

This trip restored my confidence in myself as a man. I feel now that I still got it — I was feeling real sad for myself for a real long time (30-years of substance abuse). The trip relaxed a lot of my stress; in fact, my sleep on the trip was remarkable. I hadn't slept that well in decades. The highlights for me were the thrill of going through the rapids, and my physical stamina?it was there! That paddling — maybe I can go back to work again. I now want to go back to sea. I'm a seaman — always have been, but stayed from it all these years.

And a few months later I was humbled to receive a wooden model of a boat that the veteran had carved for me, in memory of our being on the raft together, with our two first names on the side as the name of the boat: "Ray-Bob."

I found myself experiencing some of the fears and processes that the other vets had to go through on Outward Bound trips, something that confronted me with my greatest fear: of heights. Well, okay, Ray, here you are. Waiting on the

---

90. L. Hyer, R.M. Scurfield, S. Boyd, D. Smith & J. Burke, "Effects of Outward Bound experience as an adjunct to in-patient PTSD treatment of war veterans," *The Journal of Clinical Psychology*, 52 (3) (1996), 263-278.

top of this rock plateau for your turn to rappel down this 60-foot cliff (something I have never done or wanted to do in my life, thank you). You're the program director, you're along on this first Outward Bound course, and so you damn better come through...I am remembering what the Outward Bound instructor said earlier, that if you are really terrified about something on this trip that it might be best to go ahead as soon as possible and do it — because the longer you wait, the more the fear will build up and the more you will be increasingly (and stressfully!) preoccupied with doing it. And so, I am standing around on the back of the rock (as far as one can get away from the edge of the cliff!) with several other vets who seem almost as terrified as I know I am feeling. My terror welling up inside me, and I once again am wondering how I could have been so stupid as to get myself into this situation in the first place! And I know that it's too damn late to back out now; after all, I'm the damn program director, and a former Army officer: you mean that I'm not going to carry through and do my part!

And I am try all kinds of self-talk in an at tempt to pump myself up to the point where I can actually move my ass up to the front to take my turn. (Yes, I am actually trying to put into practice the very kinds of advice that I give so easily to the vets). And, simultaneously I'm giving verbal encouragement to the other vets and staff as well. Well, to get to the bottom line: yes, I actually did take my turn and rappel down that cliff. But I was so damn scared that I wasn't able to enjoy any of it until I was probably about 20 feet off the ground. Would I do it again? Not in this lifetime; although I did feel pretty good about having faced what has been my most prevailing and chronic fear since childhood.

And then on a subsequent Outward Bound trip with another cohort of vets, one of the most amazing feats occurred: one which I get to see pictures of and hear discussed in the debriefing that regularly occurs back at the program following each Outward Bound trip. A wheelchair-bound veteran is up on top of the rock. He wants to rappel down the 60-foot cliff. I can't even imagine him doing it. And, with the assistance and support of the Outward Bound staff who give him instructions and get him hooked up to the equipment, he starts edging backwards slowly towards the cliff's edge, slowly playing out the rope. And, he slowly starts going backwards over the crest and down the top edge of the cliff.

And he continues to "walk" over and down the face of the cliff. And everyone is cheering wildly in support, watching with utter wonderment as this magical event unfolds. A look of absolute and unmitigated joy and of accomplishment is absolutely radiating from him as he makes it down the face of the cliff, a physically disabled vet who has been suffering from serious PTSD for years. And that glow is still there when he describes his experience to the rest of us back at the program.

I cannot express my amazement and sense of privilege, being even a second-hand witness to this inspirational accomplishment by a man who has had extremely low self-esteem for so many years. And he was just one of many vets who participated, over the years, in our Outward Bound project.

Helicopter Ride Therapy

One of our peer counselors, Elke (Faleafine) Zeerocah, a reservist in the National Guard, and former spouse of a veteran, originated the idea of taking veterans up in helicopters flown by the Washington State Army National Guard as part of their stress recovery. The distinctive whomp, whomp, whomp sound of choppers seems to be ingrained in all Vietnam veterans. Every one of us has had memorable experiences associated with helicopters, and they are oftentimes triggered by the sights and sounds of choppers.

> Even among the enemy:
>
> In my bedroom, on many nights the helicopters attack over-head. The dreaded whump-whump-whump of their rotor blades bringing horror for us in the field. I curl up in defense against the expected vapor-streak and the howling of their rockets.
>
> But the whump-whump-whump continues without the attack, and the helicopter image dissolves, and I see in its place a ceiling fan. Whump-whump-whump. [91]

To make a long story short, we developed the only, or by far the first, helicopter-ride activity ever implemented as part of PTSD treatment. [92] Our helicopter ride project continued successfully for over three years. Over 300 Vietnam and other war veterans took a helicopter ride, with remarkably positive and impressive results. [93] It is important to note that we did not force any veteran to actually go up in a helicopter; however, each veteran in our program was required to accompany his or her cohort to the Army Air Field and to support those who wanted to experience flying in a chopper again. As it turned out, over

---

91. Bao Ninh, *The Sorrow of War*, 42.
92. Any readers interested in this subject are encouraged to read our seminal journal article: R.M. Scurfield, L.E. Wong & E.B. Zeerocah, "An evaluation of the impact of 'helicopter ride therapy' for inpatient Vietnam veterans with PTSD," *Military Medicine*, 157 (1992), 67-73.

VIRTUAL-REALITY THERAPY

There has also been exciting development of a virtual-reality therapy intervention. [a] I was contacted in 1994 by one of researchers in the group developing the program, David Ready, and provided him with considerable video footage and written materials about our helicopter ride project and protocol. While the virtual therapy intervention obviously has the potential to be accessible to a much greater number of trauma survivors than actual helicopter ride therapy, there were many remarkably efficacious aspects of our real-world or in-vivo project that it is extremely doubtful could be even close to replicated through an individually administered virtual therapy medium, such as:

- Being part of a therapy group involved in a 12-week intensive inpatient program with remarkable peer bonding
- Going go together with one's peer group to the Army Air Field to participate together in the rides
- Being at the Air Field to welcome and support one's fellow and sister veterans before and after the flights
- The visceral and experiential components of being in an actual Huey helicopter and that was piloted by Vietnam veterans.

All of these components are elements of what, together, made the helicopter rides such a remarkable therapeutic component of our PTSD program.

a. Discussed in a case report by researchers affiliated with Emory University: B.O. Rothbaum, L. Hodges, R. Alarcon, D. Ready, F. Shahar, K. Graap, J. Pair, P. Hebert, D. Gotz, B. Wills & D. Baltzell, "Virtual reality exposure therapy for PTSD Vietnam veterans: A case study." Journal of Traumatic Stress, 12 (2) (April, 1999), 263-271.

a three-year period, all but a handful of the veterans chose to take a helicopter ride. And with wonderful results.[94]

When I first heard about this ride, I was totally against it and was in a really bad mood when I woke up this morning. In the hangar, the crew chief said I could climb into that stripped Huey (it was undergoing a major overhaul). And there were no blood stains on the floor: it was nice and grey. And, that sense of incredible power came back to me, and the responsibility and job that I did on that bird in Nam [as a crew chief]. A piece of my time, of me that was lost over there...my youth...on this ride I, got to bring some of me back again.

93. Scurfield, Wong & Zeerocah, 71-72. See also: D. Largent, "Confronting the past: Vietnam vets fly back in time for stress therapy," *Evergreen* (Campqc Murray, Tacoma, WA: Washington Army and Air National Guard, January, 1989), 8-10; H.E. McLean, "A flight on the Huey 'memory machine,'" *Rotor and Wing International* (Peoria, IL: February, 1990), 60-62; and M. Wark, "Healing through helicopters," *The Evergreen State College Review*, 10 (3) (April, 1989), 1-3.
94. Scurfield, Wong & Zeerocah, 1992.

I sat there and found my hands in the position to hold my M-16, and yet it felt strange not having my gear on. It was a strange feeling to think back 20 years and remember the times of going into LZs (Landing Zones) both hot and cold, and tree-line hopping brought back the feeling of a hot LZ, trying to fire to get in, or trying to get the other recon team out. It helped me to bring back a lot of feeling and fears of going out on patrol, and the happiness of getting out without groundfire, knowing that this time I am home and don't have to go out and patrol tomorrow!

[Vietnam peer counselor on staff] This was one of my greatest experiences since Nam! The pilot, co-pilot and crew chief, Vietnam vets, they were tremendous, open, warm, and positive, experiencing with us...I had a lot of fear [on the flight]...and then it became real exciting...the LZ, thoughts of lots of hot LZs, and I was flashing on the day I was hit [wounded] in country. I actually "saw myself" being loaded onto the chopper; but, I was up there, looking down at the experience of me being hit...but from a whole different view 20 years later...I got the good part of Nam (the rush, the thrill) and not just the negative memories. It was like I had an overview of my whole tour up there...I had tears in my eyes...and I felt wonderful.

I brought along today on this ride all the young Marines who I helped to medevac in Nam, and all the ones who didn't make it...I have never felt this way before. In some spiritual way, those men were with me today...It was such a powerful experience!

All of the above activities enhanced and complemented office-based PTSD treatment. Indeed, each activity seemed to contribute in its own special way to furthering the PTSD healing process, above and beyond what could be accomplished in "the talking only" components of our treatment program, and they brought speedier therapeutic resolutions.

In addition, we had heard several stories of World War II veterans who had positive experiences in returning to former battle sites in Europe. All together, then, these "in-action" therapeutic activities created a natural basis and a rationale for a dramatic extension of the principles inherent in action-based activities: a return to Vietnam.

Chapter 6. The Controversial Plan

> Let me tell you my picture of war. It's a young boy's face. His mouth is open and I can see dirt on his teeth. His face is a mixture of dried mud and blood and a tear makes a path down his cheek. [95]

Bill Koutrouba, a heavily decorated combat medic, wanted to return to Vietnam — to exorcise that image. Mary Branham, former Army nurse, wanted to go back to where her hospital was in the late 1960s. Mary's most haunting memory is of a young soldier who had his arms, legs and face blown off by a mine. No one thought he would live — but he survived for three days before he was finally evacuated. Mary wanted to go back, because of the recurrent nightmares that began again three years ago, triggered by a divorce and family illness.

> I had just come from Kansas and was agog at all the weaponry, helicopters coming and going, patients being rushed in...You could smell infection a block from the hospital.

> I have no idea what happened to him — no idea what happened to anybody...Consequently, I see open, gaping wounds, not healed wounds.

Mary wants to return to Vietnam now, because of the recurrence of nightmares that began again some three years ago, triggered by a divorce and family illness.

> I expect [to see, now] a country at peace and rebuilding.[96]

---

95. Glamser, Deeann, "Vets: Finding peace. They'll return to Vietnam hoping to heal old wounds," *USA Today* (January 25, 1989), 1-A.
96. *Ibid.*

Bill and Mary were involved in a therapy group at the Seattle VA Medical Center for their war-related PTSD. While in this therapy group, Bill originated the idea of having their therapy group go back to Vietnam as a step in their recovery and healing process. [97] His therapist was unable to make such a trip, since she was pregnant. Bill found out about the PTSD program at the American Lake VA Medical Center, of which I was Director; we were asked to consider leading a therapy group back to Vietnam, a group that would include several members of the Seattle PTSD therapy group.

After much thought, I became convinced that a carefully prepared return trip to Vietnam could be justified therapeutically. Indeed, this seemed to be a logical extension of our long-standing and highly successful "helicopter ride therapy," along with our equally successful Outward Bound activity — taking veterans "beyond the walls of the counseling office" to help in their psychological and social recovery from the war.

And so, a new therapy group formed that combined some members of the Seattle group with other veterans with PTSD. This chapter briefly describes some of the planning and preparations for this first return trip to Vietnam by a therapy group of combat veterans with war-related PTSD.

GROUP COMPOSITION AND SELECTION CRITERIA

The 1989 group was comprised of seven male and one female veteran, representing all four branches of the service, both officers and enlisted personnel, front-line and combat support; seven were White and one was African-American. They manifested three quite different levels of severity of chronic PTSD (severe, moderate and relatively mild). All had received substantial mental health treatment at a VA and currently were linked with a primary VA mental health provider at either the Seattle or American Lake VA Hospitals. Each veteran's primary VA provider had assessed and recommended to us that they were at an appropriate place in their stress recoveries to be able, in all likelihood, to make a return trip to Vietnam a positive experience.

---

97. Leslie Brown, "Vets will face the enemy within on Vietnam visit," *Tacoma News Tribune* (December 8, 1988), B6.

This kind of trip had never been tried before. This was an "exploratory" approach to assess whether such a trip could be helpful to veterans active in PTSD treatment who were motivated to return to Vietnam. I was, in effect, performing a civilian version of my military role in Vietnam in 1968-69, that is, as an Army psychiatric social worker with military psychiatric casualties. We purposely selected veterans with a range of levels of severity of PTSD.

The trip was coordinated by Stevan Smith, a Vietnam veteran from Kent, Washington. As a former newsman at KSTW Channel 11 in Tacoma, Smith also coordinated the filming of the trip (in anticipation of a PBS documentary film, broadcast in 1990 as *Two decades And A Wake-Up*). Dan McConnell, of Seattle, was our publicist.

I kept a detailed journal before the trip, and each day during and immediately following our 1989 return trip to Vietnam. In addition, media interest in our trip resulted in numerous written and televised records, [98] including an interview by Ted Koppel on *Nightline* and on *Nightwatch* (CBS), following our return. [99] And so, in addition to my journal, the other two sources of information for this chapter and for several of the quotes from veterans are public records: the PBS documentary, and some twenty newspapers articles (from *The New York Times* to the *Bangkok Post*).

LOOKING BACK 11 YEARS LATER

On March 27, 2000, I took a look at my journal of the 1989 trip with a view to transcribing it. Indeed, this was the first time I had ever even re-read my journal! The trip had been stressful, with substantial intra-group conflict, and issues and conflicts that went on long after our return. And so, I just moved on. I assumed that this had been a once-in-a-lifetime experience, a difficult but invaluable learning experience — and one that I had absolutely no desire to repeat.

---

98. Timothy Egan, "Veterans returning to Vietnam to end a haunting," *The New York Times National* (January 24, 1989), 3-4; Glamser, "Vets finding peace. They'll return to Vietnam hoping to heal old wounds, *USA Today;* and Associated Press, "8 US veterans return to VN to cure trauma," *Bangkok Post* (January 29, 1989), 2.
99. Ted Koppel's *Nightline* (ABC), "A Healing Journey," March 7, 1989; *Nightwatch* (CBS), "Return to Vietnam," March 8, 1989.

It is essential to be aware of a number of historical and contextual factors that were present in 1989, for two critical reasons. They laid the foundation for the issues and developments that arose as part of our 1989 return trip; and very significant differences surrounded my second return to Vietnam, in 2000.

In 1989, there was an economic embargo in place against Vietnam, and the US government had no official diplomatic relations. Indeed, no direct travel to Vietnam from the US was allowed. We had to fly to a third country, one that did have diplomatic relations with Vietnam, such as Thailand or Hong Kong, and apply for a visa after arriving there, before we could fly to Vietnam.

This return visit was a unique opportunity to further the VA's and the mental health profession's knowledge about the possible therapeutic benefits of a return trip to Vietnam for veterans suffering post-war traumatic stress. Vietnam vets were starting to go back to Vietnam as tourists, anyway; if they sensed there was a need to go back, we were the logical institution to help them determine how to do it most effectively. However, The VA and the State Department did not see it that way and refused to sanction the trip or grant us official leave. [100] There was a concern that, if they were the only institution to support the mission, they would be blamed for any shortcomings and again criticized for short-changing the veterans.

The State Department was noncommittal: they did not approve the trip, but would not stop us from going, as private citizens. Their TWX dated 1.17.89, said,

> Re foreign travel. Raymond Scurfield and April Gerlock to Vietnam. US State Department advises it would be inappropriate to grant authorized absence for travel to Vietnam since the US does not have diplomatic relations with the country and there presently exists an economic embargo against Vietnam by the United States. VA evaluators note public relations activities that cannot avoid implicit role of VA in project...In view of the foregoing regret this request not approved. No objection to use of annual leave and/or leave without pay.

April and I thus became the two group leaders "responsible for the mental health welfare of all participants," with no medical, mental health or diplomatic back-up.

Some politicians and Vietnam veterans were very angry that we were going to Vietnam. They accused us of "consorting with the enemy," and con-

---

100. The VA was not the only institution to put roadblocks in the way of employees attempting to return to Vietnam. Steve Smith chose to resign from his position with Channel 11 because they were unwilling even to grant him sufficient leave without pay to make this return trip. It is not clear what motivated them.

tended that such a trip would undermine their continuing efforts to punish and isolate Vietnam. The issue of Prisoners of War and those Missing In Action (POW/MIA) was particularly contentious. MIA advocates argued for continued economic and diplomatic isolation until Vietnam had provided the maximum help in locating and returning any missing Americans, or their remains.

Perhaps the most potent opposition stemmed from the continuing unresolved war-related rage of many Vietnam veterans "against the Vietnamese." Such vets were preoccupied with suspicion, rage, fear and bitterness; and, they tended to focus such intense emotions on all Vietnamese, North or South Vietnamese, former military or civilians. Finally, many veterans were particularly enraged at the incongruity between what they perceived as special programs to assist Vietnamese immigrants in the US, and the relative neglect of American Vietnam veterans. Thus, there was a clear element of risk associated with our experiment. To our knowledge, this would be the first time that a psychotherapy group of war veterans with PTSD had ever returned to their former war zone. The same arguments were raised as had been offered earlier, in opposition to the hospital PTSD helicopter ride therapy program with the Washington State Army National Guard, and the river rafting and rappelling activities for both able-bodied and physically-disabled hospitalized psychiatric patient veterans, our decision to admit an entire cohort exclusively of American Indian war veterans to our program and the building of an American Indian sweat-lodge on the hospital grounds. The fact that our staff was comprised of about 60% Vietnam veterans (many of whom also had unresolved war-related issues) did little to mitigate the fears and suspicions raised by innovative thinking.

There was also a professional and legal risk. We could not rule out the possibility that some of the vets might psychiatrically decompensate while in Vietnam and act out in dangerous ways. If such psychiatric crises occurred, we, the therapists, could be held personally liable.

However, traditional mental health interventions appeared to be fairly ineffectual in treating PTSD. The positive results of the above-mentioned specialized interventions encouraged us to go further in what appeared to be a very promising direction. There were many veterans and non-veterans who were supportive of our trip. Even some who disagreed with our going also said that any war veteran who continued to suffer from war-related PTSD and was not satisfied with the results of PTSD treatment had the personal right to return to Vietnam if he/she thought that such a trip had a reasonable chance of promoting his/her personal stress recovery.

Media Coverage

There was a remarkable amount of media coverage and several national television affiliated film crews were on hand for various parts of the trip. The *Tacoma News Tribune* sent reporter Leslie Brown to accompany our group and write a series of in-depth articles. The media reported positively and constructively about the war-related and post-war difficulties of Vietnam vets, and the impact this trip might have.

Thus, one of our objectives was met; we had hoped to provide a small window onto Vietnam 1989, by sharing information that was not generally accessible to Americans and, most importantly, to Vietnam veterans and their families, due to the government's continuing embargo of Vietnam. National and international politics were still preventing hundreds of thousands of Vietnam veterans with unresolved PTSD issues from the war from gaining any understanding of what Vietnam was like, today. That left veterans with no image but their memories, frozen in time, stuck in the horrific quagmire of the Vietnam of twenty years before.

A few of our group members were caught up in the onslaught of media exposure, and were highlighted in the news. Sometimes, this led to tension within the group. But, by and large, the venture was so stunning that when we were in Vietnam, the cameras ceased to exist in our consciousness.

The Eight Veterans

It took courage for the eight veterans to go on this unprecedented journey back to Vietnam. [101]

1. Mary Branham. US Army. Served one year tour as a triage nurse, mostly at the 93rd Evacuation Hospital in Long Binh (near Saigon). Mary determined the degree of injury and priority of patients going into surgery. In her words, "I sent patients to O.R., war, or the Dying Room."

2. Jim Kessi. US Army. Served one year tour, assigned to A Company 3/22nd — 25th Infantry Division in the Cu Chi area. He was one of the few men in his unit not be wounded or killed during his tour of duty.

---

101. Most of this information on the participating veterans is excerpted from: "Media Advisory," February 16, 1989, prepared by Dan McConnell, The McConnell Company, Seattle, WA.

3. William Koutrouba. US Army Three tours as a medic, with Special Forces and with the 1st Air Cavalry. He treated more than 200 seriously wounded soldiers, pulling many from the battlefield under fire. One of Washington State's most highly decorated veterans. Career military.
4. Francis (Jake) Lafave. US Air Force. Korean War and Vietnam War veteran. Served one tour in Vietnam and returned on assignments for a month on two other occasions. Although assigned to Nha Trang as an Air Force advisor, he experienced a wide variety of combat exposures.
5. Edward Marcin. US Army. 33 months in Vietnam as an armorer, engineer mechanic, supply clerk, equipment operator, to include helping to build roads and bridges. Served with the 69th Signal Battalion, and with the 34th Engineering Battalion.. Career military.
6. Billy Ray Pope. US Army. Served an extended tour in Vietnam. Assigned to the 1st Medical Battalion, 1st/26th, 1st Infantry Division. Served in the Phous Vinh and Bien Hoa areas.
7. David Roberts. US Navy. Two-tours. Assigned to River Ron 13, River Division 132 as a boat gunner, coxswain and radioman as a "riverine" in the Mekong Delta. Worked night ambushes, insertions, searches and fire support. Hit by a B-40 rocket during Operation Giant Slingshot.
8. Robert Swanson. US Marine Corps. Assigned to the D Battery 2nd Battalion, 11th Marines. Gun operator; served on battalion landing team sent to hot spots in coastal regions.

CAVEATS ABOUT MY DIARY ENTRIES

First, a disclaimer about the recollections that form the basis of this chapter and many of the later sections: memories are very tricky and complicated mechanisms, and especially so when one is under stress. This, plus the fact that I did not transcribe my original journal entries until 11 years after the trip, means that I may unintentionally have misrepresented what actually happened, particularly some of the details.

Naturally, I observed and recorded many things about this trip that involve other participants. Each of the eight veterans gave permission to the media to be identified by their full names, most of them were interviewed by several newspapers, and each veteran is filmed in *Two Decades and A Wake-Up*. Thus, much of the story of this trip is a matter of public record. Nonetheless, in some instances I leave the identity of the speaker unspecified and in other ways seek to preserve confidentiality.

Finally, the journal entries have been edited slightly to provide the essence of the experience accurately but succinctly.

1989 JOURNAL ENTRIES

January 6: What would I say differently to psychiatric casualties now versus what I said in 1968?

It is 20 years since I was in Vietnam treating acute psychiatric casualties. I'm starting to get stoked about returning. What have I learned in over 20 years that I can use now, to help vets who have chronic PTSD — versus "what I didn't know then" (Bob Seger song) 20 years ago? I also am thinking about the fact that I do not remember one first or last name of any of the numerous Vietnamese people I knew in Vietnam, with the exception of "Fairy" — the nickname of my Vietnamese girlfriend. And, I only remember the names of three Americans whom I served with: James Janecek, my 98th Medical Detachment Commanding Officer (CO), Pete Lynn, psychologist, and Lyman Sales, a hospital chaplain.

What I would I do differently, in treating psychiatric casualties — knowing what I know now? What exactly do I know now, or believe, about PTSD that would be useful in being in a psychiatric role in a war zone today? I would have a quite different attitude. I would consider that 20-year chronic war-related PTSD is a distinct possible outcome of being exposed to war-trauma; during the war, we were taught that chronic war-related psychiatric problems were likely *only if we prematurely evacuated* someone out of Vietnam — versus treating and sending back to duty. In other words, that it was the premature evacuation that was more likely to result in chronic post-war symptoms than the exposure to war trauma *per se!*

What would I do and say differently to psych casualties in a war today? I still believe the three statements that we constantly reinforced with psych casualties in Vietnam are appropriate today:

- You are suffering an expectable and temporary reaction to a very serious situation you have been exposed to. That is understandable.
- Right now, you are probably feeling guilt or shame that you let your buddies down, or doubt that "you have what it takes to be a man."
- You will recovery shortly and will be going back to duty very soon.

What might I add or say that I did not do in 1968-69?

- If you get psychiatrically evacuated out of country, you may feel even more guilt and shame that you "deserted" your buddies and "failed." I want you to remember me telling you this now. It is a natural reaction; but what do you have to ashamed of, if it is medically necessary to be evacuated?

- I want to be frank and honest with you. When you do return to duty, there is the risk that by going back to your duty station, you may suffer additional psychological difficulties if you are exposed to additional trauma. That is understandable, and you should recognize if this is happening and not think that you are going crazy or are a "weak" person. However, you must pay close attention; do what you have to do to protect yourself and survive during the remainder of your tour. Let's review two of the ways that soldiers psychologically survive being exposed repetitively to terrible events:

- Use your thoughts to detach yourself more from overwhelming negative feelings. "It don't mean nothin."

- Use tunnel vision: put your attention on the next thing that you have to do, and focus on that; also recognize that you have X months or days left in country and focus on what you have to do to make it through.

- Now, when you return to duty, continue to do the above. From here on, you will be very aware of what you're doing and why — making it a conscious choice — and thus you will be able to consciously adapt your survival techniques in order to increase your chances of survival.

In addition, there are things that all war veterans need to hear, whether they are or were psych casualties or not, before they leave the war zone and after returning home. The question is whether it is better to deliver this message perhaps "prematurely," to psychiatric casualties while they are in an acute stage, and still in the war zone, or later, when there is a substantial risk that the veterans are entrenched in post-war readjustment problems and have become chronic psychiatric casualties:

After the war, you may have become so conditioned during the war that you still tend to use, to a little or a great degree, the survival skills, attitudes, behaviors, that worked in Nam but are probably not appropriate for your life Stateside. After the war, you may not want to let go of "survival mode" for several good reasons. It's familiar: an intimate companion, an old friend you're pretty good at it, and it gets you some things you want: some power, some aliveness, adrenalin, feelings of security or safety. It's frightening to let go of things that are familiar (and that you have been doing for so long a period of time). What would you put in its place — or have to look at? If you let go of the survival mode, there will be an emptiness that you probably have been keeping submerged or have avoided. You have to recognize it if you find yourself not being able to "let go" of your Nam survival mode. If so, talk to somebody about it, perhaps at a VA Vet Center or specialized VA PTSD program. But don't continue to stay in isolation.

January 7: Orientation Tips.

A veteran who had recently returned from a private trip to Vietnam gave the following orientation to our PTSD therapy group. I am sorry that I did not record his name. These pointers may seem dated, as Vietnamese society has changed tremendously since 1989 and a new generation is in place; still, they reveal something of the culture at that time.

He told us that the Vietnamese would want to know if we were Russians or Americans. Many Vietnamese do not like and don't want to connect with Russians, who are seen as not very friendly, cheap, and trying to "take advantage."

The Vietnamese are very interested in "forgetting the past," and "starting fresh" — rather than holding a grudge. This is especially so for people in the South. They sincerely want more contact with Americans. The Vietnamese in the North are not as open to Americans.

Some vocabulary:

> Toi la naguoi (I am American)
> Chao Ong (Hello, Mr.)
> Chao Ba (Hello. Mrs.)
> Chao Em (Hello, to a boy or girl 15 or under, or one who is junior to you)

General tips:

> Don't be loud or rowdy
> Don't give out things in the streets, except perhaps to small children.
> Don't mention the past so much as now, and the future. People want to forget!
> Be prepared for lots of fireworks: February 6 is the Tet New Year (actual celebrations last several days).

January 13: VA Disability Compensation Under Threat.

Sometime in the last few weeks before leaving for Vietnam, the group is thunderstruck to hear from the Seattle VA Regional Office (VARO)[102] that the records of all of the group members have been pulled, in order to re-evaluate the level of disability compensation received by each veteran going on the trip. The argument was that a veteran who was well enough to travel to Vietnam might not be as disabled as had been thought, and therefore his disability compensation probably should be reduced.

Shockwaves reverberated through the group. Several of the vets had already expressed concern that participation in the trip could be held against them. Our response had been cautious.

The trip was not VA-sponsored, and April and I were not involved as VA employees or as VA therapists. We were all participating as private citizens. Therefore, there would not be any clinical recordkeeping, nor would April or I make any report to any VA official or department about our clinical impressions about the impact of the trip on any specific individual veterans. (We would file an "after-action" report giving overall impressions about the trip and its possible utility and impact in general on veterans who have PTSD.)

Certainly, none of us had any control over what the VARO might do regarding each vet's disability compensation, and we urged each trip member to take the risk into consideration. The choice was up to them.

We only asked that, if they decided to go ahead, they not say anything false or misleading while on this trip, or afterwards, about the impact it had. Making false statements in group meetings would destroy the integrity and trust among the group members, and we would very much need each other's support. Second, false statements would give a wrong message to the many veterans and others who would be following our trip closely through the media, and give veterans a false impression about the possible benefits and risks in returning to Vietnam one day — and that could be very damaging to the stress recoveries of many other veterans.

Each veteran agreed to go forward, with all that in mind; but the threat from the VARO made some of them cautious about saying how they were doing on the trip.

There is a conflict inherent in the relationship between the VA's system of disability compensation and medical and mental health treatment that is pro-

---

102. The VA Regional Offices are the veteran's benefits component of the Department of Veterans Affairs. VAROs are responsible to adjudicate and administer all claims by veterans for service-connected disabilities. For a further discussion of the very problematic relationship that exists between the VA's provision of mental health service and the VA's adjudication and administration of service-connected claims (which, in effect, pay a veteran to remain disabled, and financially penalize a veteran if the veteran shows improvement!), see discussion about the relationship between service connection and mental health treatment in: R.M. Scurfield, "The treatment of war-related trauma: An integrative experiential, cognitive and spiritual approach," in M.B. Williams & J.F. Sommer (Eds.), *The Handbook of Post-Traumatic Therapy* (Westport, CN: Greenwood Publishing, 1994), 181-203.

vided. Clinicians and veterans always have to be cognizant of the fact that, if significant clinical progress is documented in the VA medical record, such progress may well be used by the VARO to reduce or eliminate a veteran's disability claim. This means that the system of compensation, by design, gives an incentive for veterans to remain sick and disabled. [103] And so, the VARO added a dose of bureaucratic-induced stress to the Post Traumatic Stress accompanying us on our journey.

January 18: The last meeting before leaving for Vietnam. I am both angry about the VA's unwillingness to support creative and innovative efforts to help veterans, and relieved that I can go ahead on my own — no federal strings attached. The rejections by both the VA and the State Department have renewed my vigilance — there is still much to do to change attitudes in the bureaucracy and the government. Irony: this project is "too sensitive" to international relations for us to get approval from the feds — and yet, too unimportant for Channel 11 to give Steve Smith, the project organizer, an approved leave.

[We would talk more at informal get-togethers at a restaurant after the group meetings (here, I was not acting in a role that a typical "professional counselor" would accept; most counselors avoid informal social interactions under the premise that they can complicate or erode the counselor-client boundary).] At Denny's, tonight, a vet asserted that we could have won the war, if we had only had elite troops there, fought at night, with no visible base camps. But, he asked, is the attitude and mentality in place for the US to ever fight such a war? — His comment led me to wonder what it takes to do well in war, as a soldier. Who is a "hero" and what are the values a hero holds? What is taught in Basic and AIT (Advanced Infantry Training): not love, humanitarianism, mercy! Who would I most want next to me, if we were being overrun, or attacking a formidable foe, or being dropped in behind enemy lines? Probably not the same man I would want to live next door to, or see marry my sister, or welcome as my brother or father. If the end does not justify the means, has anyone told that to the military or the CIA or the extreme right or left wing?

---

103. *Ibid.*

GUILT — WHO IS RESPONSIBLE FOR WHAT HAPPENS IN A WAR ZONE?

April [the clinical nurse specialist and co-therapist on the trip] expressed her concern that I would get caught up in my own guilt issues from the war and possibly not be very functional as a therapist on this trip. I thought it was a fair bet that I would be a little spacey when we were in the Nha Trang area, but I didn't say anymore than that.

Judging from the extent and tone of my journal entries that follow, April's comments really stirred me up. The gist of the following thoughts are integrated as one component of a very effective therapeutic technique that I have formalized, "Technique to Determine Percentages of Responsibility."

This technique assists veterans and other trauma survivors to systematically explore and arrive at a more reasoned conclusion as to the extent of their individual personal responsibility for events that happened in the war zone, and their consequences. This is essential to the treatment process; many veterans and other survivors of trauma have inordinate amounts of self-directed guilt and blame, and/or are preoccupied with blaming others for what happened. [104]

> A secondary tragedy of the Vietnam War is that people who weren't there can and do blame individual military personnel for the situations they found themselves in during the war. [Some] average citizens find it easier to blame soldiers than the government and the voters who put them there and kept them there.

> The fault, or guilt, of many in the armed services is that they are sufficiently naïve and gullible to accept what they are told by their higher-ups.

> I have wrestled with the question of guilt myself, at different times. The psych team and I did send young men back into mortal danger, time after time. Whether it was right or wrong, from today's perspective, we were doing the very best we could, with the knowledge that we had at the time; and we were very conscientious in trying to help the individual soldier to the maximum extent possible. [105]

---

104. *Ibid.*, 186-193. This technique, "Percentages of responsibilities," has considerable applicability for survivors of many different types of human-induced trauma — a category of experience that is likely to induce the survivor to attribute exaggerated personal responsibility (or, in some cases, to minimize one's self-responsibility) for having been in the trauma to begin with, for behaviors engaged in during the event, or for having problems following the trauma. See also a full description of my "percentages of responsibility" therapeutic technique in G.R. Shiraldi, *The Post-Traumatic Stress Disorder Sourcebook. A Guide to Healing, Recovery and Growth* (Los Angeles: Lowell House, 2000), 186-193.

Of course, it is not that simple. In retrospect, subsequent to the war, I came to real-ize that I was not very sophisticated in my discernment of the motives and truths espoused by the military or civilian authorities.

Over several months in country, I also came to realize that several other forces were involved. The details may be different for combat troops and medical workers, but in the military there is a pervasive and necessary drive to train and form teams that function without question in ways that maximize the ability of the soldiers to fight quickly, and effectively, time and again..

Swirling through my consciousness are a torrent of thoughts and feelings:

- how much I had let myself be propagandized by Freudian thinking that considered very early life-experiences to be the key to understanding current-life functioning and psychiatric problems
- the medical model that emphasizes the unquestioned authority of the physician
- pro-defense political forces that promoted large military forces, an active military presence throughout the world, and have a significant economic motivation to fuel the industrial complex through such activities;
- and, last but certainly not least, historic stereotyping of how "real men" should act, think and feel.

This all converged in-country to buttress the notion the military promotes of what it is to be a "real man" — someone who does not break down in battle. Conse-quently, in effect we blamed the vet, psychiatrically, rather than giving due credit to the horrific consequences of being exposed to massive and protracted trauma.

Unit commanders and at times psychiatric personnel labeled the problematic vet as a "behavior problem" and suggested that he would be having problems whether in a war zone or Stateside, rather than considering him a psychiatric casualty of expo-sure to war trauma.

A double standard seems to exist. A civilian who suffers in an accident and is trau-matized can expect rehabilitation and compensation, and sympathy; yet, many vet-erans who have been traumatized in a war sanctioned by the government and society are treated prejudicially for "failing" in a war zone. [106]

Whose responsibility is the war, itself, and all that goes on in the war? The individ-ual soldier is usually held entirely and solely responsible for all of his/her conduct, both military and recreational, in the war zone. However, this singular focus denies or minimizes the reality and dynamics of war. The stressors and horrors inherent in conducting war are such that profound negative psychiatric impact on the combat-ant would be an expected outcome. Vietnam-specific stressors like the emphasis on body-count mentality and the consequent taking and withdrawing and retaking of terrain, over and over again, created psychological conditions difficult for anyone to withstand. Meanwhile, many citizens sitting in judgment, comfortably at home,

---

105. But, as Dave Roberts noted to me on June 25, 2004): "It wasn't good enough. The military can't survive if they tell the truth. They get the kids 'to fight for their country' — just like Iraq."

106. Dave Roberts, personal communication, June 25, 2004.

kept their blinders on about the impact of the national policies and society's role in promoting and prolonging the Vietnam War:

Hey, this is a lot going on, and we haven't even left yet for Vietnam. Here I go again — wow, I really did let April push a button somewhere in me! This is really tapping into, not just me, but to the terrible burdens that so many combatants as individuals have on their backs and in their souls for years and decades. Why in the hell should I or the combat vets be carrying all the guilt?! That's what a lot of non-vets, the public, others would like: for us to continue to take the blame and for them and the rest of the nation to get off scot-free. How easy it might be for us in Vietnam and all those people back Stateside who were so very lucky that we didn't have to be front-line soldiers. We didn't have to carry a weapon and come face-to-face in repeated situations where it was necessary that we would have to choose to kill or be killed. And be in so many other situations where it was a grey area whether it was necessary to kill. And Vietnamese women, children and the elderly were protagonists, allies and victims.

And, yes, I had been able to live up to my high ethical/moral standards, in most all that I did there. I was fortunate to know that I did the best that I knew how at the time, and I my monstrous or evil side did not come out...(thank God).

No: when a nation goes to war, every citizen of that country goes to war and should and must share responsibility for all that happens — there and then — and afterwards. This did not happen in the Vietnam War — in vivid contrast to World War II. So, any guilt that may be mine from having been so naive I channel into purpose and conviction and drive to attempt to make the system and society more responsive to the real needs of vets and the real psychiatric legacies of war:

All these forces at play, that have blamed the vets for their war-related problems!

All these forces that have encouraged vets to assume 100% of the blame for their war-time decisions and continuing post-war problems. All these forces that seem to be placing roadblocks to our intention to return to the Nam, the scene of our most vivid hauntings and other indelible peak life experiences.

As I am flooded with all of these thoughts, I become even more resolved and convinced about the right and indeed the ethical imperative that each of us has to participate in this daunting return trip to Vietnam. For better or for worse, we are not going to be denied this opportunity. Finally, our 7,000 mile return trip to the Nam is about to begin...

CHAPTER 7. RETURN TO VIETNAM, 1989

January 25: On our way to San Francisco and Bangkok

At the SEATAC (Seattle/Tacoma) airport, what beautiful and celebratory vibes from all the relatives and friends who came to see us off. Wow, what a contrast from when we each were heading off to a Vietnam that was at war! Of all people, a vet who is a graduate of our PTSD program, whom we had not seen for a year or longer, showed up at the airport to see us off. It was simply amazing; the positive change in him since he left our PTSD program was profound. It appears that our program played a big part in propelling his recovery, and then he took the next steps himself by going up to Okanagan log country. He has been humping logs all day long for several months; this seemed to be a release to get rid of some things he needed to "let go of." And now he's working hard (more a white-collar type job), he is not in PTSD after-care, and seems to be in a great space! We must be doing something right in our program, and this vet obviously is doing something right!

A man in a business suit stopped me by the security gate. He had recognized me from a picture in a newspaper. He said that he'd been in MACV (Military Assistance Command-Vietnam), 71-72, and that this Vietnam trip seemed like a great thing. He just wanted to tell me that, and wish us well. Just a 30-second contact: and it was beautiful.

The Vietnamese government lumped our group of veterans together with a tour group sponsored by Vietnam Veterans of America (VVA), from the Dayton, Ohio chapter. None of us knew each other, before, but we traveled together throughout VN in the same bus and stayed at the same hotels. However, we each had our own separate ventures during most of the days. This VVA chapter had taken several groups of veterans and others back to Vietnam. These were vets at large from the community, not necessarily PTSD patients under the VA. Also, they did not receive any mental health support while in VN.

A disjointed conversation took place while we were still at the airport. Don, the VVA tour leader, told me that he had been told by a high-ranking Vietnam veteran that "it's a lot easier to run a war than to run a country." But, the US "didn't know or wasn't willing to run the Vietnam War well."

Knowing that I would be writing about our trip, one of the vets in our group turned to me and said: "Will you write about me? Just say good things." And he smiled. Wow, these guys are so hurt and suffering, so short on self esteem, it's tragic.

Don (VVA) commented that the Vietnamese in the US were very jealous of each other and still fighting the war.

"Vicariously," I noted, "just like a lot of Vietnam vets who hate the fact of RVNs or other Vietnamese being in the US. The Vietnamese in the US ought to be pushing for normalization of relations in order to better reintegrate families. The Vietnamese, including former RVNs in the US, also deny their PTSD."

Don said, "We've brought several vets back here three or four times, and each time back they seem to heal a little more."

A vet interjected, "I'm glad you got included in the dream that I had last night, Ray — I wanted to tell you that."

I observed, "Nha Trang wasn't real, as far as combat really went, i.e., watching air strikes on the nearby mountain; sitting on top of bunkers when mortar attack happened; no land-based attacks against us; almost no violence towards Americans in the city of Nha Trang; having "combat come to us" via med evacs landing with wounded personnel from duty stations outside of Nha Trang;, only several mortar attacks that landed in our compound, etc."

Note: here, I have a flash back #1 to 1968-69. "Enlisted men get VD; officers get infections." (This was a common saying at the 8th Field Hospital in Nha Trang, referring to typical notes in the medical charts; I just remembered it right now, for some unknown reason.)

January 27. Bangkok, Thailand

We arrive in Bangkok. Thailand has diplomatic relations with Vietnam so we can get visas here, to enter Vietnam. We hold a special meeting at the hotel. The only place we can find is out on the 2nd floor balcony. Most of us are really angry at the VVA tour folks, and also at being forcibly lumped in with their group and their itinerary. This, of course, will restrict our itinerary in Vietnam. We are very worried that it may shortchange our vets, who need time at various battle sites in the South.

Ray: Don't focus on your anger towards the tour staff: focus on why each of us is here.

Planning the time in VN: We want to push the Vietnamese to spend only two days in Hanoi, and not four days as the Vietnamese (government) tour company insisted on.

Reviewing the Itinerary.

Saigon area: Minimum of five full days. Many of our eight vets have battle sites to visit in the greater Saigon area. With our limited time, we have to split up the group in Saigon, in order for each vet to be able to have a full day at his/her site. Two vets want to visit the Michelin rubber plantation, 20 minutes out, possibly on the same day.

Two vets: Long Binh, Bien Hoa (close to rubber plantation), Phuc Vinh Bien Hoa.

Dave and me: Navy Base south of Saigon

One vet: Saigon. Tan Son Nhat, by cyclo

Three vets: Cu Chi tunnels, at least one day

Jake and Ray: Nha Trang: one full day. Perhaps we should skip Hue (because none of our vets served there

Steve: Da Nang

One vet: An Hoa (3-4 hours south of Da Nang) and Freedom Ridge, very near An Hoa.

We need to keep our focus and group cohesion, "our ten," that is, our therapy group members (eight vets and two co-therapists), and avoid getting mixed up with the VVA tour members.

DAY ONE IN VIETNAM

Sunday, January 29

Thai Airline Flight 682 — Bangkok to Hanoi

As we are taking off from Bangkok, finally I get the feeling that we actually will be in Vietnam within two hours. Except, it will be Hanoi, which at the moment most of us have very mixed feelings about going to. All of our "business" is in "south" Vietnam. Going to Hanoi feels like an unnecessary stop, and we resent that the Hanoi government has forced us to go there first and stay for three days! Also, it feels a little uncomfortable, as in maybe we "shouldn't" be going to North Vietnam: the political capital of communist Vietnam. Indeed, Hanoi is the last place in Vietnam that the vets want to go to. To them, an old enemy awaits in Hanoi. My issues with Hanoi Jane (Fonda) are coming up, now. I'm angry as I think about her trip to Hanoi in the middle of the Vietnam War. In my mind, it bordered on treason. Unimaginable: a celebrity visiting the capital of the enemy at the very time we were fighting them!

North Vietnam; perhaps we can use our "forced" days there as a way to get our act together as a group. Things are feeling a little fragmented right now, with concern that we are going to get so little time in the south, all of the media being here, and possibly TV shows when we get back (CBS, NBC, ABC!). Maybe this really has turned into something of a media circus after all. And I see that part of my responsibility is to get the group focused on the mission — us, and our stress recovery. Oh, oh. I'm now starting to resent the media and again I worry that individual group members are too media-focused.

Going to Hanoi also reminds me that our group could be exploited by the North Vietnamese, politically — come see our war memorial — and for four precious days, at that.

I know what else is bothering me. When I go to a foreign country, I have always gone out of my way to mix with the locals, become acculturated to some extent, establish some positive communication. But, on this trip, I don't feel that I can do that, because I need to keep my focus on each of the vets and the group as a whole. But, part of my/our experience then (1968) and now is the Vietnamese — so I must juggle these two focuses somehow, when I'm in-country.

This is one tense airplane ride. I remember how *really* tense all of us were on the flight. And I flash back again to 1968-69. The quiet on the plane is eerily reminiscent of our Freedom Bird flight when leaving Long Binh in 1969 to return to the US But, this time we are going back to Vietnam and to the capital of the enemy we had been fighting! We have no idea what the reception will be. Many of the group members fear the worst. Can you blame them? We think we may be met with some hostility.

As we are making our descent into Hanoi, several of the veterans have tears in their eyes.

Bob: "It's like going back to enemy territory, but it's also like I'm coming home...This place has been screwing me up for 19 years...But as much as I hate the place, I love it. Part of this country is just embedded in me." [107]

Hanoi Airport

What a day. We are arriving in Vietnam, after 20+ years! Ed Marcin was so right — two decades and a wake-up. [108] Getting off the plane in Hanoi. The airport looked like it was out of another time; 40 years ago, run-down, barren. No guns in sight anywhere, only a few seemingly disinterested guards in uniform. There seemed to be very little if any activity inside the terminal, other than our arrival.

As we deplane, the first thing I notice is that no hot, humid blanket immediately hits us, nor the instant perspiration that covered us when we got off the plane in Saigon during the war. It is cool. Then, I notice the Russian (civilian) airplanes on the ground. We all are at least a little tense as we make our way into the terminal — a small building that has perhaps three or so stalls with uniformed customs officials. The customs officials are just that — very official and business-like. They give no outward signs that we are out-of-the-ordinary arrivals. The first few of us get processed quickly and drift outside, waiting for the rest of the group to get through customs.

And then, the people waiting outside the entrance. There must be a couple of hundred Vietnamese standing around outside. Why are they here? There are all ages and sizes, waiting, watching, indeed staring at us, initially very quiet, with no visible signs of emotion. However, we are obviously the center of attention; it does appear that we are at least a curiosity.

As one of the first two members of our group to go outside, I get to see a lot in the next five minutes or so. I notice the rather stoic adults, especially the men (or is that

---

107. Leslie Brown, "Hanoi homecoming elates veterans," *Tacoma News Tribune* (January 30, 1989), A-1, A-10.
108. The phrase, "two decades and a wake-up," credited to Ed Marcin, is a creative adaptation of the military expression commonly used in Vietnam (and elsewhere) before rotating to a new assignment. For example, someone who was leaving in four days to go back to the States might say, "I'm down to three days and a wake-up."

my imagination?). Then, people gradually start showing more open interest and friendliness, in the way of tentative smiles and talking. Young girls start giggling and smiling, posing as vets take pictures of them. Then, there are playful exchanges and bantering by a few of our group members with some of the braver children. God bless children, the universal ice-breaker!

Dave Roberts takes the initiative with an American tradition for young children. [109] He starts passing out candy. After a brief hesitation, the children become very animated and start crowding around Dave. He is bubbling with happiness, quite a contrast to his somber gaze, scanning the environment a few minutes earlier.

Then, a most remarkable thing happens. One of the vets with the VVA tour, Hank, is 6'4." He towers over the crowd. And he starts holding up something in his hands. At first, I (and I imagine the Vietnamese, too) think he is handing out more candy. But then, they recognize that he actually has tiny American flags. Suddenly, the crowd metamorphoses before our eyes; the people become vibrantly alive. Young and old and in-between, males and females, push up towards the front, smiling and waving, outstretched hands everywhere, reaching upwards to grasp for — tiny American flags! And, then, beaming as they pin the flags on their clothes, or clutch them in their hands, smiling and laughing. It is unbelievable!

The transformation of both the Vietnamese onlookers at the airport, and our attitude from when we first deplaned, were absolutely remarkable. From wary and tense (Americans) and quiet and still (Vietnamese), to increasingly more open and friendly (Americans and Vietnamese), and then the enthusiastic responses. Absolutely amazing. We were blown away. Not in our wildest dreams. It was a most remarkable sight and experience that I am sure none of us will ever forget — and this time, it's one that we want to remember.

We found our bus awaiting, nondescript, a dull yellow and white; it looked and felt like an old military bus. No air conditioning, of course. We pulled away from the Hanoi Airport and the crowd around our bus. What then immediately drew our attention was the road traffic: cyclists on all sides, and almost no motor vehicles. Rural-looking homes stretched out for miles alongside the road; most were very small, poor looking, one after the other. In spite of the increasing chill and dropping temperatures as dusk approached, families were sitting out on the "front porch area" of their homes, all bundled up, gathered around what seemed to be candles. I remember seeing only a scattered dwelling or so with electricity. And it had gotten so cold!

And then we arrived at the Thang Loi Hotel. It was a really impressive hotel, old world, and quaint. In my room there was a linen hanging over the TV. It said (in English), "Thang Loi Hotel, Room 303, Television." I lifted up the linen and underneath sat a bright red television, Japanese, of course — Sanyo.

---

109. Smith, *Two Decades*, 1990.

First Group Meeting in Vietnam

Before the trip, we agreed that we would at least try to meet each evening or late afternoon, depending on what was happening. We wanted to insure that we regularly debriefed and shared with each other, before too many experiences and feelings had accumulated. We also did not know if we would have adequate meeting rooms at the various hotels. Sure enough, we are unable to get a room to meet in. We decide to crowd into the room of one of the group members; highlights of this first very emotional meeting are on the video, *Two Decades and A Wake-Up*. We go around the room, sharing whatever is foremost in our minds. Someone says, "I'm exhausted; let's make this a 15-minute meeting and meet tomorrow." But we find ourselves talking for two-and-a-half hours!

The emotional atmosphere at this first meeting was quite heavy. At first, there was lots of frustration concerning being stuck with the VVA tour group, logistics, etc. I emphasized my worry about the group's focus on this trip. I felt that I had a primary responsibility focus on each of the vets' own issues/healing, and not fall into blaming and projecting.

At this first meeting, it was quite evident that the group as a whole was physically and emotionally exhausted. This had been a very trying and nerve-wracking day. All of us had been anticipating, mostly with negativity, the stay in Hanoi. We felt that it was a waste of time, that it stood in the way of visiting our former battlefield sites in the South; and we had no idea what kind of reception we would receive in Hanoi, North Vietnam: a place that our planes had bombed extensively! We expected a very neutral reaction at best, and more likely hostile reactions from the "North Vietnamese."

Dave: "I was apprehensive, but something pulled me towards the kids. And I didn't even think I'd be welcome. And when that happened [the positive reactions of the crowd], I said, 'My God.' It was a wonderful feeling, you know."

Ray: "I don't imagine any of us in this room had a fantasy that it would turn out the way it did today."

Bill: "How wrong we might have been, all these years, in our hate and that we were taught to hate the North Vietnamese people, and everything that North Vietnam stood for. And I think, today, because this is the only time I ever had anything to do with it [North Vietnam], they moved me very much, and 20 years of hate for something that wasn't there, maybe, for peoples that maybe didn't really exist except maybe in our heads."

Ed: "I felt more like I came home, today — and I was never here, but this must be close enough — than I ever did, in what was supposed to be my home...I gotta go [and he abruptly got up and left the room]."

Dave: "Do you know what he is talking about? That we got more of a coming home, after 20 years, from those people, those little kids and stuff, than we...than my government gave me, when I came home...My God, they don't even have anything." [And he wipes his eyes, letting out a big heave and a deep sigh). [110]

---

110. *Ibid.*

There is a major disagreement within the group. On the one side were those who were very suspicious that the very friendly reception at the airport "had been staged by the North Vietnamese government." Group members with this viewpoint were suspicious that the warm welcome we had received was in fact a falsehood and not to be trusted as genuine. On the other side were those of us, including me, who experienced what seemed to be the very spontaneous and extremely positive reactions of the Vietnamese people at the airport as so very genuine and heartwarming. We couldn't believe that it had been staged; indeed, even if it had been staged in terms of getting people to go to the airport, their reactions once we interacted were much too genuine-appearing for many of us to consider them anything other than real. [111]

DAY 2. MONDAY, JANUARY 30

Immersion in "North" Vietnam

At breakfast we read an AP newspaper article in the Bangkok Post, "8 US veterans return to VN to cure trauma." It is a straightforward and descriptive article, with a few quotes.

Dave: "I want to come to peace with my mind, the country and the people and put all that behind me because the war's over. I want to get on with a lot of things in my life."

Bob: "There's apologies I feel I need to make to the people. There were civilians who were caught in our fire and I have had guilt feelings about that. The other thing is to try to leave the warrior part of me in Vietnam where it belongs. It doesn't fit in the United States."

Ray: "Basically, we're extending a very accepted therapeutic practice in working with trauma survivors. That is, direct therapeutic exposure to the trauma. Our assumption is that coming over here will trigger repressed memories and feelings that [they] need to get out consciously, and talk about it. In doing that it appears they come to some kind of peace. By going now, ... they have to substitute the reality of Vietnam today. It's not the way it was 20 years ago. That's a very important message for many veterans. [112]

Realization here at breakfast: I feel really solid, grounded, refreshed — and I only slept 5 hours! (I think it's mainly because we really got going in the group last night — and I got going!)

---

111. About six years later, I traveled to American Samoa and was surprised to find crowds of Samoans at the airport just to watch our late-night arrival. Apparently, the relatively few flights from the US were an attraction, and people would show up just to "check-out" the passengers coming and going on — in addition to those who, of course, were there to create a welcoming reception for arriving family and friends. This experience in American Samoa brought back to me our arrival in Hanoi in 1989 — thus creating a "flashback" to peacetime Vietnam 1989!

112. Associated Press, "Eight US veterans return to Vietnam to cure trauma," *Bangkok Post* (January 28, 1989), 2.

"Mod" Vietnamese in "hip" fashions last night at the hotel. What a contrast to the people at the airport.

Gifts and souvenirs are some bargain, here — tee shirts, $1 each; dolls, $4.80, postcards, $0.60 each.

Some of the vets are deferring too much already to April and me; they are saying that it is up to us to decide what to do. No, all of us need to be involved in such decisions.

Also, let's discuss the details of traumatic events that happened in the war zone, and of various vets' issues and emotions, in our group sessions. There may be different (more) details than what anyone wants to say in front of the media. Finally, some group members have been coming to me and complaining about other group members: it is really important for the vets (and the therapists) to be willing to confront someone in the group sessions themselves if there is any important issue that needs to be addressed. Otherwise, it will come back to bite you, no matter why you did not confront the person. One of the vets was really depressed yesterday, but he is really "up" now, on the 2nd day (expect it!).

Our Vietnamese Tour Guide: Big Brother

We are given very clear instructions by our Vietnamese tour guide. The group is to stay together at all times when we are out of the hotel, and we must be accompanied by the Vietnamese tour guide at all times. There will be no unescorted touring. And, if we want to go somewhere that is not on the schedule, we must ask the guide in advance. If it is not possible, then we cannot go.

Most of the group has a very negative reaction to this pronouncement. A few grumble and say that they may be willing to go along with these restrictions here in Hanoi, but when we get to the South and near their former duty stations, they will go where they want to — and do it "secretly" if they have to.

Our tour guide and bus driver is Dan Sung, a former political officer in the NVA. (This heightens the suspicions of those members of our group who think that we are only being allowed to go to places where there will be "staged" receptions for us, and that we will be kept away from other areas.)

Of course, even in our walks in Hanoi, where we are mostly together, a few group members "wander off" into areas that clearly were not "set up" to receive us — and the spontaneous reactions of the Vietnamese at such places where we went spontaneously was no different than in the scheduled stops — large crowds gathering, seemingly out of nowhere and extremely quickly, very friendly and enthusiastic, curious, and eager to talk and interact with us in halting English (which still was much better than our even more fragmented Vietnamese!).

Ho Chi Minh's Tomb

Ho Chi Minh's massive mausoleum. Like Lenin's tomb in Moscow, it was eerie and imposing; a life-like body (some skeptics say it is a wax likeness) in a lighted glass coffin, with a constant stream of visitors.

Soaking up the sights and sounds of Hanoi. The group is impatient to go out and find out about these people that we know as the "North Vietnamese." Hanoi is a city of 3 million people. Most seem to be in the streets. The sides of the streets are meeting places, as far as we can see in all directions, viewpoints for watching others.

We are mesmerized as we encounter the people and sounds and smells of Hanoi. We are energized as we observe and are observed and interact with the people. But yet, the group has a feeling of not being that comfortable that we can come to Hanoi and have a good time.

We go to a university. I decide to stay out alongside the street. I am absorbed/ amazed at the stream (procession) of humanity constantly flowing by. Most are on bicycles, some walking. There are very few vehicles (mostly work trucks). Just imagine Santa Monica Blvd in Los Angeles, but replace all of the cars with old bicycles and crowds of pedestrians everywhere.

There are absolutely no lights or stop signs or any other external signs of traffic control. And so, so at every intersection, traffic comes together from four directions; somehow, the traffic intermingles in the middle, people (again, imagine Santa Monica Blvd: no lights anywhere) subtly adjust (brake, veer a little, etc.) to get across and/or to make a turn. It is an amazing scene.

And I stand there on the broken sidewalk (almost all of the sidewalks are in disrepair, as are all the walls: falling down, cracked, discolored, holes, piles of rocks or dirt here and there), watching the never-ending stream of Vietnamese moving in all directions.

As we (Americans) walk by — we get two distinct reactions from the Vietnamese: absolutely no indication that anyone notices us; or looks, smiles, poses, finger-pointing, people coming up and saying something, gathering around, staying in the vicinity to just stare, and smile.

We eat lunch at a restaurant picked by our driver. Everyone seems pleased to have us there. Could it be just the old Asian "polite face?" I think not — and then comes the proof. As we are getting ready to leave, they ask our Vietnamese-American ABC cameraman to write, in effect, a testimonial, in Vietnamese, in a book — about how pleased we were with the food and the service; and two of us are asked to sign it! And all of the employees seem to be proud and happy about our satisfaction with the service and the food — and the glowing written testimonial.

Illegal parking. The bus, with the Vietnamese driver and one PBS film camera-man, are parked while the rest of us go shopping and walking for about an hour. When we return, the bus is gone, and is at least 45 minutes late getting back. A policeman apparently got on the bus, told the driver he was parked illegally. There were a lot of harsh sounding words...Then, the policeman insisted that the driver take the bus (with the policeman inside) to the police station (police, by and large, walk while on duty). Apparently, all the way there, there were loud angry-sounding exchanges, with the driver appearing to have the upper hand. When they got to the station, both went inside, with the driver angrily berating the policeman. And the bus driver walked out a little while later — with no ticket.

A large crowd and a Vietnamese policewoman. At another intersection, earlier on, we get out into a "non-tourist area" (although in Hanoi, I would be hard pressed to call anywhere a "tourist" area)! Crowds of children gather around, animated, talking, laughing, crowding, smiling, wanting their pictures taken. There are maybe 50 kids are all around three of us, and they spill out into a very busy intersection. Suddenly a policewoman comes up, and gently directs the kids off the streets. She then starts a conversation (which goes on for a half hour) with one of the vets, starting off in Russian. She knows a few words of English. She obviously is intent to communicate something. Meanwhile, all the crowd is still around, laughing, pointing, enjoying themselves. The policewoman is very polite, smiling. Finally, we think we get the message; it is dangerous to have the kids and us (standing) on the street next to the curb, and the film crews should not be in the middle of the street filming. And so, we eventually move: and all this time, she is smiling, polite, attempting to communicate.

In the middle of this crowd of kids, one particularly beaming girl (8 or 9 years old) stands out. Suddenly, she says in English: "What is your name? My name is ___. Yes, I study English in school."

Some of the children begged, persistently and plaintively, tugging at the veterans' arms to the point where they had to be (gently) pushed away.

Jim: "I have a very hard time with this. You want to give and give and give, but it would never be enough." [113]

Hanoi Hilton

We saw no reminders of the war, until we approached the infamous Hanoi Hilton. This, of course, was the prisoner-of-war facility that held captured Americans, including Senator John McCain. We are told that it is still a prison, and that no one is allowed to stop in front of the building and take pictures. However, the driver agrees to drive slowly, so that we can take pictures from inside the bus. We are appropriately subdued as we pass by. Suddenly, the "touristy" feeling that many of us had, to some degree, dissipates. Each of us seems to be caught up in our own thoughts. The Hanoi Hilton, where so many American POWs suffered so much, for so many years.

Bill: "I can remember, as a boy, thinking how great it would be to drop an atomic bomb on Hanoi and kill them all...And it's so painful when you start to see the enemy as a people." [114]

DAY 3. TUESDAY, JANUARY 31

A Myth of Hatred. Can We Let "By-Gones Be By-Gones"?

We stop to see the monument at the Lady of the Lake outside of Hanoi. It was built, we are told, because an American B-52 bomber had been shot down, eventually ending up at the bottom of the lake. The plane was still in the water, partially submerged, until a few years ago when the lake was dredged and deepened. The memorial includes "USAF," a description of the plane and pilot, and a figure in a "surrendering" position (although the figure of the pilot is blended into the plaque, to a degree). (Bob Swanson told me just recently that this memorial depicts former POW and US Senator John McCain.) Our group starts taking pictures of the memorial, and posing in front of it as a group. Suddenly, I feel angry and do not want to have my picture taken in front of the memorial. It reminded me of Jane Fonda laying flowers at the tomb in North Vietnam. A memorial to an event where

113. Brown, "Hanoi homecoming elates veterans," A-1, A-10.
114. Smith, *Two Decades*, 1990.

the American was shot down, and parachuted out, and is "surrendering." A picture of the memorial, fine — but not with us in it, I thought.

A lively discussion ensued [after we got back on the bus, which was the only place other than our hotel rooms were we had any privacy]. Some of the group agreed with me, and others saw nothing wrong in what they were doing. Some of the group looked upon it as a monument to all who had served and returned home.) Part of my reaction was due to something still fresh in my mind from this morning. I had bought this large picture book with text in English about Vietnam. This morning before breakfast, I had leafed through it. Everything seemed fine and I thought — this would be a nice memento or present for the PTSD program at American Lake. And, then, I found the section about the war.

"The People's Army of Vietnam completed their victorious offensive...yet another group of Americans are leaving Vietnam forever. In conformity with the agreement between Vietnam and the USA, these would-be conquerors were given a chance to return home. They have been lucky. During the years of the 'dirty war' against the people of Vietnam, thousands of American soldiers went back home in regulation Army coffins. The great victory of the people of Vietnam over the US aggressors and their flunkey was a glorious page in the history of the world national-liberation movement."

Whoops. Better not give this book to the PTSD program: it would really make a lot of vets mad! (And I guess I didn't want to keep the book, either; I don't know what happened to it.)

And I didn't feel comfortable now, smiling in front of a memorial celebrating the downing of US planes and the surrender of a pilot. I would be almost equally upset and would find it inappropriate if we stood smiling in front of building bombed out by the Americans.

Anger and Grief Over Loss — How Can the Vietnamese People Welcome Us So?

And now I realize what else I have tapped into: my feelings of anger and grief over all of the losses during the war. All of the losses to Americans and their families (including, perhaps especially, the continuing trauma of families of MIAs/POWs) — and the incredible loss of life among the South and North Vietnamese.

How can the Vietnamese be so welcoming and happy to greet us, who did invade their country, and especially in the north caused so much death and destruction? The war only ended a short 14 or so years ago. And then, a disquieting thought intrudes into my consciousness. Maybe the Vietnamese in the north/Hanoi area could be so friendly and forgiving because they won! Would it be the same in the South; would many in the South see us as having deserted them and thus be bitter?

I find myself worrying whether the South will be a great contrast to the North: would Hanoi vs. Saigon be like East vs. West Berlin? Was the South still "free wheeling," much more lively, colorful, cleaner, better developed, and the people even more friendly than in Hanoi? Or had the South deteriorated to look as drab, dirty and poverty stricken as Hanoi and the French-built (or inspired) grand, old, mansions and museums built in mid-1800s? They must have been a wondrous, inspiring sight in those days, when the French were here in occupation. Versus now: crumbling, dirty, exteriors all dirty (except for "embassy row"). City buildings

139

almost seem to be dying and crumbling, and yet there is a vibrancy, pride, aliveness, and strength clearly evident in the people.

Being here in Hanoi destroys the myth of "hating" the North Vietnamese/Viet Cong. That isn't the source of my hate at all: it's the horror that war inflicts on both sides. This is a major discovery that almost all — if not all — of the vets seem to make while exploring and experiencing Hanoi.

Today, one of the vets, the NBC Filipino cameraman and I went off into a poorer district. We went down a crowded, narrow market-lined street. After slowly weaving our way (100 yards?) or so through the crowds of people, we discover that the street did not go through to the left and back to the main street, it dead ended; and I immediately felt a stab of concern: if these people were hostile, we could be in deep trouble — and I walked back out a lot quicker than I had entered! This was one of very few times on the entire trip that I experienced any fear. Indeed, walking around Hanoi felt much safer than many cities in the US.)

Group Meeting #3: Last Night in Hanoi

The vets, by and large, are experiencing seemingly nothing but positives, one after the other. The warmth of the people and the chaotic but vibrantly bustling crowds everywhere really move us.

Jake: I wish we could bring 50,000 vets in here to see these faces...Because this has been one hell of a day.

Bill: I'm high, I'm high as a kite. [115]

If we experience only positives here, will that be sufficient for stress recovery? Because a successful stress recovery also means giving up negative memories; the reality of the Vietnam in our nightmares doesn't jibe with our experience of Vietnam now.

Along with the joy being experienced, an amazing and unexpected feeling and theme emerges among a number of the group members. Several say they are feeling proud to be an American — and for the first time in a very, very long time. That being here, and interacting with the Vietnamese, and the way we are being received and treated — in the midst of all this, an underlying feeling is emerging: We're really proud, again, of being Americans!

Group vet: "Once again, it really hurts again to realize that we've been treated better by our former enemy nation, indeed by the 'belly of the beast' — Hanoi, of all places — that suffered the brunt of terrible destruction from [US] bombings — than we ever were treated by our own country!"

Another vet says that his terrible, long-standing and almost nightly Vietnam-related nightmares have disappeared, so far. Is this because, perhaps, the Vietnam in his nightmares is terrible, and the Vietnam he is now experiencing is friendly, receptive, accommodating, non-threatening?

If this is central to relief from enduring PTSD symptoms, then maybe it is true that to add the reality of Vietnam today into our consciousness will force us to realize fully and emotionally that the Vietnam of our memories is of the past, and is only

---

115. Brown, "Hanoi homecoming elates veterans," A-1, A-10.

alive in our minds; if we let ourselves experience and remember the Vietnam of today, it will force us to a different level of accommodation and perspective vis-a-vis our troubling memories of 20+ years ago.

My God — if an entire nation (not just the government) can apparently let go of 10-12 years of terrible conflict with us, can there not be hope that we as individuals (or as a group) also can let go of those old horrors? Or does the "country" (whatever that is) first have to fully recognize the sacrifices and the valor and the triumphs of our warriors in order for us Vietnam veterans to let go and integrate the past in a positive manner into the now? Is the "losing" of a war the critical factor that prevents us from making the transformation and break the chains of the trauma that still haunt us?

If we won't get that from the country, can vets as a collective group heal ourselves — through, partially, people-to-people contacts, despite government policy? This people-to-people contact is healing, on one level, and quite perturbing on another — when contrasted to the reactions of the US government, and the reactions of many extremely angry Vietnam vets. Also, the role the US played is explicit in Vietnam history books; the war is the final chapter of the incredible legacy of Ho Chi Minh. He died in 1969, and his inspiration before and after that time is inextricably caught up in the US military intervention in Vietnam. Perhaps it is easier for the Vietnamese to let go of the trauma we inflicted on them, while US Vietnam veterans still harbor a vitriolic hatred towards the Vietnamese; perhaps we remind them of the "invincible power of the Vietnamese people" and of Ho Chi Minh. Or, is it because we vets are a very likeable, genuine and caring group of people, and that shines through?

Do The Vietnamese Really Like Americans?

I cannot believe that the Vietnamese people we have met are responding warmly primarily because it is in their best economic interests (that is what some, back in the US, were saying). Am I gullible?

During a tour of buildings in Hanoi, we are proudly shown a large and impressive wall hanging depicting a large navy battle from several centuries ago; we are told that this scene depicts Vietnam defeating a much larger invading armada of Chinese warships.

Also, Vietnam has the fourth largest standing army in the world (following the US, Soviet Union, and China). Where does that fit in? (Vietnam is regarded by some of her neighbors as quite militaristic and a threat.)

And why am I being so shy or, should I say, holding back, in my contacts with the Vietnamese people? I find myself avoiding making full eye contact, my smile is not spontaneous — in contrast to several of the vets who have waded in with open arms among the crowds of Vietnamese, who congregate almost everywhere we go. That is how I used to be, when traveling in any other country — and when I was in the war.

Perhaps I feel somewhat of a transgressor now, as if I don't have the right to "intrude" into the daily life of the people here — and yet, they are so friendly to me/us. One vet suggests that I may have picked up some of the negative attitudes of the countless angry, troubled vets that I've counseled over 20 years. Perhaps. But I think that what may be at the core is guilt, 20 years of guilt — for buying the Government line while I was in Vietnam and even for several years after the war. Years later, I found it amazing that I had been so naive as to accept the notion that "non-Communist" South Vietnam was "superior" morally and politically to the communist North. In addition, that we should be "stopping the spread of Communism," even when it meant supporting a corrupt government. Indeed, a government that apparently did not have the support of most of the people (contrary to the lies we were told).

My belief these days is that because of the US intervention in Vietnam, the Vietnamese civil war essentially was artificially protracted by as many as eight years or so. Without our intervention, and the accompanying tragedies inflicted on so many Vietnamese (North and South) and US troops, the war might have been over as quickly as 1966 or 1967. And so what, if the communists support the other side; maybe there is an imperative there, or the commies would have taken over everyone; or, would they have? At least, that certainly is what the government and military would have had us believe.

But is, for example, supporting a communist totalitarian government inevitably of much greater threat to the very ideals we espouse? I thought I was not going to be political too much in my journal; but one can't separate PTSD of war vets from our nation's political actions. Otherwise, I as a clinician would be ignoring the most critical intervention — prevention. How do you resolve and eliminate PTSD, if you are continually being re-exposed to unnecessary war-trauma? That would be maintaining denial and avoidance of (1) the ultimate and true cause of war-related PTSD — not the individual deficits in soldiers who become psychiatric casualties, and (2) my responsibilities as a citizen, mental health professional and citizen of earth.

And is not strength of a much more powerful nature maintained (against even vastly superior military forces) by purity of conviction and ideals — as perhaps reflected by Ho Chi Minh and the Vietnamese people?

DAY 4 WEDNESDAY, FEBRUARY 1, DA NANG

Pain, Joy and Meeting Former Adversaries

The Flight From Hanoi to Da Nang

Up at 4: 00 to go to the airport for the flight to South Vietnam (Da Nang). On the way out, in the bus from Hanoi to the airport, discussion ensued regarding the North Vietnamese people, who seemed not to have been particularly indoctrinated against Americans. In the rural areas, they are more shy and reserved, and initiate contact less, but they do respond positively when approached. Perhaps this is the difference between city and country folk — or the difference between former hardcore NVA recruitment grounds, e.g., the rural areas, and the city?

"People-to-People" Versus "The Government" — a recurring theme

In fact, the kids are learning English in school. And the people seem to go out of their way to distinguish between the people and the government, both in Vietnam and in the US, e.g., the "US government" is the bad guy, not the American people. In contrast, in the US we do not seem to differentiate between the people and government of countries where the US has no relationship, or hostile relations. We aren't oriented to think, well, the Vietnamese people are fine, it's just the government that is following bad policies. And that's the tragedy of not having normalized relations with Vietnam; we are conditioned to keep our prejudices about Nam. And that conditioning holds, because we have so little contact with the people. And then, we judge the people by the government's stance (propaganda?)!

Do the people really make the country? In spite of, or reflective of, "the government"? Quite frankly, I find more and more that the US Government perpetuated myths in the 60s and 70s about the North Vietnamese. And that myth continues to be reinforced in 1989, through refusing to normalize diplomatic and economic relations. Did we refuse, after WW II, to normalize relations with Germany, Italy, or Japan until 1960?

We've just landed at Da Nang.

There is a myth among a number of combat veterans that they have so much unforgettable pain that they can never be happy again.

Antidote to pain — it can start with allowing yourself to feel joy. Most vets with severe PTSD issues find it immeasurably difficult to enjoy life anymore.

Myth: The enemy aren't human in every way.

Myth: The enemy hated and still hates me.

Myth: I don't deserve to be happy, and I never will be.

Are these myths being shattered by the profound joy our group is experiencing, in Vietnam, in 1989? Euphoria-like joy is hitting practically every member of the group. Here we are in Vietnam, in the capital of our former enemy, expecting the worst — and instead, we find warmth, smiles and laughter and positive attention everywhere we go. What a shock for the vets, most of whom have been leading very isolated and, in some cases, embittered lives!

Are these joyful reactions at least partly an emotional release of long-standing and accumulated sadness and lack of positive experiences and expression? Are these joyful reactions partly an escape or avoidance of the pain? "How can I feel my pain when I'm being treated so wonderfully by the Vietnamese people?"

This stimulates my thinking about two quite different tactics to treat PTSD: getting into the pain, and relieving it, etc., or putting your attention on positives, on joy, on love. Is it really possible to ameliorate PTSD solely or dominantly by ascertaining and experiencing the positives, the love, the joy?

In the field of mental health, we know very little about how to consciously structure a therapeutic program that would do just that, focusing on positives and strengths. Usually, that's a little piece...What can we do to build on more joy?

Maybe this people-to-people joyful experience is just what it takes to break down the negative conditioning of basic training, AIT (Advanced Infantry Training), and war-trauma.

Whenever I/we think of Vietnam past, I/we tend to feel pain. Now, we are adding positive, joyful visions of Vietnam today. The big question is, will this positive memory transcend to some degree the painful memories of decades ago and help us move beyond them? Only time will tell.

If the joy continues, a tactical clinical decision must be made in the next several days: whether to dig for the pain, or just go with the flow?

Tet Offensive, Fireworks and the 4th of July

American memories of the Tet New Year's celebrations are indelibly grounded in the Tet offensive of 1968. And for me, that became generalized to a negative reaction to all 4th of July and New Years fireworks displays. Firecrackers and explosions always used to remind me of the Vietnam War. I avoided them like the plague, since Vietnam. It has only been in the past several years that I have lightened up somewhat. I guess this is at least partly due to having three children and a wife who like to partake in such celebrations. Now, we are here in Vietnam during Tet (1989), facing an unceasing barrage of firecrackers for several days, everywhere we go. And, what do we see: joy and celebration, and no fear of being attacked. In spite of our initial startle reactions to the fireworks, we seem to have adjusted fairly quickly to the new reality of a Peacetime Vietnam. We can stand around as groups of Americans, and not feel targeted; indeed, we feel very welcome. And gradually, we start being able to partake in the celebration mood. Is this truly joyful celebration that we are witnessing and are immersed in, today, a new memory that will endure — one that might even supplant intrusive, painful memories?

Group vet: "It's real significant being around Vietnamese graves here. When I was in Nam, on a Listening Post (LP), I had to dig into a cemetery, and man my post lying on top of graves. Also, I had a traumatic experience with fire on the beach in Nam, and ever since I have associated bonfires on the beaches with this Nam experience..."

Group Meeting in Da Nang

The group gets into an emotional discussion about whether we are acting too much like tourists and blindly accepting that the Vietnamese are genuinely friendly towards us.

Billy Ray: "I still see them as the enemy. And I have never accepted them as being that friendly, you know, because to me I feel like it is nothing but a facade for them, and it's scary...and in Hanoi, I seen a lot of bad, ugly stares. But some of you guys, you walk around like these stares are not there. All of us are here because we have PTSD, and everybody is trying to walk around like it's peaches and cream. People over here have PTSD, too, just as much or more than we have. Sometimes, I wonder why I came on this trip. I'm scared, I'm very scared."

Ed: "When you see, or when you perceive, that we're just freely running around like it's a picnic, understand, for some of us, it may look that way, but it isn't, it really isn't. We have many of your concerns...we try to deal with it a little differently...What do you do, what do you do? I can't spend the rest of my life bunkered in my home. I gotta get out, or I'll just dry up and die."

Dave: "When I flew into Hanoi, I was scared. There's no doubt about it. But, after the reception that we got, and the people, why, they seemed to be friendly. I'm going to give them, as an individual I'm going to give them the benefit of the doubt and say 'hi.' I'm going to meet them half-way."

Bill: "You want to talk about the fear I feel from these people, with no guns, when 20 years ago I'm going down the trail in the middle of that jungle out there. And there was someone waiting there with guns and booby traps to kill me dead. Now, if all I have to fear is their pain at us, at the American people, that maybe they're looking at me — maybe, some of it is justified. I feel a lot more positive with what they're doing to me here in these few days, than I have felt for an awful long time in my life. Anything that could happen to me here is worth the chance that I could put some of this to rest. [116]

Vietnamese Veterans' Center in Da Nang

We asked a day or two earlier if there was a veterans' center of any kind that we might be able to visit? We were taken to the Nam Mgai Veterans Factory in Da Nang, a regional operation that employs about 1,000 physically disabled veterans. What transpired there was extremely emotional and controversial.

We walked into a small, rickety wooden building, and met the director, Iek Thach, a veteran of the war ("The American War"). Other veterans are there, and they all look aged. One had lost his leg in the war; he had also fought in their war with the French; and there was a veteran disabled during Vietnam's 1978 invasion of Cambodia. This really brought home to us why they refer to the "American war" and the fact that they have many veterans from several relatively recent wars — almost all of which have happened on their home soil.

We were greeted and sat down, and shared a warm *ba maba*, a Vietnamese beer. We drank to the end of war. As we were sitting and sharing with this group, I was filled with sadness. We were killing and maiming each other for so many years, and for what? Here we were now, listening to stories (through translators) about how three of the Vietnamese vets were wounded (one in an American attack on the Cu Chi airfield by a M-79).

Vietnamese vet: "The government was at war with the government, but you and I are people..."

Once again, I was struck by the ability of the Vietnamese to distinguish the US government from the US people, and to not carry grudges against the "American people."

We collected $100 among our group as a cash donation to give to the veterans' organization; in return, they gave us a large bag of coffee — grown on land that we once had fought over. Meeting with former enemy soldiers, even to share a toast to the

---

116. Smith, *Two Decades*, 1990.

end of war, brings a rush of deeply held feelings. I suddenly felt awkward, as the one pushed forward by our group to present the $100 to the Vietnamese. Suddenly, with cameras rolling, I felt ambivalent. On the one hand, I feel really good that we were having this friendly interchange. On the other hand, I was concerned that this would be used as a propaganda ploy by the Vietnamese. And, wouldn't many vets back in the US be enraged that we, indeed, were "consorting with the enemy"?

The factory Director, Mr. Thach, was appropriately polite and not too talkative — until we started specifically asking about his own status, and the veteran status of his two associates. Suddenly, there was a transformation. He became animated and engaging when he found out that we all were Vietnam vets. He told us that we were the first group ever to visit their factory. And then, he started talking about his eleven wounds, and how and where he had gotten them.

Spontaneously, two of our vets, and the other Vietnamese vets, started pulling up their pants legs and shirts to show their battle scars! It was a moving scene. And I became very sad. I just knew that many of the vets back home would be furious to know we met, shared beer and tea, war stories and handshakes and good wishes with each other — former soldiers, former adversaries of 20 years ago.

"The Nam" versus "Vietnam"

As I was walking out into the street from the meeting at the veteran's factory, I had the melancholy realization that my experiences with Vietnam 20 years ago were from another time, and that I would never again connect the Nam of 20 years ago that I had been carrying all these years. I feel a loss, even though it was at least partly a tragic time in my life and the lives of so many Americans and Vietnamese.

This trip is now starting to change "the Nam" into "Vietnam." And, now that I am back in Vietnam meeting Vietnamese veterans, I notice myself referring to "US veterans" to distinguish from "Vietnamese veterans."

And then another wondrous thing happened. Immediately after we had said our goodbyes and boarded our bus, the Director came rushing out. He climbed up in our bus. He started going down the aisle, shaking hands with each of us, animated, and very smiling and expressive. He thanked each of us for coming and visiting. It was a very emotional sight (especially in contrast with his very formal demeanor during the whole first half of the meeting, before he found out that we were not just tourists but veterans of "The American War").

It hits me now. It really hits me, what this trip is: a journey, not back into the past, but ahead into the present.

We are told that last year there were 5,000 Soviet tourists in Da Nang, and 3,000 Westerners (mostly Europeans) — and perhaps 400 Americans.

Evening Group in Da Nang

We discussed our meeting with the Vietnamese vets earlier today. Once again there are lots of strongly expressed and mixed feelings. Some of the vets were very suspicious that we "were set up" at the veteran's factory; that it had been a carefully orchestrated meeting that would be exploited by the Communist government for political propaganda purposes.[117]

Billy Ray: "Some of my friends told me before we left home that our group was being made a pawn of the Vietnamese government, which desperately wants to regain diplomatic relations with the United States. This is going to come back to haunt us.[118] That was strictly propaganda, that's all that it was, propaganda. And you guys enjoyed the hell out of getting it done to you."

Bill: "We came here, and the purpose for this was to heal within ourselves. Now, if healing within myself means that, I'll go to a former enemy and shake his hand, and admit that the war is over and I don't want to have hard feelings. That's the whole thing of my PTSD, all this anger and hatred that I have built up, and I got to let it out. And I gotta stop it."

Billy Ray: "You were puppets, that's what we were today, puppets on a string. And they played us like that."

Jim: "I have two choices. I can say, hey, I don't want to talk to you, go away; or, I can say, okay, let's talk. And I can take those grudges and I can hold them in my heart forever. Or, I have choices, and my choice is I can let it go. I can work on that."

Ray: "A whole lot of Americans are going to be very angry about it [our meeting today at the Vietnamese veteran's factory], and part of me says, 'they're going to be angry, who cares?' And, part of me got very sad over the fact that there is no way this won't cause some very hard feelings."

Dave: "When does the whole war end? Does it never end? Do we keep carrying on, year after year after year, with hate?"

Ray: "The purpose of this trip is to help you, the group members, find some healing from the wounds still being carried. It is not a political mission. And yes, there are vets back home who are very angry about our trip...The last thing you guys need is another unwelcome home."[119]

If we are to truly heal from the war, must not the healing include supplanting Vietnam war-related trauma thoughts and emotions of yesteryear with Vietnam Peace-time thoughts and emotions of today? These people are no longer gooks, chinks, slopes, the enemy, are they!? And if they are no longer the enemy, what does that mean to what so many veterans have been holding onto for so many years?

These Must Be Real

We were very surprised at how friendly all the Vietnamese people are to us. I am convinced that the positive and warm feelings that we are experiencing are quite genuine. It happens everywhere we go, with and without our tour guide, on both spontaneous and planned contacts, in one-to-one, small-group and large crowd

---

117. *Ibid.*

118. Leslie Brown, "Symbols cry out as veterans journey through time to yesterday's battle-fields," *Tacoma News Tribune* (February 4, 1989), A-5.

119. Smith, *Two Decades*, 1990

interactions. The only time I have felt otherwise is in a couple of contacts with what seemed to be hard-core Communist government officials.

DAY 5. THURSDAY, FEBRUARY

Highway 1, Hai Van Pass and East To Hue

From Da Nang to Hue We spent an entire group meeting last night, discussion at breakfast this morning, and the first hour of the bus trip venting and discussing our emotions and fears regarding meeting the Vietnamese vets here, and the likely negative ramifications of the media coverage of these meetings and negative reactions from angry vets back home.

The problem in all this is that we are focusing on the external world (media, people back home, etc.), rather than on us and what this experience is triggering in us. For me, what is being triggered is:

- Refreshed painful memories of the losses of the war on both sides
- Fear that I may be duped, somewhat, by some Vietnamese officials for propaganda purposes
- Worry that we will get another unwelcome home, when we get back after the trip, from vets and others who are opposed to anyone having contact with Vietnam/Vietnamese.
- And yes, I must admit it to myself, a fear that I will lose some of my credibility with the hard core combat vets because I came to Vietnam, and have been meeting with former enemy Vietnamese soldiers
- Why is the PBS documentary so personally important to each of us? Payback to others, by making our individual and group stories open to the public, thus giving others the opportunity to see what we have experienced on this trip — versus being totally self-centered on this trip
- Its our own "permanent picture of the now of 1989" — which makes it that much more likely that this will become indelible and really overpower the residue of our trauma memories!
- The US media were still emphasizing stories showing individual vets blaming themselves, and continuing to be blamed by others, which allows the voters, the government and military officials to avoid responsibility for when our nation goes to war. Come on, Ray: focus on us, and what is underneath our concerns about the media.

All long Highway 1, we saw signs of the war we had fought here: a signal van with the words "US Army" still on its side; a tank, immobilized, back from the road, but now converted to a home.

Ed: "It's hard for me to accept the sight of so much of our equipment still remaining here. It dredges up so many feelings of loss. I realize I'm not the one that left all this behind, but it's still here, like so many other things, and I can't help feeling I could have done more to prevent this loss. [120]

Group vet: "I am really concerned that my disability pay will be cut off because of the government's opposition to us going on this trip and their objection that we may be seen as 'unauthorized representatives of the US' over here in our meetings with the Vietnamese vets."

Riding by, on the bus, we saw a very positive and recurring reaction when people alongside the road noticed us. They all almost instantly smiled, pointed, waved, and pointed out to anyone near them that we were passing by. Such reactions were consistently positive everywhere we were traveling, and were in such great contrast to our negative pre-trip fantasies. Furthermore, we quickly learned that being identified as Americans rather than Russians would immediately bring positive response.

Consequently, our group started feeling much better about being identified as Americans, and at some point a number of our group put American flag decals on the bus and on their luggage, and one group member even hung a US flag in the bus window. The group now wanted to openly communicate to all that we were Americans. This was another sign of the significant positive impact of our experiences, renewing the sense of pride among group members.

Children would yell out, "Viet Nam," "Viet Nam" and smile as we drove by ("pride in country?"). Could you imagine a tourist bus driving by some children in the US and kids shout out, "USA," "USA!"

I hope I carry through on my intent to write an article about this trip after we get back. How about this for a title: "Go To Vietnam: if your Vietnam had/has any significance in your life."

Phu Bai, Camp Eagle

It's not "the Nam" to me anymore, it is "Vietnam" now — well, mostly.

Hai Van Pass

We leave Da Nang on Highway 1, ascending the steep mountainous route to the top of Hai Van Pass, the gateway through the mountains into central Vietnam and Hue. We stop near the summit. The deserted ruins of bunkers are there. Amazingly, discarded M-16 ammunition casings, an old black army boot, a rusted helmet, a 105 mm howitzer projectile and a Ho Chi Minh sandal cut from the rubber of an old tire all are lying around on the ground in plain sight.

Ed: "We need to put war and the memories of it in the same place where this helmet is. Gone."

Dave: "Gone. It's not reality, today."

---

120. Leslie Brown, "Symbols ...," *Tacoma News Tribune* (February 4, 1989), A-5.

Ed: "The war's over."

Dave: "It's gone. Forever."

Ed: "Do you know the significance of this [M-16 ammo casing]? It's all used up, like the war is. It's gone. You can't reload it."

Dave: "It can't do any harm anymore. It's gone."

And both Ed and Dave are laughing with glee. [121]

The group mood tonight (in Hue) was much more somber and contemplative than any time since we arrived in Hanoi.

Group vet: "I remember writing to my mother when I was in Nam. She had been so worried that I was dead, because it had been so long since I had written to her. She just died about five months ago."

Hearing this, I got real sad and teary, myself, being reminded of my mother. She was so worried about me coming on this trip; indeed, she told me for the first time, just before I left Tacoma: 'I remember how much I worried about you every day you were in Vietnam. But I didn't say anything to you about it. I didn't want you to worry any more than you must have been doing, already.'"

Even among the enemy:

"Oh, my son, since receiving word of your brother's death from his unit, then having his commemoration ceremony in the village, and getting the Patriotic Certificate, my dear son, I have worked night and day in the rice field, ploughing land and transplanting. And I pray always to Heaven, and the ancestors, your late father and brother, to bless you in that distant battlefield, praying you and your comrades will return safely..." Kien read and re-read the letter. His hands trembled, tears blurred his eyes....[122]

As the co-therapist, I find myself not in the mood to "push" the vets to work in the group sessions the way I do back at our American Lake PTSD Program. One of the vets is avoiding any deep work on the marked changes in his demeanor; he is very sad and serious today. This appears to be closely connected (at least partly) to his meeting a legless Vietnamese veteran in a wheelchair earlier today. I was more "up" today, walking around the market area with one of the vets. Indeed, I noticed that both he and I felt somewhat more relaxed among the crowds — at least a little!.

I'm now taking more notice of the run-down "modern" facilities: the hotels with fixtures missing and wires still hanging out; no lids on toilets, doors that don't close well, bullet holes still in the glass block in the lobby, the "tour boat" that was old and decrepit, windows that are broken in half or that don't open — or close.

---

121. Smith, *Two Decades*, 1990.
122. Bao Ninh, *The Sorrow of War* (London: Seckekr & Warburg, 1993), 20.

At this juncture, some of the group members mention that, not only are they starting to feel proud again, and lucky, but they are even missing home; not me — yet.

We see an amazing sight. There is, in effect, a massive "junk collage" sculpture of machinery and vehicles, including a canted small jeep trailer-sized box with the white US star on it. It is just there along the road, with the rest of Vietnam all around it. It reminds me of scenes in the *Planet of the Apes*, with the ruins of the Statue of Liberty and of subway tunnels, viewed from the future.

It is beginning to grate when our guide repeatedly says, "after being liberated from the Americans..."

Fears — And Courage

Group vet: "I still have many fears, and I am experiencing them on this trip, of bodily harm from any Vietnamese who have PTSD and are bitter about the war. I notice negative stares all around us; how can the rest of you go running around and ignore these signals?[123]

Others of us, too, mention fears that have popped up, especially when we are immersed in crowds of Vietnamese.

Group vet: "I don't have too much courage, I'm really afraid. I'm staying in my hotel room a lot during our free time."

Ray: "I don't agree that you don't have too much courage. In fact, I say that you have considerable courage: to be as afraid as you are, and even with all that fear, you have been willing to come to Vietnam! Now, that's courage!"

Le Nhu Tu, Telex Office, Huong Giang Hotel, Hue.

Ray: "How can the Vietnamese treat us so nicely now, after what happened during the war?"

Response(in English): "When enemies become friends, let bygones be bygones." (And she certainly seems very sincere in what she says.)

However, this "let bygones be bygones" attitude appeared not to extend towards former Saigon-regime soldiers.

The Land Is Recovering From Agent Orange

The land is reclaiming its territory: the defoliated mountain pass from Hue to Da Nang is now growing back, some 20 years later. The vegetation is only a few feet high in most places, but it looks healthy, and next to the stream the growth is perhaps 4-5 feet high.

---

123. Smith, *Two Decades*, 1990.

DAY 6. FRIDAY, FEBRUARY 3

Hue and A Flashback

We take a boat on a 45-minute ride to a temple in Hue. It strikes me as really familiar, and I ask if there is a golden Buddha in the temple. Sure enough, there it is. Just where it was when I visited my college roommate and fellow ROTC cadet, Angelo Romeo, who was stationed in Hue while I was in Nha Trang.

I'm excited; our guide seems to know the former Army compound where Angelo was — near our hotel, which used to be the MACV (Military Assistance Command Vietnam) compound.

It's possible that part of my reaction is because I want to see some visible signs that America was here — any signs. Wouldn't we be absolutely depressed if all signs were gone?! And yet, in another way, would it not be wonderful if all signs of the "American war" had vanished and Vietnam had moved on! Where are all the soldiers? They seemed to be everywhere, in great numbers, in Hanoi: all with green pith helmets or caps and uniforms and red stars, everywhere. And here, hardly any military uniforms. In retrospect, part of the Hanoi somberness was the ever-present dull green military clothing and hats: that is not the case in Da Nang and Hue.

I go back to the bus at the Citadel; I want to sit and write and think. I have discovered a new word: I am "monumented out" (after visiting just two). That is not why I'm here, at all.

Our sixth day, in three cities, and our first traffic light in Vietnam is here in Hue.

Hoa Hotel. We really are very lucky and fortunate to have the standard of living we have in America, especially in comparison to what we see here.

[Here, there are only two pages of notes for an entire day. I may have mislabeled some of my notes for Day 6 and placed them under Day #5 and/or under Day 7.)

DAY 7. SATURDAY, FEBRUARY 4

Da Nang and Highway 1 South.

Marble Mountain and LZ

This not experiencing "negatives" or numbing; instead, allowing ourselves to experience JOY. Is this an avoidance, or moving to another level in our stress recoveries?

Some vets, including me, don't have "trauma" related to specific events that happened in the war zone (such as having a buddy killed in front of us). Rather, we felt the impact of simply being in the war and exposed to wounding and dying — in terms of our values, outlook regarding war, government, etc. Memories come back of what was perhaps my most stressful duty in Vietnam: taking rotations as AOD (Administrative Officer on Duty at the 8th Field Hospital). AOD duty starts in the late afternoon. My repeated experiences removing valuables from acutely wounded soldiers in the ER remain anguishing memories. For me, it's the tragedy of war for all who participate, and the shock of going through college and then going to war.

Why do the Vietnamese people really seem to enjoy Americans? I know that this keeps coming up. But it so critical to our entire trip so far; we have returned to a land in which we had been the primary military opposition that resulted in killing some three million Vietnamese. In our most optimistic fantasies before this trip, none of us had expected joyous acceptance and greetings from practically everyone. US greenbacks and American generosity, being "soft," are certainly part of it. Our tour guide, Mr. Dang Sung, mentions that the Russians have the reputation among Vietnamese for being "very strong," but not nearly as friendly as Americans. Indeed, the Russians give the impression that they dislike having to be in Vietnam. In contrast, Americans offer gifts and souvenirs, and also some Vietnamese see them as possibly having information about places in America where their relatives have gone to live.

Today, a Swiss tourist told us, "Thank you, Americans, for having put your foot down and fought here in the war — no matter the outcome, it let the Communists know that the US will not just stand by. That message is critical." It is not clear that most of the world shares that view of US intervention, but it was a welcome comment.

One of our vets had a birthday, today. Two Vietnamese hotel employees, a manager and a desk clerk, came in and gave quite a speech, the gist of which was, "We are honored to have you here as a guest on your birthday. We know you miss your home and friends, but you have friends with you now, here. As a memento, here is a trinket for happiness and long life."

If all the vets get out of this trip is a renewed pride in being American and a feeling that we are fortunate to be living in the US, and to be who we are — this trip is worth it. I get into a conversation with one of the vets as we are walking along the beach, someone who has had a history of severe mood problems. He says to me, "Do you know what it is like to be [psychiatrically] disabled, and feel totally useless? That's how I have been feeling for several years. I worked so hard to get my VA disability, because I am disabled from the war. But not to be able to work, to have a purpose day to day, to be worth something, to give to others — it's terrible. But now, standing here on the beach, I believe that I will be able to do, to be, useful to some degree — and that feels good!"

Constant references are being made to our war perspective and the necessary updates to a peace-time Vietnam:

- Look at this hotel (in Hue): It has such a commanding view (and field of fire)
- Being next to the ocean (in Da Nang): Wouldn't this be scary, with all the noise of surf, to be on sentry duty when it would be just about impossible to hear anyone sneaking up on you? (Nothing seemed so dark as a starless and moonless night in Nam.)

- Here we are, standing around in a group in Hanoi, attracting all kinds of attention and crowds. This is the last thing we wanted to do, before!
- We are purposefully going into crowds: to face our fears and to meet the people
- The firecrackers of Tet repeatedly reminded us of the Tet offensive: and yet this is not the Tet offensive, 1968 — this is a Tet celebration, 1989!

There was a burst of fireworks within 20 feet of several of our group members, who were window-shopping. I was sitting on the bus, another 20 feet away. As the rockets exploded, I thought of terrorist attacks on groups of Americans in the street during the war.

Marble Mountain

Marble Mountain is an area south of Da Nang that was a VC stronghold. As we huffed and puffed up the long series of marble steps, little Vietnamese children (6-12 years old) walked along effortlessly beside us, constantly trying to sell us their wares; we were having a tough time just making the climb! How incredibly difficult it must have been to take Marble Mountain when it was infested with VC (who, we understand, stored lots of munitions in these caves).

Walking from Marble Mountain back through the village towards the hotel was like walking a gauntlet, a gauntlet of outstretched hands, empty ones, begging for dollars, showing us their wares for sale — and walking alongside us for perhaps 200 yards and making the same pitch over and over. I did "okay," trying to numb myself from the pleas of those begging, except when the kids looked (particularly) forlorn. And then, a one-legged man with a stick for a crutch grabbed at my hand, pointing to his absent leg and begging. He followed me and kept at it. I actually started feeling fear; or was it anxiety? I had to get away from him. And I abruptly turned and walked off — to be accompanied by the "more tolerable" pestering of the kids.

As one vet in the group had pointed out, the kids in Da Nang (where there was a massive American military presence) are very persistent and assertive about selling items, or begging: "Hello — you buy?" "Baby, no money, you help." This is in marked contrast to Hanoi, where older children and adults would push smaller children aside if they started begging or being pushy.

The Americans had been gone for a whole generation, yet it was as though somehow these kids were picking up what their parents and other adults must have been doing 15-20 years ago. Is that not incredible, and sad? It seems that a significant presence of the cash-rich among an impoverished people inevitably breeds this degrading relationship.

When we get to Saigon, we will have five days in the same hotel. Until then, this whirlwind schedule, this pace of moving from one hotel to another almost daily, and to ever new locations, allows us to avoid heavy feelings. There is so much external stimulation, and we are absorbing it everywhere, drinking it up, not wanting to miss anything. But in Saigon, we will have a designated mission each day, for a specific vet, and we will stay at the same hotel. It will be an entirely different experience.

From Da Nang to Qui Nhon

We headed off south on Highway 1, leaving Da Nang and going to Qui Nhon. Quang Ngai is a small town about halfway down the coast of Vietnam. A near-riot broke out after our bus parked on a street full of tiny, open-air storefronts. Indeed, the crowd was so dense that we could hardly move. Children ran their hands over our arms, laughing as their hands touched our arm hairs. They pounded on the sides of the bus (in a very friendly, laughing manner).

We stopped to take a break alongside Highway 1. Suddenly, a Vietnamese man looked up from where he was working in his garden in a churchyard. He rushed over, beaming, and began vigorously shaking hands with all of us. It turns out that he was a Protestant minister, pastor here for about 35 years, with a congregation of 150 people. He stated, in rudimentary English, that he had not seen any Americans since 1975. And, indeed, almost all the Vietnamese who gathered around reflect the same feeling — all curious and smiling.

We made a brief stop, for Bill, two hours south of Da Nang. This obviously was not a tourist spot. And the locals were very curious, but shy, with not one hand out begging (a refreshing change from Da Nang).

We drove around in the town of Bong Son. We were discovering that, while the Nam consisted mostly of villages and hamlets, and small towns dominated by military bases, the bases are mostly gone now and the villages and small towns have grown considerably. Bill was looking for LZ Two Bits, which had been at the edge of the small town of Bong Song during the war. It was not easy to find. Finally, our driver got directions.

After several turns and queries, we drove down a little road through the edge of the town. And suddenly, we rode up onto a long runway that stretched as far as we could see in either direction. And it looked to be in reasonably good condition. But, that was all that was there, in stark contrast to the bustling town immediately adjacent. It seemed empty and ghost-like. And it seemed so incongruous: the Vietnamese, with such terrible roads, seem to have "forgotten" about this runway. Was it forgotten on purpose?

And then, I noticed the obviously defoliated areas on the side of the runway. Saplings were now growing, but the gravel and grass seem manicured. And absolutely no one was around, with one exception. Squatting in the middle of the runway was an old peasant woman, with a basket of some kind of fruit or vegetables. She was making a use of something long since rendered non-functional. She was using the runway to grind food. And, remarkably, she continued pounding on the pavement, seemingly oblivious to the large group of foreigners who had suddenly and noisily appeared. It was surreal. [124]

---

124. Stevan Smith told me later that the villagers also dried rice on the runways.

And then, within a matter of minutes, a sea of villagers flooded in. The noise level was raised several notches. The villagers crowded in closely, watching everything we were doing. And that solitary peasant woman continued squatting, pounding vegetables on the abandoned runway...And I knew that, within five minutes of our leaving, the runway would be deserted again.

We were surrounded by Vietnamese. Perhaps they huddled so close to us at last partly due to the possible danger of unexploded mines, as our guide mentioned to us. And they listened and watched as Bill talked about LZ Two Bits and what happened there, so many years ago.

"It was New Year's Eve, 1967. The Americans fired weapons, to make noise as midnight was approaching.

"But in the morning, the people from the village brought out seven small packages wrapped in plastic, seven children who had been killed. And I remember one guy from the group looking up at us on the hill, and I said to myself, 'We just made another VC.' And some of our guys said that they had received some fire from the village, and so they had fired into the village around midnight. But it was awfully coincidental that they fired into the village exactly at midnight [Bill was convinced that the Americans had fired into the village at midnight to "celebrate the New Year" and not because they had been fired on].

"I always considered myself a soldier, and I never ever could make war on children. And it hurt me that we fired on kids. I started to have, for the first time, to have a different feeling about what we did...we used to go into the village and do sick call with the kids...and to think that our own people fired on them."

Bill's sense of pride and purpose died that day, with those seven children.[125]

Metaphor of the War: The Fate of Former American Military Bases

This scene of the abandoned runway seemed to be one metaphor of the US presence during the war. We finally found a tangible presence that the Americans had actually been here 15 - 20 years ago. And it was almost deserted — yet adjacent to the town — and being used for an entirely different purpose than during the war.

There were two recurrent findings during our return trip: (1) installations that were being used for the same purpose as during the war, such as a former American military base, or (2) places that had been so transformed as to be unrecognizable or impossible to locate — even for vets who had been thoroughly certain that they would be able to find their former duty station site — no matter what changes had occurred.

Bong Son and North Dakota

I couldn't help but smile at an image that popped into my mind. Picture the contrast between the scene at the "deserted" runway at Bong Son, and what might happen if a

---

125. Smith, *Two Decades*, 1990.

group of Asian tourists showed up in a town or city in, say, North or South Dakota. How would the Americans in that locale react to a busload of foreign tourists?

The abandoned, yet perfectly good, runway in Bong Son was an echo of the past and a sign of how archaic and out of touch our vivid 20-year-old memories were with the current reality.

Our guide informed us that the Vietnamese war vet gets 2,000 *dong* a month for a missing limb (66 cents) and an annual military benefit of $160; and physically-dis-abled vets can go to clinics for treatment or medications; they get angry because there is no money or medication there for them.

I'm feeling somewhat disappointed, at this moment. The "exotic" memories of Viet-nam seem quite in the past — or is it because I am 20 years older? The rush, the fas-cination, of being in the Asian country of Vietnam does not reflect in my experience today. Today, I am more conscious of the poverty, the lower standard of living than we in the West are used to, the rather poor "tourist" bus transportation.

And how cut off these people have been from Westerners. They seem spellbound when we stop. I spot many people, of all ages, staring back, intently watching one or more of us. And doing that for 10-20 minutes, or as long as we are there, without moving — except to smile, laugh, or comment to each other.

Lush, verdant, neat, beautiful, and tidy fields of crops, dikes, and irrigation channels stretch in every direction; everything obviously has been painstakingly accom-plished by hand labor. And, in vivid contrast, the yards and houses right next to those picture-perfect are muddy, dirty, often decrepit, untended and somewhat junky looking. Is it that so much energy must be put into the fields all day long that there is little left to do the same to the houses and yards and streets? Or, is there a different sense of what is important?

Every once in awhile (maybe one out of 30, 40 or 50 women), I notice one (of vary-ing ages) who looks very well-groomed, neat, nice outfit, amongst the teeming num-bers who look so much poorer and dirtier. And I wonder if their homes are as different as their clothes; they all seem to be riding the same quality of bikes.

And I just love the remarkable friendliness being expressed to us, everywhere. A vet and I were just getting into our hotel room. There came a knock on the door. An older (50+) *mama san* came in with our sheets, as we were both lounging on top of our beds. As my roommate moved to get off his bed, she tossed his sheet on his shoulder, laughing at, and with, us. She left my sheets, and laughing, backed out the door. And we looked at each other, and laughed. A very simple but delightful moment.

Just got into Qui Nhon. Will try to locate the 67th Evac Hospital after breakfast.

Well, Jake and I got good news: we will spend two nights and one full day in Nha Trang, so I will get to go to Xom Bong Hamlet where I had led many MEDCAPs! (Jake and I were both stationed in Nha Trang: Jake at the Air Force Base and I at the adjacent Army Hospital).

I notice that our mosquito netting is beige, not Army green. Also, I remember that the VC and NVA were never described as cowardly, or lacking the will to fight. In contrast, a number, but certainly not all, of US soldiers had negative things to say about some of the RVN forces whom we were aligned with.

We learn that Russians in Vietnam have to use US dollars, and have to speak to shopkeepers in English! Of course, they resent it.

Qui Nhon. I feel a sense of "ownership" about my experience here. In a way, I do not want to share it: especially with non-veterans. Most non-Vietnam vets probably don't even know that there was a 67th or 85th Army Hospital. We vets do, and I want to see it and take pictures of it for medical personnel vets in the US.

I feel obligated to get these pictures. And it would be okay for a medic or nurse to go with me, but I don't really want anyone else to come along. [Looking back at this note, in 2000, I am surprised that I felt this so strongly!]

Well, I just had a 2,000-dong (66 cent) "cyclo" ride to one of the two former Army Hospitals here in Qui Nhon. I won't know which one until I show the pictures to someone who served there. It was gratifying to see that it is still a hospital, albeit a Vietnamese civilian one. It's the first US military remnant that we have seen on this trip that is serving some reasonable, and civilan, purpose. Others we have seen are still in military use, but some are tourist hotels, or are totally abandoned, or have been converted to bizarrely different purposes (like the Esso gas station in Bong Son that was now some kind of shop — with the Esso Gas sign still hanging).

I am now hopeful that the 8th Field Hospital in Nha Trang (where I served) also will still be a hospital. Again, somehow, it would be gratifying that a resource for helping people was still being used for that purpose even 15 years after the war. Would the war have been worth it, if most of the larger US military hospitals were still hospitals? Of course, not. However, somehow it would contribute a small yet beneficial legacy that would make the co-existence of the Nam and Vietnam much more palatable.

I am starting to get really serious and really antsy about seeing Nha Trang today. Jake, who also served in Nha Trang, seems to be having the same reaction. I want "alone time" there, to be with Nha Trang and me, past and present. Yes, I do want to and will share my experience with the others, but first I want to experience my own healing.

I also find myself feeling resentful that the US government is so adamant about keeping Vietnam in diplomatic and economic isolation that it would try to discourage veterans from experiencing this return trip. There is a relationship between politics and war-related mental health recovery.

With our arrival in Nha Trang imminent, a set of old memories are triggered. The bus ride from Qui Nhon to Nha Trang begins shortly. This will be a trip that I made a number of times by air, but not by land. And now, it is not only safe to go by land, I really want to go by land. Still, a Huey chopper ride between Qui Nhon and Nha Trang, with the doors open and my feet dangling towards the edge, just like in 1968-69, would be a rush! We used to fly periodically to Qui Nhon to consult on psychiatric casualties at the Evac Hospital. And we, of course, would always fly. You never went overland if you had the option to go by air, which was comparatively safe.

DAY 8. SUNDAY, FEBRUARY 5

Nha Trang

Finally, we arrived in Nha Trang. I felt great as we were coming across the bridge, a bridge that I remembered quite well from the many times I drove across it. Jake and I were indeed coming to our former home in the Nam.

Also, perhaps, my memories of this bridge were anchored by a couple of photographs that I still had. In fact, I have been thinking that having pictures to look at from Vietnam during the war facilitate anchoring one's memories. The events and context that surround each such picture seem to predominate in several of my most frequent mental images of Nam: perhaps even more so than they would if I did not have the pictures. When vets come in for PTSD treatment, I counsel them against holding onto war pictures of violence, such as photos of dead enemy personnel, or war-trophy necklaces of ears taken from the enemy. Constantly refreshing the images can only reinforce their intrusive traumatic memories of the war, and keep alive and frozen in time the images of decades ago as if they were still true today.

Once we got into the city of Nha Trang (population about 500,000), nothing looked familiar, anywhere, except for the boulevard and beach. But in the city itself, a city that I was in several days a week for a whole year, there was nothing that looked the same. I found myself getting somewhat depressed; where were all the restaurants where I ate, the places I would go for a drink, Fairy's home? There was nothing. I hold onto one last hope: that I can find and recognize the site of the 8th Field Hospital.

I don't remember ever going into the ocean, but I have a crystal clear memory of being on the beach, and bargaining to buy fresh-as-you-can-get coconuts from *mama-sans*: I'm on the beach in Nha Trang. Mama-san comes along, carrying fresh coconuts and pineapples in baskets tied to the two ends of a pole draped on one shoulder. She smiles widely and kindly, with betel-nut stained and deteriorated teeth. We begin bargaining, usually with fingers to indicate the price. We quickly agree; the mama-san takes a machete and slices open a tip of the coconut and hands it to me. I greedily gulp down the juice, and may hold on to the coconut to reap the bounty of the white coconut meat later. Wow, what a Kodak moment, with full visceral effects of taste, sweat, heat, thirst, and then delicious thirst-quenching satisfaction.

And, I remember the old school house on the beach where I used to teach English to Vietnamese children. Will I find it? Probably not, as it was not a very sturdy structure even in 1968. I remember the wonderful combination of innocence and enthusiasm of the students, young and old alike, as they faithfully came to the English class, week after week. It was a most rewarding and humbling experience, as I struggled to learn how to "teach English as a second language." However, I knew that, no matter how amateurish my approach might have been, the students were getting the opportunity of interacting with a native-language English speaker — rather than a local instructor who spoke accented and, perhaps, flawed English. And, they were getting to know American humor! I have watched almost no Vietnam war movies, but when Robin Williams is shown teaching English to Vietnamese students in *Good Morning, Vietnam*, I find a poignant reminder of my "school" on the beach in Nha Trang. And along with the pleasant memories of teaching English on the beach, off in the distance the war was still going on...relentlessly.

I'm getting real emotional. On the spur of the moment, I bought a black bamboo elephant head walking stick last night for Billy Ray, one of "our" vets who walks with a cane. It was him: black, shiny, impressive, proud. I gave it to him this morning, and got all teary doing it.

One vet in the group is paranoid, and he has not been taking his prescribed medications. Some of them are sleep-inducing: and he is intent on staying on alert at night. Why? Because we are in Vietnam, and who knows what may happen. But, of course, now he can't sleep, is scarcely eating. He's afraid that someone could be adulterating (poisoning) the food.

Some details of this vet's Vietnam story strain credulity. He states that he carried a machine gun in Vietnam, plus a rifle, a pistol and a straight razor. That, in and of itself, may not be unusual; many combat vets carried all kinds of weapons. However, he functioned in a role in which we had never heard of anyone carrying a machine gun.

But, of course, one thing you learn about Vietnam is that unbelievable and far-out stories were often very real. And so, this vet may well have carried a machine gun, paranoid as he was. He saw danger everywhere.

We approach the Vietnamese Air Force base and see the wire fence that borders what is now a Vietnamese Air Force Base and runway, and Jake notes the changes.

Jake: "This was the runway. This has grown up so bad I can't tell where the hell I'm at. There was no woods here 20 years ago. Nothing. This was all open country. Beach. We missed our turn, we got to be looking for a left turn, because...See this stuff over here (pointing), that is where I belong..."

Even though this is where he "belongs," Jake will get no closer.

It is a Vietnamese air base now.

Russian helicopters are in the hangars.

And we Americans are on the outside, looking in...It's very frustrating to travel 7,000 miles and be stopped 200 yard short, as Jake is, here in Nha Trang.

Across the Nha Trang Bay bridge, my past is now only miles, and not decades, away. And on my first full day in Nha Trang, I stay in bed an extra hour or so, a little depressed. I'm not finding the familiarity that I was looking for.

Yet I'm anxious to get going, and irritable: just like one of our group members had been when we were in Da Nang, where he had served. This may be a pattern to be aware of for the remaining vets: as each vet gets close to his/her former duty station, he/she also may well become agitated and irritable.

Again, a bittersweet experience. Here's the Air Force Base and the runway that Jake and I can only look down along from outside the fence. We are not allowed on the airbase itself, because it is an active Vietnamese military base. We may not be able to get close enough to see the hospital!

The beach is all grown in; new buildings, new trees, and the people can't remember an old wooden building on the beach. It is gone now, just like the "Alliance for Freedom" is gone (the joint American/South Vietnamese coalition). I'm so close and yet so far away: from the hospital, the terrain, the memories.

It's like the jungle, the inevitable growth of vegetation, 20 years later. All that the Americans did and built here, all of that is disappearing and gradually but relentlessly being reclaimed by the vegetation and by the Vietnamese people And stories two decades old feel more and more like nostalgic and distant memories, memories that I am desperately trying to touch more fully. However, my ability to recall seems to be failing me; or is it that the events and memories of the Nam are now fading to a position of less importance now, as we are being immersed in a Peacetime Vietnam? I do and I do not want that Nam time to be of less importance. We've gotten as close as we can get to the 8th Field Hospital (looking from the north end of the runway). This is anti-climatic, a real let down.

Well, that's that: we're not able to even see where the 8th Field Hospital had been, let alone being able to walk on the grounds.

Coming up next: we'll see if Xom Bong Hamlet brings anything back. So close, and yet so far. This is a theme that several of the vets are experiencing in regard to returning to specific sites. There are many sites that, even when we can actually find them, we cannot get close to. Somehow, not being able to go that last few hundred yards makes it feel tantalizingly and frustratingly far away, after traveling 7,000 miles.

A Vietnamese man asked, "Why did you Americans leave us?"

And one vet answered: "Because the government made that decision, damn it!"

Yes, we did abandon the South Vietnamese people — the RVNs and their families, the CIA operatives and their families, the Chu Hois and their families, all who opposed communism. And yet, who feels the guilt for abandoning our Vietnamese friends? Certainly not the government. Certainly not most Americans. But, a number of vets do. It's the veterans who are the ones who are left holding the anguish from the wars they are sent into.

I meet the American husband of a Vietnamese woman from Nha Trang. He tells us that the government sent former RVNs to labor (e.g., "re-education") camps — and that some are still there (19 years after the war ended). When former RVNs get out of the re-education camps, they are not allowed to own any property. Many live with their parents. The only kind of work they can get involves physical labor, no matter what their level of education or job skills.

I expected lots of feelings here at the 8th Field Hospital site; and I got more, as we were approaching Nha Trang and I was thinking about it, than when we actually arrived. Why? Perhaps because here, I really was "an observer" — from several hundred yards away; standing by, increasingly frustrated, hearing and watching the interpreter trying and failing to find any locals who remembered where the Army hospital was. This just reinforced the idea of how fast and far the past has receded, left behind by these people and this place — and, increasingly, by me?

In my frenetic quest to find Xom Bong Hamlet, I was of course on a tight time-line. The group spent the day enjoying Nha Trang. I took the opportunity to focus totally on something for myself: finding that Hamlet, the fishing village where I had participated in many MEDCAPs during the war. Since I couldn't find the 8th Field Hospital, now my hopes rested on finding Xom Bong Hamlet. While we were going into various neighborhoods and asking if anyone knew where Xom Bong Hamlet was, I encountered a former RVN Air Force lieutenant. He told me that he had been in a re-education camp for three years. And, he was very pre-occupied with wanting to get to the States. He had an uncle in America, he said, but had not received a letter from him in four years. Vietnam was no place for a former RVN to live; could I help him get to the US? With his family? He pleaded, looking into my eyes. But, I could hardly hear what he was saying, let alone come up with any satisfactory response. I have no idea what I said; but I clearly remember my internal reaction. I was in distress, myself. I couldn't find the 8th Field Hospital, and other than the bridge I didn't recognize anything in Nha Trang City. Here I was, at the location where I served 20 years ago, swept away in a crescendo of thoughts and feelings, desperately searching, trying to find a familiar sight amidst all the new housing, new trails, new growth.

[Note: reading what I wrote and was feeling at the time in 1989, I am a little ashamed that I was so cold, ignoring and indeed resenting this former RVN "interrupting" my quest. My reactions, as expressed in my journal, are a sign of how frenetic the other vets and I were, as we got caught up in the moment, each of us trying to zero in on the "end" of our 10,000-mile and 20-year journey.]

Nha Trang and Qui Nhon: The details of the downtown areas look only vaguely familiar, and not even the beach looks the same because it is now overgrown. Only the bridge rings a bell. What has stayed familiar, what remains indelibly imprinted in the mind is the intense emotion, the momentary, singular experiences on the one hand, and a more amorphous sense of overall experiences. But the in-between: no! It seems to be gone from my memory banks.

Three of us were invited to the home of a Vietnamese family in Vinh Tho, Nha Trang, to celebrate Tet with them. And I got loaded. We were toasted numerous times by our hosts, and we had been told before we went that it was considered very impolite to not drink when a toast is offered, especially in someone's home. I have an overall memory of a very pleasant and touching visit, lots of laughter, and graciousness on the part of our Vietnamese hosts.

The next morning, I finally found someone who said he knew where Xom Bong Hamlet was. In fact, he said it was actually right about here, where we were. But, this didn't make any sense to me. We were in the midst of a congested neighborhood, houses everywhere, going all the way to the water and to the bridge going into downtown Nha Trang. But, the Vietnamese insisted; he was taking me to Xom Bong Hamlet, which was very nearby. And I got into Xom Bong Hamlet, and it was a mob scene.

It took about a half-hour discussion (through a not particularly fluent translator) to find a family (Catholic) who knew about where the old village square was located, where we used to set up our MEDCAPs. And now we were going through narrow streets with a teeming population. I find that I cannot get into nostalgia or sadness because I am overloaded, indeed, saturated, with sensory inputs. As we are walking towards the old village center, kids that we pass all along the narrow streets are chanting, literally, a friendly chorus of "Hello Americans," in Vietnamese. That is something to experience, as we are walking along; I get goose bumps.

Finally, we arrived, and stopped in front of one particular house. I was told that the family in this home had lived there a long time and were very familiar with this place when it was just a fishing village. They tell the family inside who I am, and why I am here. A very special encounter then ensues. We are quickly invited inside and seated, the family gathering inside the room. In addition, a number of the entourage of Vietnamese who had been tagging along as we were walking on this recon crowded into the edges of the room, by the front door.

It takes several more minutes of conversation before the family fully understands who I am and why I am here, looking for the village square of the fishing village where I used to run MEDCAPs. One family member slips out of the room as we are talking; he comes back a short while later, holding about a five-foot long, grey wooden boat oar, smoothly worn from use. It is offered to me as a memento. I am stunned, trying not to accept it; but they insist that I take it. This is the first tangible and tactile moment in Nha Trang where I actually feel that, yes, this is from 20 years ago, this is very familiar, this is real, it is validated, then: my memories that there was a fishing village called Xom Bong Hamlet, on the outskirts of Nha Trang, here in South Vietnam.

However, I also become extremely frustrated. As best as I can decipher from the translating, we are perhaps within 150 meters of the old Hamlet square. However, only one of the older villagers would be able to help pinpoint the exact location. But, there is no time left. We have to go back to the waiting bus, and I can hardly make it in time. To find where the square used to be would have entailed tracking down one of the older locals, and following a winding 150 meter path that could have gone in any one of several directions through the urban sprawl. There was absolutely no way that I could have found it on my own, and there was no time to find a guide.

163

Once again, a recurring theme for several of us on this trip. We travel 10,000 miles and two decades, but are stopped a few hundred meters short — or can't recognize or find our former duty sites, which must be right around the corner — or under our noses. As a side-note, I took very good care of that oar during the rest of the trip. What happened with the oar after our return to the US is perhaps symbolic of my "forgetting about" this trip for many years, or my "forgetting about" many memories of Vietnam during the war. When we first got home, I hung the paddle on a wall, like an art piece. Later, I took it down and I think it went into a closet. Later, I put it out in the garage. Although I might have had a "special relationship" with it, it was just a "beat up oar" to most viewers. It was shunted from one corner of the garage to another, until after I retired from the VA and took a position at the University of Southern Mississippi. Then I moved a number of books and mementos into my new office, and I "rediscovered" the oar and placed it right next to my bookcase. And soon enough, I found myself transcribing the diary, finally, and planning another return to Vietnam.

I find myself flashing back to the Vietnam War and to the irony and contrasts, between 1968 and Vietnam peacetime today. A small fishing Hamlet, now transformed into an urban sprawl, Vietnam style.

An American Army hospital cannot be located. An American Air Force base is now a Vietnamese Air Force Base, and entry is denied. An American runway in Bong Son, now abandoned and desolate, yet only a few hundred yards away from a bustling town. With these peacetime and wartime images of Vietnam juxtaposed, there go my sadness anchors, e.g., my 1968-69 memories of the fishing village and of the 8th Field Hospital. Have they disappeared, or just gone to some other place from whenever they might reappear one day? And what will my images be when PTSD-laden vets are still eating, sleeping, dreaming, talking the Nam and I'm sitting there, with fresh memories of Vietnam 1989; will I become impatient, and attempt to "persuade" them how much the realities of Vietnam have changed?

In fact, I have become even more impressed with how vivid and fixed are the recurring traumatic memories of war vets; and, to attempt to "convince" a vet that his/her images are now obsolete is a futile effort — and, indeed, is often anger-producing. The war memories are one's images of an indelible time and place, and will remain so. But, what we can hope for is to allow a new series of experiences to take up residence alongside those views — whether by flying in a helicopter as part of a therapeutic program, or returning to Vietnam, or watching a video of such a return trip: and then, possibly, being able to generate "new" and "safe" and "positive" experiences of Vietnam to juxtapose alongside the old ones .

I just had a flash. Is it possible that I will be less "driven" or motivated to stay in the field of PTSD, because I will have let go of many of my Vietnam-related issues?

Or, will I have a renewed vigor and drive to promote what we've learned from this trip throughout the VA and among mental health professions?

I truly do not know, at this moment. Of course, I may go back to being just as I was before I arrived in Nam. But, that seems improbable; this trip is certainly changing me, even if I do not yet know in what ways.

And yes: having that oar from the former fishing village (which is still called Xom Bong Hamlet) was and is very important. It is a tangible experience today, something I can touch, feel, see, and smell, of yesterday. And, it still was functional and used in the hamlet today, even if "the hamlet" is now part of Nha Trang as it sprawls across the Xom Bong bridge.

The Tragedy of Vietnamese Supporters of the US

As I remembered it (both then and now), Nha Trang seemed to be full of Vietnamese who were genuinely pro-US: many were raised as Catholics, many were well educated, many were former RVNs. And so many continue to dream of getting to the US — somehow, someway, someday. That is a big part of our legacy to the Vietnamese: we have, in essence, had many of them branded as allied with the old Saigon regime and with us; we pulled out and the Saigon government went under; and these people (former military and civilians alike, whole families and especially Amerasian children) are now prisoners in their own country. The country has changed and is hostile to them, and the people who got them in this bind —the people who made up the US government, in particular — and many US Vietnam veterans too, for that matter — feel absolutely no responsibility about it. It's a tragedy of immense proportion and suffering, just as the PTSD that US Vietnam vets have is a tragedy of immense proportion and suffering.

"I Don't Need Money — I Need Friends"

As for the former RVN who interpreted for me as I was searching for the old fishing village, he went so far as to close up his shop to try and guide me to the village square. I attempted to give him some money for his trouble, but he said, "I don't need money, I need friends." And, he obviously needed both.

In a conversation, one former RVN said "10,000 piasters," referring to the monetary unit that was current before and during the war. It has long since been devalued, and rendered entirely worthless by rampant inflation — calculations are now made in dong. This seems to reflect the fact that he, and no doubt many older Vietnamese, are living in the past, struggling since the war ended, feeling little hope for the present or future — except, perhaps, for the dream of getting to America — whatever they imagine America to be. And by the same token, many US vets with Vietnam-related PTSD are living in the past, struggling since the war ended, feeling little hope for the present or future — except perhaps for the dream of returning to Vietnam; but of the latter category, many strongly resent those Vietnamese who do manage to live out their dream of getting to America.

We had originally planned on a five-day transition in Bangkok, after leaving Vietnam; we hadn't wanted to replicate the "48 hours from foxhole to front porch" that left so many in shock during the war. However, having been in Vietnam for several days, many of the group members now think that we don't need such a transition. Most of us want to get directly home as soon as possible, when our "business" is done. There is a critical difference between going home after being in the war, versus coming home from peacetime Vietnam: we are eager to talk about this Vietnam experience to everyone back home!

Some differences between the Tet New Year now, versus during theWar —

1969: The year after the 1968 Tet Offensive, no Tet celebrations or fireworks were allowed in Vietnam.

1989: Big Tet celebrations. You absolutely would not believe the amount, the duration and sheer loudness of the fire crackers; now, I have a much better appreciation of how perfect an occasion Tet was for a sneak attack by the Communists.

The former RVNs came out of the woodwork all over Nha Trang to talk to us. This is the first time on our return trip that this has happened. All of our contacts with former RVNs in Nha Trang bring back memories of the many Vietnamese living in Nha Trang in 1968-69 who were truly anti-communist and heartfelt supporters of the US. Many had already fled the communists in the north.

Jake had a recurring Vietnam nightmare. Now, Jake gets to recreate his recurring dream in the exact location in Vietnam where it was set! A psychodramatist's fantasy fulfilled We get Jake to do the scene: he helps to build the fire, set up the seats, select who sits where and who plays what part in the drama. He is sitting around a campfire on a beach in Vietnam, with other Americans. They are giving Jake a really hard time, accusing him of having hesitated when the Viet Cong woman suddenly appeared in the tunnel and knifed the American soldier standing next to him. He let her do it, they say. The dialogue between Jake and the rest becomes very emotional, and this time it ends differently than in his dreams. The other Americans accept Jake. [This enactment is shown partially on the PBS documentary, "Two Decades and a Wake-Up."] And I get to sit back and observe, rather than being an active therapist, as April facilitates the re-enactment.

Once again: we have American drama going on, with a large and very curious gallery of Vietnamese gathering around to watch with fascination. Jake and the rest of our vets on the beach at Nha Trang, at night, fire blazing, video cameras rolling. Steve tells some of the onlookers that we are celebrating Tet by letting go of sad memories; and indeed, we are. Two of the vets toss letters into the flames, letters that other vets back home had given them to burn or bury in Vietnam.

Amerasian Sisters in Nha Trang

Amerasians, off-spring of US soldiers and Vietnamese girls, are called "Bui Doi." Literally, this means something like "Dust of life," but we also hear that another way of translating would be more like the "fallout" (or "debris") of life. We wince as our guide keeps referring to them (in Vietnamese) as half-breeds. American soldiers fathered an estimated 50,000 Amerasians. Today, the thousands who remain are reportedly are among the poorest of the poor. Many live in gangs, in parks, hustling for money, selling postcards and chewing gum, at best. In the middle of a sea of Asian-looking Vietnamese people, we are introduced to two Amerasian sisters, probably twins, who look very American and who apparently have their own families. They have obviously lived in Vietnam all these years, they speak and act "Vietnamese," yet they look startlingly American — the cognitive incongruence is bewildering. How did they survive, following the US withdrawal — amidst the anti-American sentiment that must have been present and active. How did they withstand the racist comments and prejudice — or perhaps it was not as bad as I imagine? I pray that it was not.

As difficult their lives must have been over the years, these "living reminders" of our presence in Vietnam were obviously very happy to see and talk with us, and one or two vets exchanged addresses and promised to write. I hoped that this wasn't a replay of what happened in Nam during the war: many vets, as they were getting ready to leave, promised to stay in touch with comrades remaining in Vietnam. And oftentimes such promises were not fulfilled, and the promised letters were not forthcoming.

Is It Dangerous in Vietnam Now For Americans?

Vets had wondered, back home, whether it would be dangerous here in Vietnam on our return trip. Perhaps angry (North) Vietnamese veterans with severe PTSD might act out when they saw us. During our time here, so far, walking around in the cities has proven remarkably peaceful and safe. Indeed, there appears to be practically no danger of Vietnamese hurting American vets with PTSD who return to visit Vietnam — and the Vietnam of today is proving to be an incredible eye-opener, entirely free of the terrible or terrifying scenes in the traumatic war memories of veterans with PTSD.

DAY 9. MONDAY, FEBRUARY 6

Saigon And Long Binh

What To Expect When Visiting One's Old Duty Site: Lessons Learned in Nha Trang

There is a marked difference in my attitude today versus yesterday. Now I am relaxed, at peace, calm, content, satisfied. In contrast, coming into Nha Trang I was really antsy, getting angry, was self-centered, and was operating with tunnel vision, that is, intent only on getting to Nha Trang and the former site of the 8th Field Hospital. Last night in our group meeting, based upon my personal awareness of my own experience in Nha Trang, I emphasized the following:

1 Be assertive, and do what you have to do to get your experience here in Nam.
2. The rest of us should realize, as we get close to someone's "area" of service, that the vets whose former duty station we are approaching will probably not be in a frame of mind to let others know what is going on with them.
3. Expect that you will be experiencing tunnel vision, at first merely intent, and then probably desperately searching, for a familiar site; introspective, and with a spectrum of internal thoughts and feelings that will be speeding by
4. You will almost surely want some alone time, there, at your former duty station
5. If strong feelings and issues come up, we must make time to deal with them immediately. And the bus may be the only relatively private place to do that. In fact, if you wait even 30 minutes, that flooding-in surge of feel-

ings and emotions may be gone, and not come back (like my internal reactions when Jake was in front of his old billet — and I could not find mine)!

[As I am transcribing the above, I note with some amusement how, on this day, I was "the calm, reasoned voice of wisdom." I had just gone through it, so I was describing what "would" happen to the other vets when they got to their old duty station sites. Of course, these were my own feelings and reactions, and only time would tell if this was a "universal" or typical experience that other vets would share.]

Just went through Cam Ranh Bay, about a 70-minute drive from Nha Trang. I flash back to thinking about the psychiatric casualties that we assessed on our regular mental health sick call trips to Cam Ranh Bay, versus the veterans we assessed from combat units. And a reflection on the many chopper rides between Nha Trang and Cam Ranh Bay to do psychiatric sick call. Now, that was a trip; flying down to CRB where people would actually sign up for a psych sick call. In my memories, it seemed like the soldiers would be lined up, waiting for the arrival of the head-shrinkers, parallel to waiting in the sick call line to be seen by the medic for some medical treatment. (The psych business was brisk enough in Cam Ranh for our unit to eventually off-station a social work officer there full-time. As I recollect, substance abuse was particularly problematic.)

This reminds me of the fact that, when we were treating psych casualties in Nam in 1968-69, it seemed that the majority of the psych casualties who had been evacuated to us were rear echelon personnel, as in CRB, rather than front-line personnel [again, very similar to US troops in Iraq today]. At the time, we thought that this was because rear echelon troops had too much time on their hands and/or were perhaps less stable and more prone to acting out. Later, after treating hundreds of veterans over many years, I realized that another factor must have been involved. When you are out in the bush, fighting for your life on a daily basis, you must remain alert and in survival mode all the time. Strict adherence to this survival mode was what made it possible for you to get through the daily horrors, or through the daily routine and boredom in a context of constant threat — attack all around — interspersed with the momentary madness of combat action. In such circumstances, almost any person will function in order to survive; thus, actual psych breakdowns on the battlefield are extremely rare. And it is only later, back in base camp or back in the US, when the danger is past, that emotional reactions and dysfunction typically occur — the so-called "delay" in symptoms.

Over the last couple of days, one vet who has been quite quiet, soft-spoken, and less animated, has been hanging out the bus door as we are truckin' down the highway. He has been yelling "hello" to just about everyone we pass. He must have said several hundred hellos in two days! And he is constantly getting back grins, smiles and greetings; probably 80% of the people we have passed have greeted him in reply. And the remaining ones simply stare or show no reaction — but never have I noticed an angry or hostile expression. Vets will enjoy Vietnam today, as we are discovering, if for no other reason than the fact that Americans are still seen as very special here (or many Vietnamese are faking it extremely convincingly!). And that is a very seductive attraction, especially for individuals whose self-esteem has been so damaged for so long.

Dave is a brown water Navy vet, one who served on or near the muddy rivers of Vietnam's Mekong Delta. One day he and I, along with a cameraman — Phil Sturholm, a fellow vet — took a cyclo ride from our hotel in Saigon to visit the site of his former Navy base in Nha Be, south of Saigon. [126] We had split up the group on this day, so that other vets would have the time to go and visit their former duty sites all around in the vicinity of Saigon. Dave calculated that it would take us about 20 minutes to get where we were going. It turns out to be more like two hours, one way, a bouncing and very hot cyclo ride, directly into the sun. And that's not to mention the physical exertion on the cyclo driver pedaling us. That should have been the first clue that our journey to Nah Be was going to be full of surprises.

The cyclo driver does his best to muster the vocabulary to establish communication. He tells us that he is a former RVN and opens a conversation with us, stating, in quite broken English, that the North Vietnamese "don't know if Americans are coming back to make war or peace: so they are suspicious." I note that we had found almost all the Vietnamese we had met to be very friendly and full of smiles; and the small number who didn't smile would simply look at us. He said, "If Vietnamese smile at you Americans, they are happy to see you — or, they could be sad behind the smiles. But if Vietnamese are angry at you or not happy to see you, they will not smile and probably won't say anything." No doubt, the emotions brought up as we passed by were far more complex than we could perceive from a fleeting glance.

Vietnamese Colonel Outside of the Nha Be Navy Base

At the Navy base, which became a Vietnamese Navy Base in 1975, we walked up to the sentry gate, pressing the cyclo driver into service as a volunteer amateur interpreter. He had told us that we would stand a better chance of gaining entry to the base if we presented a slightly modified story, namely, that we were Americans with Vietnamese wives in the US. He recommended I say that I was a doctor, and not a former GI, and that Dave was my patient and a Vietnam veteran (which he was). The sentry guard said that he did not have the authority to allow us onto the base, and to wait. He then went out of sight, and returned awhile later with a man, in civilian clothes, who looked like he had been disturbed on his off-duty. He was introduced to us as the Captain.

The Captain talked to us a little and then took us into a building outside of the base perimeter wall (we later found out that it is the Colonel's home). There, we sat down, quite an assorted crew: a Vietnamese military officer, five NVA veterans, a cyclo driver who had fought for the South, a cameraman and two American Vietnam veterans.

We talked for a while, and the Captain then offered a toast of Russian vodka: "For friendship." Vietnamese protocol compelled us to drink, although a shot of vodka might not seem so refreshing on a hot summery day. In any case, we hope that by appreciating the hospitality and sharing the goodwill, Dave ultimately will get permission to go onto the base.

Then, the Captain tells us that he does not have the authority to allow us onto the base, and he walks out. He returns a short while later, and introduces us to a Major. Once again, we go through our introductions, why we are here, etc. Several more

126. Smith, *Two Decades*, 1990.

toasts are offered and drunk. Finally, the Major says that he does not have the authority to allow us onto the base, and states that he has to go get the Colonel.
The Major and Captain then leave. A while later, the Major returns with the man whom he introduces as the Colonel — the same man who had been introduced to us as the Captain! After we got over the initial shock, the Colonel and we all burst out laughing. And, he explained that he had wanted to observe us — without us knowing that he was the Colonel. We then sat down again, and yes, drank several more toasts. The Colonel then told us about his life and his career in the military. He was quite pragmatic about the war. "I was a soldier, you were a soldier, and we fought. Now, the war is over, and we can be friends." [127]

While all of this was unfolding, Dave and I intermittently interjected our request to be allowed on the base. At some point, it occurred to me that Dave might have a better chance of getting the nod if I stayed behind. And so we change our negotiating position, and only request that Dave be allowed in —with much emphasis on the importance of this to Dave. Of the Vietnamese, the Colonel and Major dominated the conversation almost entirely; only they were interacting and asking questions and making comments. The Colonel observed that the war entailed shared decision making. "No one [officer] made the decision; it was me [the Colonel] and the Navy, and who knows who [there is always someone else, higher in rank, involved] — who makes the decisions. All three together, not one; and we don't know who #3 was, do we?"

It seemed to me that the Colonel was trying to defuse any tendency among us to personalize the question of who was ultimately responsible for what happened during the war, or for that matter, during this little visit; to say that we all were just soldiers doing our duty and never knowing why or who all was involved — "nothing personal."

We continued to talk, and through several rounds of discussions and toasts we continued to hope that they would eventually let Dave in for a brief visit. They gave him a pin of Ho Chi Minh as a symbol of friendship, and pinned it on his shirt. And Dave reciprocated, pinning an insignia on the Colonel's shirt. But Dave did not get permission to go onto the base. Instead, a most touching thing happened as we were leaving the Colonel's home. As Dave and the Colonel were walking back by the gate and the cyclo, two former enemies, they spontaneously put their arms on each other's shoulders as they continued walking. What a sight to see. Dave's former enemy had become an ally, giving support to the best of his ability in Dave's trek to heal from the wounds of war.

In retrospect, it was insanely naive to think that two men, recognizable as foreigners from a mile away, and one's former enemies to boot, could simply knock on the gate of a secure military base, in a country that their own government has refused to have diplomatic relations with and against which it has instituted an economic embargo — and hope to talk their way in! We could as well have proposed that two Russians who spoke no English arrive at a guarded military facility in the US, during the height of the cold war, and explain that they are veterans and want to come in. Nonetheless, we tried, believe me we tried; and in the trying, we had a priceless experience.

---

127. *Ibid.*

The following are reactions and impressions that I noted in my journal on the way back to Saigon on the cyclo. I was full of emotions, heightened by the innumerable toasts, and struggling to absorb the incredible shifting dynamics and nuances of what had happened at the base.

Even the Colonel, who ended up sitting with us at the building outside the base walls: it's not that it was so difficult for him to give permission to let us on the base, but the thought of what would happen when his superiors heard about it, after we had left!

He masqueraded in the first sit-down discussion with us as the Captain, but he was really the Colonel. And he was afraid/reluctant to let us go onto the base.

Did he believe we were CIA or...did he not believe us, at all, as to why we were there; and, in any case, what would he tell his superiors?

Did I miss any other possible options in my negotiating? Dave had been so intent on getting onto the base, and was so very disappointed while we were there. Perhaps we could have negotiated to have Dave just to stand directly inside the main gate, without going any further? That couldn't be the extent of it, to only to sit in the building outside the walls and not be allowed any closer than 20 feet outside the front gate.

So, people-to-people (e.g., the group of us sitting here and interacting today outside the Vietnamese Navy Base), did it have any impact today? I just don't know!! But my gut tells me that a people-to-people connection had indeed been made.

Am I feeling despair at not getting Dave onto the Navy Base, or is that just the way it was going to be, no matter what we had done?

There is government-to-government, and there is people-to-people. Surely, this was one of those circumstances where the people-to-people transcended (to a degree) the government-to-government...Of course, we have no way of really knowing the "Colonel's" real rank. But, judging by his demeanor and the obvious deference shown to him by all the other Vietnamese in the room, he obviously was the highest-ranking official present.

And now, both Dave and I are sad, notwithstanding how illogical it was to expect to be able to get onto the base.

After all, Jake couldn't get onto the Air Base at Nha Trang, and I couldn't even find the 8th Field Hospital! So close and yet so very far to getting on the base. What do they really think about us and why we were there?

One drink, two drinks, three drinks. They are professionals, both at drinking and at checking us out. But, of course, we knew what they were doing. Both of us had decided, independently, that our best chance was to get a little high, and talk, and obviously tell them everything, hoping that this show of openness would get Dave onto the base.

But, Dave and I, we're amateurs at this political dance; we got as close as we were going to get.

You know, if there was a shred of doubt in the Vietnamese military persons' minds that we were CIA, or conversely a shred of belief that we were actually who we said we were, then it was worth it. Were we able to convince them, at all, that getting on to the base was important for what David was trying to accomplish on this trip? I do hope so.

As we were riding back to Saigon from Nah Be, an insightful and revealing conversation ensued with our cyclo driver. He said that they believed us, but they were afraid. What would happen after we left? But they believed [that we were Vietnam veterans wanting to return to a former duty station].

During all the toasts to our respective countries and military forces, to former enemies who were enemies no longer, the Major even offered his rank insignia to David as a gesture of goodwill. We saw that as a show of "soldier-to-soldier" comradeship, but to our cyclo driver, it was a great deal more.

Cyclo driver: "If we take his rank, we beat him."

Ray: "So, he offered to let us beat him? I guess we went further than any American before (or are we fooling ourselves?)."

Dave: "I'm happy we went to Nha Be. The Vietnamese are professionals. The Colonel gave permission to the Major to give us his rank. He gave us soldier to soldier, once we admitted we had been soldiers...Today is as close as we would get."

Ray: "Yes, and that is in spite of the fact that they probably thought I was a spy or CIA, not just a *box xi* (doctor)...After a series of toasts, the Colonel said: 'Let all of us former and current military raise our glasses in salute!'"

Our cyclo driver then got very teary; and so did I, over the next several minutes of talking.

Cyclo driver: "For what? What do I have? I have nothing. All I have, I have xxxx [can't decipher the word in my journal] and there is peace in Vietnam. Dr. Ray, I need some family and friends. So I can be alive in the future; I must be with God and my Buddha.

"Why do foreigners put their cameras in my face for money?

"If you aren't friends, I be quiet.

"I say I have no feelings, but I am not a beggar.

I found myself at a loss for words, feeling his pride and angst. Hopefully, I showed him, by my quiet attentiveness, that I heard what he had said, and that what he had said was important. Unfortunately, we had been oblivious to the fact that he was much more than a disinterested bystander during our interactions at Nah Be. After a little pause, our conversation continued.

Ray: "Hey, he did let us know he was the Colonel — why?"

Cyclo driver: "A Colonel is as far as we would ever get. He gave us his soldier's life, he told us his story about his military career. That is what he give to us: his story in the Army for 19 years, for 19 years. He gives this as friend to friend, that's what he said.

"Now, I have nothing. This cyclo I borrow. But do not tell police, or cyclo (owner) and I will get in trouble!"

I think the driver was saying that as a former RVN he was not allowed to have a cyclo business, but that he had borrowed this cyclo to make some money. And that this was illegal both for him, and for whomever he had borrowed the cyclo from. And he made a statement that jolted me out of my preoccupation with Dave's and my own stories; he eloquently communicated the plight of former RVNs in Vietnam. He literally was a non-entity in the experience that happened at Nha Be! (We later learned that the communist government refuses to recognize that the former RVNs ever existed in the first place. There aren't even any cemeteries for deceased RVNs.) At the very least, it helped me to put our disappointment at not getting onto the Navy Base into proper perspective.

Cyclo driver: "You are sad you cannot go the last little distance to get inside Nha Be Navy Base. This is my country, and I cannot get inside."

Lesson Learned: The Value of the Predetermined Objective Versus What Actually Happens

The episode of our trek to Nha Be reflected the odyssey that each of us has taken in returning to Vietnam. And, in the end, it was the new experience of today that far surpassed the expectations of seeing it again as it once was, and the disappointment at not being able to fully re-experience the place as we remembered it. Getting on the base was the predetermined objective. But the whole experience of getting within 25 meters turned out to be far more meaningful.

Dave: "All the money in the world couldn't buy this experience."

Quite frankly, Dave got it right. And that is all the justification that I need to feel very good about what we did, and what I did, in the Colonel's home, regardless of the subsequent controversy that arose over our camaraderie at Nah Be Navy base.

Controversy Over Nah Be And Drinking

Later, this did become a big issue with two vets in our group. Dave was accused of making a fool of himself at Nah Be, and I was accused of violating my professional responsibility to take care of Dave by "allowing" him to drink and then participating in drinking, as well.

My only response is that I decided on the spot to do what I could to try and help Dave to get onto the Navy Base. I had deliberately participated in the toasts, with our ultimate goal in mind. I consciously metering my drinking to the extent possible, in order to prevent becoming too tipsy; and in the end, it is my impression that they came to believe us at least partly because they perceived us as being willing to loosen up, and unlikely to be hiding anything, as we accepted the drinks. And, genuine goodwill really seemed to transpire in the room.

Furthermore, I do not remember that Dave ever had a problematic drinking history, so that medically there was no special concern. Finally, there is no way I could have stopped Dave from drinking without causing a major incident in front of the Vietnamese military. Dave had come 7,000 miles and was doing what he thought best to finish his mission, which was to get onto the base.

I only had two realistic options at that time. I could sit there and partake in the toasting, or else I could put off, or outright insult, the Vietnamese by not drinking — thus surely destroying any chance Dave had of finding any satisfaction at all. Alternatively, I could have left Dave alone with the Vietnamese and waited outside, but even that would undoubtedly have made them much less hospitable and much more suspicious. I chose to not make a scene with Dave over the drinking, stay and nurse my toasts in relative moderation (relative to everyone else, that is!).

Desensitization; New and Old Images Co-Exist

> Talk about desensitization: three full days and nights of firecrackers, in Vietnam, during Tet, and most of our associations of Tet had been of the bloody 68 Tet offensive! Does two weeks of a very positive high throughout VN compensate for, substitute for, override, resolve, one year of fear? Are the new images and experiences going to co-exist with the old, or will they recede over time and the old traumatic memories surge back again, as strong and as frequent as ever?

Mary and the 93rd Evacuation Hospital

> While Dave and I went south to Nah Be, Mary and April had gone to visit the site where the 93rd Evacuation Hospital had been located. Mary had continued to be a nurse after the war. (In contrast, many Vietnam nurses found it impossible to go on as nurses afterward.) Mary had been a workaholic: trying hard to stay ahead of the trauma of Vietnam.

> Where Mary's Army Hospital had once stood, where she had treated a never-ending flood of acutely wounded and dying men, day after day, nothing stood. The hospital no longer existed. Instead, thee site now was filled with a young orchard of trees.

Mary said,

> "I'm glad it has changed. I think it would have been too much [if it had not changed]. It doesn't feel like it's here and now, but something that had been, and it's a long time ago. It's very sad. Couldn't be anything else but sad. There's just no way you could see thousands and thousands of kids, shot to pieces, and not have it be sad and not have it effect you.

"They were kids, like my kid brother. Full of life, full of energy, and trying really hard to be brave. And they were; they were very brave.

"I never looked around when we started getting a lot of incoming (casualties). That's the first thing I learned. Never look around. Don't look ahead, don't look back, just keep moving from one to the next. Because it was overwhelming if you looked around."[128]

As Mary was getting ready to leave the former site of the 93rd Evacuation Hospital, she added:

"I wish I had brought a plaque back and put it here where the 93rd evac had been, saying, 'We the people of the 93rd wish the Vietnamese people peace and happiness.' Because so much pain passed through this spot. I'm really glad it's changed here...it helps. It helps a lot."[129]

A Combat Medic's Return

Bill returned to a rubber tree plantation area where he had served as a combat medic. He discussed how traumatic it had been, especially the combination of dealing with so many casualties and ultimately coming to see that he had to kill the enemy in order to protect his men.

"And I used to get so angry at God. I felt like he abandoned me there. I felt like he put all this friggin' weight on my shoulders. I've never forgiven me. I've never forgiven me that I could be so heartless and take a human being and kill him and not think. I'm sorry for what I did. I really am. But that doesn't bring nobody back, or undo what was done. I joined the Army to be a soldier, and I did a lot of things that I never thought that soldiers did.

"I don't know where sanity ends and war begins."[130]

An Armorer Returns to Than Sahn Nhut

Ed returned to the location where he had served as an armorer for 33 months, in Than Sahn Nhut. He was able to recognize the base at Than Sahn Nhut, but much had changed physically in the Saigon and Than Sahn Nhut areas since 1968. Things looked very different from how they were then:

"It was a little distressing, contrary to the images [in my mind's eye] that are still alive."

During the war, especially in the earlier years, Than Sahn Nhut and the greater Saigon area had been considered a 'safe' area in the rear — until the Tet Offensive of 1968.

"The Tet offensive, 1968. That was when the reality of war came to me. When we picked up the bodies, they were there, they were dead. It seemed somehow to become real [the war]. When I picked up this one body, the arm came off...I laughed

---

128. *Ibid.*
129. *Ibid.*
130. *Ibid.*

and threw it in the hole and said, 'Now, he's not so heavy.' But, it wasn't funny. I laughed because I couldn't deal with what I was doing...

"I couldn't be...happy, I couldn't have fun [since the war]. I don't remember enjoying life. And I would like that to change.

"But here it is. It's still here [Long Binh]. I can see my friends, and I can see the people I buried. But there's no marker, there's no grave. There's only the ground.

"For what, for what?"

That night, Ed left the hotel alone and secretly went to the airfield. He snuck in under the fence and past the guards. He dug a hole at the end of the runway, and buried a marker — and said his goodbyes.[131]

DAY 10. TUESDAY, FEBRUARY 7

Cu Chi Tunnels: Returning to Face the Nightmare

The following notes are related to our group going to the Cu Chi tunnels, where several members of our group crawled through the tunnels — the scene is on the PBS video.

Jim served in the Cu Chi area with the 25th Infantry Division. Jake had a horrific experience in a tunnel, including the tunnel collapsing on top of him after a GI was killed by a VC girl. Jake has blamed himself for hesitating a moment before shooting her, thus "allowing" the girl to knife the GI. Several times a week, over the past five years, Jake had had a recurring nightmare of this event, where he wakes up with the tunnel collapsing on him, claustrophobic and terrified. Today, Jake will confront his fear.

We hooked up with a woman who could guide Jake the tunnels. She told us her brother had been Viet Cong, and she had lived in the tunnels herself for years during the war. She said they had a mantra when they were living in the tunnels, in order to stay safe and secret from the Americans above ground:

- talk with no sound
- walk with no footsteps
- cook with no smoke
- don't know more than two other faces

In other words, they covered their faces when they met people in the tunnels; only three people or less could recognize each other, in case someone got captured.

---

131. *Ibid.* Ed did say, on *Two Decades and a Wake-Up*, that he had returned to the airbase that night, but there is no way to confirm whether he actually did; the consequences, for himself and the group, of being caught secretly entering an active military installation are difficult to contemplate.

After our guide explained a little about her connection to the Cu Chi tunnels, we explained why it was so important and challenging for Jake to go through the tunnels, today. When she heard this, she took a particular interest in shepherding him through. I wanted to remember to emphasize to Jake, later, the irony of the details. Today, he went through the Cu Chi tunnels, with a Vietnamese female who would have been an adolescent back then, whose brother was VC, and she had lived in the tunnels for several years.

Considering his frightful memories of being buried alive, it was a very brave thing for Jake to do. Down he went into the tunnel, crawling on his hands and knees, the woman from Cu Chi in front and April going along, behind.

Other group members went to meet them at the other end of the tunnel. We shouted words of encouragement down the exit hole to Jake. It was a very anxious few moments. Suddenly, there he was! Jake pulled his upper torso up through the tunnel exit; several of us were standing there to welcome him.

After we helped him get out, Jake was immensely relieved. But I was thinking therapeutically; I was concerned that he really come to terms with his recurring nightmare and claustrophobic fears. It would be important for him to go back into the tunnel, if he could, and further reinforce his "mastery" of this situation. I ask him about that. "Jake — how about going back down in the exit and looking at where you came from?" And then, I gently suggest going all the way. "And, Jake ... can I close the trap door for a little while?"

That must have sounded just great...But, Jake came through the tunnel okay, and this was his best shot at defeating his demons forever.

Jake agreed, and down he went again into the hole. I closed the trap door. A minute later, I opened it up, and Jake climbed out once again. Now, he was radiating pride, not just relief! Yes, Jake emerged successfully, again. The group gives him well-deserved kudos. Way to go, Jake! And Jake now has pictures of going into and exiting from the tunnels, Vietnam 1989, and he will write it down as a new memory to keep beside his bed to look over, any time the nightmares come back.

All right, Jake! I sure hope that Jake is doing okay these days, and that he isn't bothered much (or not at all) by nightmares.

Our tunnel guide posed for pictures with Jake afterwards, and asked us to send her a copy. Later, back in Cu Chi, we said our goodbyes, and the group got on the bus. As we were waiting to go, very unexpectedly our tunnel guide came up the steps, and she had her child with her. She wanted us to meet her child, and to say a last goodbye! It was a very special and quite emotional moment. I feel honored that she has taken this extra step to connect us with her family. This further confirms what we had been experiencing with her throughout the day at the tunnels. Her graciousness is genuine and sincere; it is heartwarming. She went out of her way, with great sensitivity, to help former enemies to cope with our long-standing traumatic war memories.

As we drove away from Cu Chi, one vet was looking out the bus windows and said: "The war really is over. I have been bothered for 23 years, and now I have peace. I realize that I can feel good that I never got to kill anyone [during the war]." This statement marked a great contrast to his post-Vietnam years. He had been preoccupied with the fact that he had never had the "opportunity" to kill the enemy because his particular role in the war kept him out of the battle.

In Dong Tam, we stopped at a café. A Vietnamese lady there came over to tell us that she had a sister in Alabama.

We encountered a Russian man; no smile from him. Real serious!

DAY 11. WEDNESDAY, FEBRUARY 8

Ending A Curse, And Piloting A Boat In Vietnam — Again

I had promised to undertake a certain mission for a vet back home. Dave and I arranged to take care of it this next day. One of the men in our PTSD program had been having increasingly recurring nightmares over the years. He believed that it was due to a wooden block, some eight inches by eight by two inches thick, that he had stolen from a deserted Buddhist temple south of Saigon during the war. He had brought it back with him. He had concluded that the wood block was "cursed" and that was why he was having his nightmares. He had requested that I take it back to that temple near Saigon, if I could, and return it. He hoped that this act of restitution would end the curse and his nightmares.

We were told that we needed to rent a car to get to the place where the temple was located. Somehow, we managed to get a black Russian automobile (with driver), and set off with the directions the vet had given me. After driving for quite awhile, we arrived at a large river. We asked around, and were told that the only way to get to that temple would be to go on the river, by boat. However, we would not be permitted, because it would mean passing close by a Vietnamese military base that was next to the river. The only alternative would have been to drive for hours, if not a whole day or more, to get around the long way; and we did not have that kind of time. What a let down! Disappointed, I asked where was the closest Buddhist temple that we might be able to go to instead? We were given directions, and decided to give it a try.

Dave was also determined to see if he could once again experience piloting a boat on the river, something that he had done many times as brown-water Navy man so many years ago. Thus, these two objectives were our missions for the day.

The Vinh Trang Pagoda and Breaking a Curse

We headed out to what we understood was a famous temple in Tien Giang Province, the Vinh Trang (Long Life) Pagoda. There we went, bumping down narrow dirt roads. Based on the size and condition of the roads we were traveling, I thought that what they called a "Temple" was probably just a dinky little out-of-the-way shrine. But then it suddenly rose up, right in front of us. It was, indeed, a very large temple and was surrounded by sprawling grounds. The very atmosphere was charged with special feeling. Yes, this was the right place to fulfill my promise to return the wooden block.

178

We asked the Vietnamese translator who had accompanied us to introduce us to the head priest. He was surrounded by children, conducting a ceremony. After we showed him the block and explained the circumstances around it, he explained what it was: a Buddhist prayer block, an offering, a charitable gift that is given by the family of someone who has died and is buried near the temple. They are supposed to burn the tablet on a particular day for the memory of the deceased ancestor, and place the ashes in the ground. The priest went on to explain that, while this prayer block was supposed to be burned to complete the ceremony and offering, in this case it obviously had not been. Thus, the departed soul had been left "floating," alone in the void, unable to rest or complete his/her journey. And so, he told us that he would complete the ceremony today, a ceremony that had been delayed for over two decades. Then, the deceased would finally be able to rest in peace. He gave us incense to offer, too, and had us stand in front of several Buddhist statues while he chanted a song and beat on a drum-like object.

The head priest also told us that today was the first day of the New Year (we had totally lost track of time on this trip, and had not been aware of this). And so, it was a very special day, indeed. For us to bring this tablet on this, the first day of the New Year, must mean health and happiness for him and his temple. The priest was very warm and cordial. He wished us peace, happiness and prosperity.

After I got back home to Washington, I contacted the veteran who had given me the prayer block in the first place. I explained to him everything that had happened, and what I had learned about the prayer block and its significance. The veteran felt immensely relieved. A few months later, he told me that ever since I had returned from Vietnam, he no longer felt cursed for having stolen the prayer block. There is an immense relief available in setting things right, in creating a sense of completion; and in so many ways, that is what this trip was about. How wonderful that we were able to extend that gift even to those who could not travel with us!

The only wrong note in this came from the tour guide who had gone with us. After the ceremony at the temple was completed, the guide insisted that the priest write down the details of what had happened, and what we brought to him. The guide indicated that this had to go into his report back to the (government) tourist agency. Here it is again, big brother government, Vietnam style!

The Legacy of the War Continues

I guess that none of us is meant to have a complete catharsis here in Vietnam; two weeks does not wipe out a year of vivid experiences and a subsequent two decades of related memories. Indeed, some of the legacy we carry from the war will and must and should be with us, forever — should it not?

At least we have some comfort after the prayer block sojourn today. And here we are, Dave and I, returning to town in a chauffeured black Russian sedan.

In addition to wanting to visit the site of his former Navy base, Dave had been hoping to be able to get on a boat and pilot it, on the river. He had been over so many Vietnamese rivers before, during war-time. And he got that opportunity today. We approached a Vietnamese man on his boat, one with a motor. After some bargaining, we get him to give us a ride. Once on board and out on the river, Dave gets to work persuading the fellow to let him actually steer. And he does it. It is quite a sight, watching Dave piloting a traditional Vietnamese work boat, nothing fancy, on the Mekong Delta. He is beaming, behind the wheel, putt-putting down the river, grinning, looking all around, joy and contentment emanating from him. I can only begin to imagine the procession of mental images, thoughts and feelings that are coursing inside Dave as he navigates, again, in the Mekong Delta. It is 1989.

And now, when Dave and I look back at this experience, we will have some peace; but, always with the alternating flashes between 1969 and 1989 — the boat, and the happiness in peacetime Vietnam today, and the contrast with the sadness and anguish so close even though they are from the memories of 20 years ago.

Dave: "I never thought that I would ever experience being a pilot on a boat in the Mekong again...I'm really sad, and happy, today."

Behind the Scenes: Negotiating with Big Brother as We went to the Temple and the River

Everyone in tourism here (who, we understand, are government employees) is very concerned whenever we want to deviate from the prearranged itinerary. "I must ask my supervisor." And then, when we arrive near to our destinations, "I must ask permission of the local communist leader." This was the first response when Dave and I first announced our plan to go on this trek to find the temple. The guide was not at all happy about having to field such a request; however, I was particularly insistent.

When it became clear that we were going to get to Dom Tam with or without official "help," with or without his permission or assistance, he grudgingly arranged for the boat, and he allowed the guide to take us to a Buddhist temple. However, he insisted that I had to give the wooden block to him, for him to give to the priest. So, to some extent we had to play by "their" rules; but our goals were met.

The Nastiness of War

We still have bitter memories, of course. One vet in the group recalls a red-haired boy (a US soldier) who was brought in. He had been almost totally de-skinned by the VC. Imagine the pain of being skinned alive!

But, this is the nastiness and horror of war that is part of "going into harm's way;" the nastiness that politicians, the Department of Defense, many non-vets and society at large seem to find easy to minimize or deny, let alone begin to acknowledge as part of the painful post-war healing that many combat vets must deal with. And, as in all combat situations, those affected are many: in this particular case, obviously, the vet who was skinned, those who treated him, his comrades who became further enraged and "kill-crazy" towards the Vietnamese, and later care-givers, family and friends who come into contact with that vet (if he survived) and all the others during their long and arduous physical and emotional rehabilitation.

I have flashes of anger:

- seeing an American helicopter painted a carnival blue and white, for kids to play in

- the war museum in Saigon, playing up American atrocities. Of course, there is no mention of those who were the masters of inflicting horror and atrocities on both Vietnamese civilians and on the South Vietnamese and American military forces: the Viet Cong.

DAY 12. THURSDAY, FEBRUARY 9

Emotional Ending In Saigon — And We Gotta Get Out Of This Place

Encounter With a Former RVN Working in an Art Shop

We started talking with a Vietnamese man working in a small art shop. Turns out he was a former RVN captain; now he is a civil servant, employed in a government-owned art shop. He cannot become a supervisor or director of the shop, although he has a formal education and certification in art. As a RVN captain, he spent six years in a Hanoi re-education camp; he stated that lieutenants typically spent three years. And, he believes there are now about 20 colonels still left in camp.

I asked about how much killing there had been after the war ended in 1975 — were former RVNs executed? He denied it, unequivocally, and emphasized that, to his knowledge, there absolutely was not any killing of RVNs or RVN-sympathizers after the end of the war in 1975. He went on to say that things were getting better. "Five years ago, I would have not dared to sit and talk in English to a Westerner; I would have been in deep trouble. Now, it is encouraged. And, there is no killing."

His brother, who had been living in Hanoi during the war, was able to join up with the rest of the family here in Saigon after 1975. Now, he is the Chief of this shop!

And so we sat in the shop, having tea with a former RVN and his brother. The cyclo driver who had brought us there said something to the owner. What did he say, I asked the shopkeeper. He wanted a 10% cut of the sale, for bringing us to the shop. "No," I said; "we will pay him off ourselves."

Former RVN: "No, please, don't. The driver still would come back later. And, although we are a government shop and thus really can't be coerced to pay (like private shops), the driver will make it tough, and never bring any tourists by again."

Ray: "Why don't we give the 'extra' ten dollars to you, and you can give the extra money to the cyclo driver and still be able to keep the entire amount we actually agreed to pay for the art."

Brother: "No, you don't have to do that. We'll just give him the 10% out of the sale."

We left the extra money with the former RVN, anyway, and hoped that he could then just pay that to the driver as we walked out. Okay, we're softies. But we really liked and appreciated the candid conversation with him and his sister.

Our cyclo driver then stopped at a little café. He said that the *mama san* running the café was the wife of a former NVA officer. She got this café because it had belonged to a RVN who had fled the country. (It is our understanding that this happened all over South Vietnam; former RVNs lost their property and it was given to communist party members or former NVA soldiers or their families.) How little we had known before this trip about the plight of former RVN soldiers and their families.

Our Last Group Meeting in Vietnam

It is our last night in Vietnam, and we have one final meeting together as a group. One of our goals is to communicate to viewers of the PBS video our impressions and feelings, as we are getting ready to leave Vietnam. Most of the group, but not all, express satisfaction that this trip has helped them confront their PTSD.

Ed: "In one respect, I feel happy. I believe I forgot what that felt like [he laughs]. And I like it, again."

Bill: "The Vietnam that I knew and the Vietnam that's been haunting me is gone and it's not here anymore."

Bob: "I lost a lot of the fear that I came here with. Fear that I'd carried around for many years. I gained a comfort here; it's one that even I'm surprised with."

Billy Ray: "I don't know. I feel like my time is wasted here. And I have nothing good to say about it. It's a real bad experience, worse than the first time [during the war]."

This is how Billy Ray has been talking in front of the cameras; however, we have all noticed that off-camera he has been having obviously very enjoyable interactions with Vietnamese people in many of the locations we have visited. While not wanting to deny his negative feelings, I do want to confront him with the apparent incongruence of his totally negative closing statement today.

Ray: "Billy, who was that guy I've been seeing smiling, and making those connections with the people?"

Billy Ray: "That has nothing to do with it. My feelings are worse now than the first time I was over here.

Ray: How can you sit here [and say that] and have that contact you've been having with the Vietnamese?"

Billy Ray: "I've been closed up for 23 years and I still am. Nothing's happened."

The group continued.

Dave: "The Vietnam war for me is over. It really is. It honestly is."

Ray: "And how does that feel?"

Dave: "It feels good, it feels good. I feel like I can go back home and get on with my life."

Mary: "I'm really glad I did it, and, uh, I think a lot of issues here have been settled. And I'm ready to move forward, I hope (smiling)."

Jim: "The war is over. The war is over for me. The other thing, I've been looking at the people, at the damage, because my guilt was over what we had done to the enemy while we were here. And so I was asking about Charlie, and I feel like I have met him, and it felt good (smiling)."

Ed: "If you haven't done this, you're no different than I was three weeks ago, before I came here. You're living with memories and ideas and perceptions that are no longer valid today. They don't apply; it's gone. The war's over." [132]

DAY 13. FRIDAY, FEBRUARY 10

Heavy Emotions: Departure And Return Home

Saigon to Bangkok

At the Saigon Airport: One Last Adventure Trying To Leave

The scene at the Saigon airport, when we arrived en route to Bangkok, bordered on chaotic. People were pushing and shoving at the counters (what lines? there were no lines). When it came time to present our luggage, we were ordered very briskly to get our stuff up there immediately. Then, it was a rush to go through the ticket gate. Indeed, everyone started running; I think we were even told by an airport official to run! I was left standing there, waiting for the official to return to me my ticket and boarding pass, as everyone else ran to the boarding area. However, there is no boarding pass for me. There seems to be quite some confusion as to what possibly could have happened to my boarding pass and ticket. Consternation!

Of course, my anxiety meter shoots up, with flashes of being stuck in Saigon by myself until the next flight — which is not until four days later! Now, I'm having the typical on-alert and hyper-vigilant mindset, like before in Nam (although not quite as marked). I do have one amusing thought, in the midst of feeling that I may be being abandoned by the group; hey, at least I have my wooden oar (memento from Xom Bong) with me. So, I won't be up the creek without a paddle.

Look at this, the group is deserting me: leaving the officer behind! Well, at least I'm not being fragged.

And then the truth comes out — some 15 to 20 very long minutes later. The authorities are holding one ticket from our group as insurance, to make sure that all our final bills to the Vietnam tourism authority have been paid.

As I remember, there had been some arguments with the customs officials at the airport over the value of various items that members of the group were taking with them from Vietnam. This was crucial to the calculation and payment of duty. We were also required to present proper receipts for certain types of artifacts to prove that we had indeed bought them through legitimate government shops. And, of course, there could be no argument about the charges; this is the amount of additional duty that must be paid, so pay it, now.

It was a harrowing 20 minutes before this relatively innocuous, merely annoying, circumstance was explained. Finally, everything was straightened out. Some of our vets have to pay more duty; and then and only then am I free to join them.

---

132. *Ibid.*

A completely unexpected shift has occurred over the past several days, and now it has reached a climax. Most of the group members do not want to go to Thailand, and certainly not for six whole days. Most of them just want to go directly home; they are homesick, missing family, people and American food, and they want to share their experiences while they are still fresh. Thus, they no longer feel that we need a transition period in Thailand. Unfortunately, during the planning stages for the trip, we all had agreed to avoid re-creating the re-entry shock that complicated our original homecomings from Vietnam during the war.

I had similar thoughts; however, my wife Margaret was waiting to rendezvous with me as part of a long planned holiday that we were going to have in Thailand. At this point, I had no desire to go sightseeing, to fight the crowds, struggling with the constant come-on to tourists, the baggage, the currency exchange rate, ad nauseam. My gosh, have I become Americanized to the point where I'm not appreciating exotic third world conditions? Well, at least I am not appreciating such these few weeks after the physical and emotional exhaustion from two weeks of riding nonstop on school-bus type vehicles all over decent to very bad roads, one hotel to another (many about a one star, at best, by US standards), feeling the responsibility for making this project work, constant interaction with the media, constantly retelling our/my story as to why we/I are here...However, there is no way that we could change our Thai Air tickets at this late notice, and we are not allowed to fly directly from Vietnam back to the US, anyway.

We obviously had to return to Bangkok, and then try our best to see if it would be possible to get earlier connections back to the US (sure to be a daunting task, judging from our prior experience with the airlines).

The Thai nation/people have to be the most hospitable and food- and service-oriented and delightful nation in the world. Still, once we got to Bangkok, the stress multiplied. There was considerable pressure from the group to try to get earlier flights out.

Over the past few days in Vietnam, and continuing into our time in Bangkok, personal and intra-group tensions continued to build. Six of the veterans were adamant that they wanted to return home immediately. Two others want to stay, as planned, in Thailand. April's husband had flown to Thailand to vacation with her, as my wife had come to meet me; personally, we were not in a position to cut the stay short.

For my part, I was feeling absolutely exhausted, and torn. It had taken a big effort for Margaret to get to Bangkok to be with me, and she was looking forward to a rare and exotic vacation. I wanted to be with her. Also, in retrospect, I was suffering from some mental exhaustion. Simultaneously, I was preoccupied with trying to continue to be a care-giver for the group. All of this meant that I was just "not there" emotionally or physically for my wife in Thailand. And that led to further personal stresses. And this was on top of all of our individual and intra-group stresses and very emotional states from having just left Vietnam.

Ultimately, we were able to arrange for an earlier flight out of Thailand. April decided to stay on, with her husband; and that was my initial inclination, as well. However, I had begun to feel that I would be "abandoning the group" before the sojourn was completed; at least one of the two therapists would have to accompany the group back to Seattle. It was going to be a very emotional journey and "welcome home" (not to mention a media circus). It would have been completely unacceptable for us both to separate from the group at this point. (Was this Ray the therapist, or Ray the vet, or both, who was experiencing this angst?!)

Can the psychiatric social worker Army veteran "abandon" the psychiatric casualties during their flight back to the US? During my tour in Vietnam, of course, I had never accompanied any psychiatric casualties back to the US — and never knew what became of them. I just couldn't to that again, here in 1989. And so, with agonizing apologies to my patient wife for ruining her own long-awaited travel plans, I decide I should return with the group; and Margaret decides to stay on, for the remaining time in Thailand, to enjoy it as much as she can.

Did I make the right decision? I still am not sure...

Thus, I was in a very emotional state as we were waiting to get on the plane to head home. I was still reeling and in great personal conflict at having decided to leave Margaret. What else could happen to add to my stress? Well, two things. First, a confrontation with one of the two vets in our group who had complained about Dave's and my visit to the Navy Base in Vietnam. As we were in the terminal, getting ready to depart, he accused me of deciding to go back with the group in order to "be the center of attention" with all the media, rather than out of concern for the vets. I blew up; I let him have it, and shouted some choice words right there in public. And then I walked away.

Yep, spouse Ray and perhaps Vietnam vet Ray lost control; and therapist Ray responded unprofessionally. A vet with severe PTSD who was making an unfounded and inappropriate accusation. I was used to that; but for the first time ever, I had let a veteran "get" to me. In my anger, I believed he "deserved" this response from me. Of course, I regretted my verbal response to him — and I still do. And I apologize. But an apology can only go so far, and an act cannot be undone.

What else could possibly happen? About two hours out, we are told that we must turn back due to mechanical trouble. During a very tense turnaround to Thailand, I am assailed by thoughts and fears. Will we make it back at all? Will we crash and burn in Vietnam, of all places? Will we ever get home? I am anxious to see my children and my wife — only, she's still in Thailand!

SEATAC. The arrival in Seattle, when it finally came, was very positive and emotionally overwhelming. Family and friends are there to greet and welcome home the group members. Staff and vets from the American Lake PTSD program had come out for our originally scheduled arrival at 10: 30 AM; and then, after our aborted flight, they came back at 11:30 PM. It was so heart-warming, seeing them there to greet me/us.

Banners and signs and cheering. Wow! Now, this is a welcome home! Very bitter sweet for me, however. What an ironic twist of roles: here I am, Stateside — and my wife, Margaret, is in Southeast Asia.

Chapter 8. Aftermath and Reflections

After we returned from our trip, the emotions kept running in high gear, and not least because:

- Two of the vets lodged official complaints about my behavior in Vietnam.
- It was reported that a VA psychiatrist observed one of the veterans making a serious threat to kill me in front of another VA staff member.
- The group made an emotional return to the Vietnam Veterans Memorial in Washington, DC and filmed a tension-filled special with Ted Koppel on Nightline.
- Vets back home reacted strongly to our trip, many of them negatively
- The editing process to finalize the PBS documentary took over a year — with every decision as to what to keep and what to cut affecting each one of us very deeply.
- Several filmmakers contacted us to express their interest in procuring the rights to produce a movie about our return trip. The discussions among the group members inevitably tapped into our various self-centered interests about having our lives featured in a major film.
- Oh, yes, and we each had our professional and personal lives to pay some attention to...

I did much reflecting about the trip, about what I had learned — and not learned — about taking vets with varying levels of severity of PTSD back to Vietnam, and worked to refine my conclusions and recommendations for any veterans contemplating such a return. We had a one-year reunion of the entire group to see how everyone was doing and to celebrate being back one year.

I continued keeping a journal for the first several weeks back, although not daily. This chapter is largely bsaed on my impressions at the time.

POST-TRIP JOURNAL NOTES

Two Days Back.

> Exhaustion rules the day. I'm also staying somewhat incognito, as we are being bombarded with local and national media inquiries. This is the time for the vets to be center stage; after two decades, they deserve it!

> Wednesday, I had flashes of Vietnam 1989, today: smiling faces, many people; scenes of war are not very visible. And I think and hope that the vets in the group are having a similar reaction. I am thinking about the possibility of making a "travel documentary" on Vietnam gleaned from the video footage of our trip. It could be just as useful as the documentary that is in the works, because it would expose vets to many more images of peacetime Vietnam. Peacetime images that they could, possibly, set alongside their long-held war-time images, and help them balance the old, traumatic memories of war — without having to make this difficult journey in person.

> Memories. I had a series of flashbacks about Ho Chi Minh.

> Many Vietnamese reverently describe Ho Chi Minh as having been dedicated to children. Ho Chi Minh insisted on living in a simple two-story wood house, rather than living in the palace built by the French. "Uncle Ho" stocked goldfish there, and he took great pleasure in feeding them.

> Hanoi Hilton: still is a prison, only for Vietnamese. I remember the police who were stationed alongside the intersection next to the Hanoi Hilton, so the bus could not stop as we approached and passed by.

> We heard, several times, that about five years ago the communist government made a big change in attitude, and were starting to be somewhat less repressive.

Ex-SS Nazi Visits Austrian Home

> I met an Austrian American who wanted to talk about our trip to Vietnam. She told me about an experience that she had in Austria after World War II, before she had moved to the US. "I have a great deal of difficulty," she told me, "believing the Vietnamese could have been so friendly to you veterans, their former enemy. Our family's home in Austria was unexpectedly visited by an ex-SS soldier in 1952, after World War II. He had occupied and lived in our home during the war; and he came back to visit out, of nostalgia. Basically, he pushed his way into our home to look around. We were very cold and resentful that he was there. No, we didn't tell him

that. I know how we felt, having that German come to our home; why wouldn't the Vietnamese feel the same about American veterans visiting Vietnam?"

I'm sure that some do. I'm amazed that we weren't confronted directly by at least one Vietnamese who felt this way.

The Austrian woman's experience reminded me of a conversation that had taken place in Nha Trang after our group heard the tour bus driver mention "the American occupation" several times. The word "occupation" aroused considerable reaction from several of the vets, and reinforced for me the impression that many American veterans tend to feel a claim, a sense of ownership, a possession of Vietnam, the country, certain places there — and especially the bases and areas where we had been stationed. "I'm going back to the place where I belong."

Hey, there's my place, the old base — right over there. But it never was mine, or ours, was it? Nha Trang, Xom Bong Hamlet — they belong to the Vietnamese. Perhaps the word "occupation" is accurate!

Vet: "Going back to Vietnam was like going to your home and a stranger answers at the door."

2nd Vet: "But, it wasn't your house."

Disgruntled Group Members

I was asked to meet with about 10 VA and veteran's service organization officials. The PVA (Paralyzed Veterans of America) officer noted that the VA should not have sanctioned this trip. I clarified that the VA had *not* sanctioned our trip. The only "VA sanction" was that we were allowed to use a VA meeting room for our pre- and post-Vietnam trip briefings and debriefings.

He then said that two vets from the group had accused me of getting drunk in Saigon. "They witnessed it." (Some of the scenes of Dave and me sitting outside of Nha Be Base, having toasts, were on the video and had been viewed by the group.) I explained the circumstances of Dave's and my trip to his old Navy Base site.

The *Nightline* show filming was coming up; the PVA was concerned about fallout if the two disgruntled vets aired their complaint on national TV. It could jeopardize Congressional support of PTSD programs. "Maybe," they said, "the two had already called someone at the TV about this."

As it turned out, either the two vets did not go through with their threats, or they did tell the TV crew and nothing was done with the information. I don't know. However, from this moment until the show was actually filmed, we were operating under the threat that accusations had already been made to Ted Koppel (or to other news stations) and that this allegation could spring up, without notice, during the filming. National news loves to get dirt on federal employees! And we would, of course, have to respond to whatever accusations were raised. Nothing came of it, but I cannot express how stressful it was to be going on nationwide television with Ted Koppel and anticipating that I would be broadsided with negative accusations.

Another official took exception to the fact that, while being filmed on national TV, one vet had made a comment about "shooting a gook — and leaving him with no

189

face." Apparently he thought I should have anticipated and prevented such taste-less expressions in the veterans' war stories.

A rumor came up, after we returned, that I had been asked by the VA Regional Office to write up an evaluation of each trip member about our PTSD service-connected disability. There was no truth to that; I never received any such order or request, and I would not have complied if I had. It was just a measure of how much everyone's nerves had been frayed by the notion that the VA Regional Office had pulled the files on each vet before the trip, with a view to reviewing their disability claims.

The disgruntled two decided that, as far as they were concerned, the American Lake VA Medical Center group was "destroyed" by this trip. They didn't even want to get together with the rest of the group to look at pictures. And so, they dropped out of the post-trip group sessions and were referred to the Seattle VA (the next closest VA facility) for counseling.

Back to Washington

The group went to Washington, DC, on February 22, about ten days after our return from Vietnam, to visit the National Vietnam Veterans Memorial (which most of the group had not previously seen). [133] This was to be a symbolic connecting and "completing" of our Vietnam trip. While in Washington, three veterans from the group and I ended up being interviewed and televised on Ted Koppel *Nightline*.

On the plane, one vet showed me some 30 photos of him in Vietnam that had been taken during the war. However, he hadn't yet had his Vietnam 1989 pictures developed. When he did, just think: along with the 1960s Nam photos, he will also have Vietnam 1989 pictures to show — and a lot more!

We went to the Vietnam Veteran Memorial today. After our visit, it appears that the mourning process should have occurred to a significant degree before the trip to Vietnam.

Bob: "We stepped into the present when we went back to Vietnam, and coming here is like going into the past. It just doesn't fit. The wall's been a place where a lot of people get in touch with their pain. But I have already gotten in touch with my pain, and I left a lot of it in Vietnam. [134]

---

133. Stevan Smith sold video footage of the first meeting of the group to NBC for $5,000, and paid for the trip. With Dan McConnell's help, Stevan and Dan got the group to the Wall for that $5,000.

134. Leslie Brown, "Veterans' quest for healing leads to 'the wall.' US should heal rift with Vietnam, too, group urges," *Tacoma News Tribune* (February 22, 1989), A-1.

For most of the vets, going to the wall and statue after the trip was somewhat anti-climatic. (Does that mean they lost an opportunity, or leaped ahead, in their healing?) Also, the Wall and Statue seemed in a way to be a nostalgic "return to the past" rather than an emotionally healing experience in the now.

However, there was one important exception to this generalization. One vet had been to DC before, with his family. At that time, he had not allowed himself to feel and experience grief and loss. This time, with a group of vets, he allowed that grief to be expressed much more. Of course, this was after several years of therapy and a Vietnam return trip, as well, since his first visit to the Wall; but the difference was very intriguing.

Another vet said, "I'm finding that I now seem to have to go through the new and positive memories of Vietnam 1989, just to be able to then connect with the 20-year-old memories. And it is much harder now to make those 20-year-old connections!"

This reaction would suggest that, at least for this one veteran — today — positive memories of Vietnam as it is now may have now become the primary, or central, associations with Vietnam — supplanting the painful and destructive old, mostly negative associations. If true, that alone would have made this trip worthwhile.

Welcome Home

An NBC cameraman was filming us at the wall. After he was finished and was ready to leave, he said, by the way: "I'm a US citizen, and I just want to express my appreciation for your service to the country." Thank you, sir. I'm sorry I did not record your name. This is a wonderful example of a real genuine and spontaneous personal welcome home that most of us did not get 20 or so years ago.

Question: Could one have truly experienced profound joy in Vietnam on this trip if he had not already, to a substantial degree, accomplished any significant mourning? Or are the two not necessarily tied to each other? I suspect that the latter is more true than the former.

February 14: Vets' Comment on the Trip

Mary: "The most healing thing for me was getting a different perspective on the Vietnamese people. I really enjoyed the children and I'd always avoided them before because they had such sad eyes, and it drove me crazy to look at them."

Ed: "I went with visions of being stoned, at worst, or at best being ignored. Instead, we were met with open arms. It wasn't the walls of Jericho. I have spent most of my life with Vietnam buried in me because no one knew or cared. It's too early to tell how well this worked. But my initial gut reaction is that it's going to help. But I have lived with images that are up to 23 years old. They're sort of frozen in time. You certainly can't change 23 years in two weeks."[135]

---

135. Rob Carson & Leslie Brown, "Back from 'Nam: Welcome arrives 20 years late," *Tacoma News Tribune* (February 14, 1989), B-2.

Many of the vets in our American Lake PTSD treatment program, both current residents and outpatients who had graduated from the residential phase, were interested in seeing some video footage of our trip. I showed an early rough cut of the film "Two Decades and A Wake-Up," at a special meeting, both to share our experience with them and to get their reactions.

The first overall response was real curiosity to see what Vietnam looked like today, quickly followed by several getting angry. Then, a highly productive discussion ensued.

Vet 1: "The Vietnamese got over it and we/I haven't; the waste, the loss; had a violent impulse, lots of feelings, hard to sort out. I saw those people — sadness for destroying their land, anger at my country (again), some jealousy... They [the Vietnamese] seemed to get on down the road, and I'm stuck. And so much waste — me, physically [amputee], and my friends dying."

Vet 2: "So. the Vietnam during the war 'never existed?' Apples and oranges. I heard from the vets on this return trip that everybody had healed over by going back. And my first reaction is, is this what's happening? And then anger — at the waste of the land, the people 20 years ago — for no outcome. And the screen showed a new land that looked so different, but I saw it 20 years ago, ripped apart."

Vet 1: "My mind's eye is trapped in 20 years ago, whereas my eye today saw the film [of peacetime Vietnam]..."

Ray: "Aren't both true: then and now?"

Vet 1: "Yeah, but I can't seem to shake that empty feeling. My first instinct is that I'm being lied to, right now. I don't want to believe it, that 'it's over,' sure. But until I really see it with my own eyes, step on that soil myself..."

Ray: "Yeah: it was unbelievable."

Vet 1: "We've been taught from grade school: you can't trust communism!! So we think it's a lie; but the country too — the government, whom to trust?! Amazing to me; our country caused so much pain and death there; and they [the Vietnamese] have forgiven us. I want to bend over and have them kick me in the ass."

Vet 1: "Yeah, in the field, they didn't care who was in charge — why are we here? When we win, we go in and help set up an empire. And when we lose (like in Cuba and Vietnam), and the government is again in my face — blocking my stress recovery [by isolating Vietnam from Vietnam veterans]..."

I elaborated to the vets that it had become very clear to me, while we were visiting the tunnels, that Cu Chi had been very heavily saturated with VC and with VC sympathizers. This was demonstrated by the complexity and extent of the labyrinth of tunneling, and the number of persons who apparently had been living in the tunnels in what was supposedly an area was supportive of the US. Indeed, I came away from the Cu Chi Tunnels convinced that the VC in Cu Chi would have fought down to the last man, woman and child, no quarter asked and no quarter given. Period.

Vet 1: "Ray, I appreciate what you said about the VC in Cu Chi. It was a bitch there; never knew where VC would be or disappear to."

Vet 2: "I came back to —, it was all for nothing. There's no way to rationalize it, to make it 'okay' — except that on the video we can see that now the land, the country is okay."

Ray: "As the vets really found out on this trip, the Vietnamese are real people, not gooks, chinks, slopes..."

Where are those 60s anti-war protesters? They should be at the front of normalization of ties with Vietnam — and aren't. So I'm even more suspicious of them!

Vet 1: "I wanted to go back and live there, later."

Ray: "My feeling also had been to want to go back and live in Vietnam. But on this trip I lost that feeling, and was quite content to spend only two weeks there."

While on this trip, we only had as many group sessions as we were willing to have (which came to one meeting every two or three days); before we left on the trip, we had planned to have group sessions daily.

Talking about the ABC *Nightline* broadcast, [136] Steve Tice noted that Jake really showed courage in facing some issues. He observed that this would be a good film to use in showing vets the courage it does take to deal with this stuff — so that they could see that maybe they, too, could do it [Vietnam trauma work in focus groups].

Two of the vets reported that another vet who had gone with us on the trip had been carrying pistols to the group meetings. April and I confronted him on that, and he agreed to stop bringing any weapons into group. (Note: this is not an extremely unusual behavior. Indeed, part of assessing war veterans should include discussion of their present-day habits with weapons. Some vets carry weapons in their cars, or on their person, or they keep them on hand at home. Finding out about that is particularly critical in assessing whether there is any substantial risk of suicidal or homicidal behavior.)

March 13

Bob: "As far as attitude goes, they [the Vietnamese] are far ahead of Americans in the healing process...I got a good sense of what is present and what is past; the Vietnam I remember from twenty years ago does not exist anymore. I found forgiveness by their acceptance and attitudes towards us." [137]

---

136. "A healing journey," *Nightline* (ABC, March, 1989). Three vets interviewed by Ted Koppel in a special expanded one-hour segment. Also: "Return to Vietnam," *Nightwatch* (CBS, March, 1989); interview with two veterans about our return trip.

March 28: Film Offers Inundate Our Group

We finally decided we had better separate group therapy and "business" discussions. In our post-trip group sessions, a lot of the discussion had centered around the several offers from film makers to produce a movie about our trip. And much discussion ensued regarding the economics of the various offers, the pro's and con's of each offer — one was a commercial feature film, one a made-for-TV film. These topics monopolized our time and side-tracked the group sessions.

Furthermore, issues related to such offers had an unpleasant impact on the group's bonding. Our various egos got quite involved; after all, each of us was going to be featured in the film. The discussions even got to the level of detail as to what actor each of us might want to have play our individual roles in an ensemble-like casting where there were more than one or two principal actors.

Very strong opinions emerged about which offer was most appealing, on various grounds: to make us the most money, as individuals; to have the biggest impact nationally; to stand the greatest chance of actually being finalized into a product — versus something that sounded wonderful but might never come to fruition. And so there also was much discussion about the sincerity, track-records, financial backing, media clout of the people behind the various offers. And despite our efforts to weigh and assess the offers, we accepted a substantial cash advance from a film producer that tied up the rights to filming our trip for several years. And then, that agreement lapsed and nothing else ever materialized. Consequently, in spite of the enormous amount of video footage from this trip, only one film was ever produced: the original PBS documentary in 1990.

Follow-up Group. April 14, 1989 Two-Months Later: The Impact On the Vets.

One vet said: "My feelings of self-worth have really gone up. I had a finalization of some issues while in Vietnam on this trip; I accepted less guilt, I guess because of feeling forgiveness by the Vietnamese, and the decision of the Vietnamese to move ahead with their lives. So, now I'm more serious, determined to move ahead."

A second vet: "I have been much more decisive, much more able to make decisions now, than before the trip."

Jake reported that his nightmares were about 50% less severe and were far less frequent. He has suffered the nightmare only about once in 6 weeks; before, they had occurred about twice a week for three to four years!

Another vet: "I participate now in 'crazy behavior" [playfulness]. I like that; I was always so serious before our return trip."

Another vet: "I'm now finding it much harder to get numb than before Nam."

Another vet: "I felt really good in Vietnam, 1989. And then, when we went to the wall in DC two weeks after our return, I felt my losses more than ever before! And I

137. Damon Rosencutter, 'Vet perceives growth in post-war Vietnam," *The Collegiate Challenge* (Tacoma Community College, March 13, 1989), 8.

had been pretty stuck with them before the trip. I still do realize a part of me came alive in Vietnam [on this trip]. I'm struggling to find it, again — although I know it is there inside me now...and I was not able to get into loss at the wall in '82."

Ray: "I really felt a serious responsibility over there, on this return trip. I felt I was not a 'therapist' so much as I was being an XO (executive officer) and CO (commanding officer). Along with Steve, I felt like we were carrying full and complete responsibility for a unit of about 10 people and assorted film crews. And when I did 'play' some — like in Dom Tam — it's been thrown back at me as unprofessional behavior. That hurts."

Obviously, from the above comments two months later, several vets found that they had let down or let go of their numbing-detachment while back in Vietnam, and that it had been hard to erect those barriers to their feelings again. That meant that we had reached a crucial time to move along in therapy. However, several of the members seemed to get stuck with these in-rushing emotions and did not deal with them in therapy.

Vets Continuing to Claim "Ownership" of Vietnam

No country has the right to feel or claim or take ownership of another country, or of any part of it. Yet, at the personal level, some vets continue to hold onto feelings of ownership of Vietnam (like the Nazi visitor to the Austrian home?), because they gave their blood, their limbs, their friends and their youth, there. But that is something that one can never in actuality attain and as long as this feeling continues we will be stuck with resentment and frustration. One of the tragedies of the war is that yes, we "lost" parts of ourselves over there. We will never be able to reclaim them from the Vietnamese — only from within ourselves!

RVNs and American GIs: An Unfair Competition

I had a talk with Sue Burns, a Vietnamese-American who married a Vietnam veteran and immigrated to the US several years ago. I met Sue in 1988 at a conference on healing from Vietnam in Eugene, Oregon. At this conference, Sue gave a very emotional presentation about her guilt related to having witnessed a cousin being killed in Vietnam, and her struggles after Vietnam. I have a ten-minute video clip of her presentation that is extremely powerful.

Vietnamese women went to US troops; there was no security with the RVNs. Needless to say, RVNs resented Vietnamese women for seeking relationships with US soldiers, and resented US troops for attracting the Vietnamese women.

As I looked back, years after leaving Vietnam, I realized that a similar dynamic had been in place while I was stationed in Okinawa in 1969-71. US troops had "buku" money, were viewed overall as friendly (and naive!), and physically attractive to many Asian women. We also were a possible ticket out of

Nam, and out of Asia. Most Vietnamese men could not compete with the Americans. Resentment would be natural.

Interaction At a Convenience Store. "My Husband is a Vietnam Veteran"

Stopped at a convenience store on the way home from work to buy some junk food. The lady behind the counter, who seemed to be around 50, was kind of staring at me and I felt a little self-conscious. Maybe I looked out of place here? Then, she said, "You look like that guy who was on TV last night."

I took off my glasses and said: "Yes, that was me."

Store clerk: "Well, it was really interesting. You know, my husband never talks about it, but he and I were really moved by the show. In fact, he told me afterwards for the first time that sometimes he will cry about Vietnam when he's alone. He never told me that before. I asked him, 'Why don't you talk with me about it!' And he said, 'But, I don't have problems about it like those guys on the TV.'"

And, as I was walking out the door, she asked me, "And so, how was the trip for you?"

I gave a partial answer: "It was truly wonderful."

(And now, if she reads this book, she will have some idea how complex the trip was, and how complex and confounding her husband's feelings may still be.

One Year Later: Reunion Dinner

The travel group held a reunion dinner one year later. All eight of the veterans and the two co-therapists were there, along with Steve Smith and many of our wives and partners. All of the vets made evaluative statements about the trip and its impact. [138] Yes, even the two who had lodged complaints against me came together with us. Everyone was friendly with each other, at least on the surface.

Jake said, "All in all, there's just one hell of a lot of improvement [nightmares are less severe].

Dave: "I have nothing but positive feelings. In fact, I want to go back so bad! [He felt that the trip was a healing experience.]

Bob: "Making it through two weeks of Vietnam without a rifle, I almost feel safe in the streets of Tacoma." [Bob is now a VA PTSD peer counselor.]

Billy Ray: "A lot of nightmares, flashbacks, things like that."

Mary: "Well, I have been wishing to go back. It was an adventure."

---

138. Susan Gordon, "Veterans hold reunion after difficult return to Vietnam," *Tacoma News Tribune* (January 29, 1990), B1.

Ed: "I'm having a hard time right now. I'm remembering a lot of things that I'd forgotten. I don't like a lot of what I'm remembering."

Jim: "I think I'm a different person now, today. And it's helped me get going, get back on my feet."

Bill: "We all got something important out of the trip. We all did, every one of us, down to the letter. There's life after Vietnam. [No longer feels suicidal.] [139] I went to Vietnam three times and I left my heart there. I'm gradually going back to take pieces of it home.

Ed: "It was a very significant beginning to turning the past around...I can't say that things have changed to any great extent with the PTSD. However, it's given me something different to confront old memories with."

THE LAST PAGES OF THE JOURNAL

Avoidance

I really am having mixed feelings, now that I finally finished transcribing my diary — only 11 years after the trip! First, I am relieved and excited to have all this material on the word processor. I am struck that I could avoid looking at this diary until about a month before a second return trip to Vietnam.

I needed to review the 1989 experiences in order to prepare for the trip in May, 2000; in order to revisit the conclusions and see what more could be learned from a bit of distance; to plan again how best to help the other vets; and to make sure that my recollections of the first return did not become infused with memories of the return trip in 2000.

I am sad that I did not "get around" to doing this earlier. There is much in this diary that I believe is very important regarding implications for PTSD treatment and recovery that I could and would have been able to integrate and add to numerous publications since 1989. Many care providers, vets and their families might have benefited from reading those ideas. What kept me away from it?

At the same time, I am feeling re-energized by the powerful and remarkable experiences that we had, during and related to the 1989 trip. How utterly stressful that trip was! For many reasons: including the fact that it was almost a direct reprise of my role in Vietnam in 1968-69 as a psychiatric social worker working with military psychiatric casualties.

I am amazed to think that I "laid aside" a number of memories and points I thought I had learned from that experience — and just seemed to move along with my life almost as if I had not returned to Vietnam. And that, too, is a reprise of the approach I took following my active duty in Nam in 1968-69 —and that many veterans have

---

139. All of the immediately preceding quotes are from the video, Stevan Smith, *Two Decades and a Wake-Up*. The last two comments, by Bill and Ed, are quoted from Susan Gordon, "Veterans hold reunion after difficult return to Vietnam," *Tacoma News Tribune* (January 29, 1990), B1.

taken. After the war, I "set aside" much of my identity as a Vietnam vet and many of my memories and what I learned from the war. I just seemed to move along with my life for several years — not particularly identifying or dwelling much (consciously) on my Vietnam history. But, why is that?

Looking back, I believe that several specific sources of stress that hit me toward the end of the trip and immediately following our return kept me from looking at this more closely. They include accusations made by one veteran of racist comments and racist attitudes on the part of some other group members; accusations that one veteran was playing to the cameras in order to enhance his disability compensation; and the quandary I was confronted with in Bangkok, when I had to choose between "leaving my wife" or leaving the group. Then, the accusations of improper conduct continued regarding Dave's and my "guerrilla" efforts to break barriers at the Vietnamese Navy Base (by dissolving them with vodka). Then, the two "disgruntled" members of the group threatened to go to the media about their issues, and angrily split off from the group — and last, but certainly not least, one of those two was reported to have made a serious threat on my life, in front of his primary therapist, thus invoking the "duty to warn," that is, to notify me in writing of the threat. Knowing the veteran in question and his collection of weapons, I had to take the reported threat seriously. He was prohibited from entering the American Lake VA Medical Center grounds. It is important to note that the veteran denied the seriousness of his threats, and did not make any subsequent threat or act of violence against me. However, I continued to be quite apprehensive for my personal safety for several months. Later, at the veteran's request, I did agree to allow the VA prohibition against him to be rescinded so that he could again receive his medical treatment at the American Lake VA.

Caution against Generalizing What Happened On This Trip

Our 1989 trip was a unique undertaking and may have been much more problematic than one might expect, and perhaps more problematic than others. There were all sorts of additional pressures on our group, compared to other returning-vet groups, as we were the first-ever PTSD therapy group of veterans to return to Vietnam. We were pressured by the VA not to go, and coming back home we were the targets of spill-over anger from a number of other Vietnam veterans who were, understandably, still upset about Americans still missing in action in Vietnam. We were traveling despite a US diplomatic and economic embargo of Vietnam, and had to handle the physical rigors of traveling in a less-developed country; and we did not have any mental health backing for the trip. These negative factors were coupled with what turned out to be a rather volatile and extremely heterogeneous mixture of personalities, most of whom were psychiatric outpatients who evidenced a remarkable range of severity of PTSD.

Stevan Smith has mentioned to me [140] that since 1989, he has taken another 100 to 125 veterans back to Vietnam in the course of 16 different trips. He ran 1st Cavalry Division tours of Vietnam for five years. Steve states unequivocally that there have been many dramatic successes and just a handful of problems throughout. In fact, Steve still hears from vets and their wives who tell him that the trip saved their lives and marriages. Indeed, my second return to Vietnam as part of a University Study-

---

140. Personal communication, June 25, 2004.

Abroad course (that is described in my forthcoming book), was dramatically different than this 1989 return trip.

A Very Important Silver Lining

Our journey of healing turned out to be much more stressful, for me, personally, than I had ever imagined it would be — both in-country and for several months following our return. And yet, not by any means was it all negative. Bob Swanson was eventually hired as a peer counselor in our PTSD program, another vet, Jake LaFave, and I continued to communicate over the years, even getting together several times in Hawaii; and several of the other vets evidenced benefits from the trip (see the reunion dinner on the PBS video).

So, again, why did I avoid looking at my diary for so long? Of course, I have my own issues about my experiences in Nam in 1968-69, when we knew little about PTSD — even though I was there in the role of an Army psychiatric social worker. To return in 1989 as a "nationally recognized expert" on war-related PTSD — and to be unable to ensure an overall positive experience for at least two of the vets in the group — was quite painful. Anything short of being perfect in my role as care-giver was bound to provoke feelings of guilt. Perfect, I was not. And yet,

- Nothing catastrophic happened to any of the vets during the trip or following their return that seemed in any way connected to the trip (although, of course, many significant issues arose and were not necessarily resolved or handled optimally)
- We all did return safely
- There is no evidence that anyone came back worse than he or she was before the return trip
- All the group members appear to have come back with significant positive benefits that may never have been possible if they had not gone
- We all did have remarkable and indelible positive experiences during our return trip — and they will remain in our minds, to juxtapose with the traumatic war experiences that we carried for decades.
- A PBS documentary was produced that is a permanent resource that anyone can view: both those who never will return or go to Vietnam, and for those who may return.
- I, personally, continued to learn about my own unresolved Vietnam-related issues for a whole decade after the trip, and I am the better off for it
- And last, but certainly not least, this experience in 1989 turned out not to be an ending point — rather, it turns out to be the second leg of a Vietnam trilogy.

Sigh: Finishing this transcription of my 1989 diary feels like a lot of closure, finally, about an important chapter in my life that had retained a lot of unfinished negatives — as well as some wonderful positives.

This return trip fortified my strong impression that nationalism was an extremely powerful force during the Vietnam War, much more so than communism. [141] Or am I still being politically naive? The information that the government and military make available to the general public will always be slanted to motivate civilians to enlist, and soldiers to fight — one can hardly expect to be told all the nuances of why, and for whose benefit, and what the full extent of the risks both short- and long-term really are.

Well, this return trip was quite an experience. As lots of vets say about Nam: It was a remarkable experience, and I absolutely would not want to do it again, ever!

[Little did I know!]

---

141. Dave Roberts (personal communication, June 25, 2004): "Vietnam was a civil war — no way to win. What about the French — we never seem to learn from history. We were sold a bill of goods on the threat of Ho Chi Minh, communism and the Falling Domino Theory.

CHAPTER 9. THE PSYCHIATRIC AND SOCIAL LEGACY OF WAR AND HEALING: A VIETNAM TRILOGY

And then came an amazing series of events. In the decade after my return from a peacetime Vietnam, 1989, circumstances conspired to form the backdrop for an evolution of my understanding about the longer-term impact of war and healing — and my willingness to consider returning to Vietnam yet again.

There was a profound impact of the Persian Gulf War on Vietnam and other war veterans, dredging up long-buried hurts. Dave Roberts verbalized this quite vividly.

> We came home one by one, just like mortar rounds, just dropping in all over America. One by one, with absolutely no help or understanding! Random hits, but no help! They trained us psychologically, but can you still train that dog to do new tricks! Oh, to live happy. You have that family of brothers in Vietnam always in your thoughts. But, you left them there in Vietnam, kind of like a divorce, forever! Divorce from war/trauma/life/pain/hurt/death/loneliness. A void that sucks on your life's blood. To come from Hell and walk in to an American Party; but make sure you check your mind at the door! [142]

There was the discovery that critical lessons learned during the Vietnam War concerning evacuation of medical and psychiatric casualties from a war zone had been forgotten.

There was the discovery that the powerful collusion and sanitization about the true and full impact of war was resurrected.

---

142. Personal communication, June 25, 2004.

There was an upsurge of racist attitudes and behaviors against Arabs and people from the Middle East. These were a manifestation of how we dehumanize the "enemy." This, in turn, resurrected profound issues of racism in and about the Vietnam War — towards the Vietnamese people and between and among US military forces.

There was a powerful and controversial series of face-to-face interchanges that took place between former adversaries — US Vietnam veterans and Soviet Afghantsi veterans — that raised echoes and reminded me of lessons regarding US veterans who had gone back to Vietnam to face former adversaries.

Finally, there was the discovery that a group of combat vets from the state of Mississippi, like the combat vets from the Pacific Northwest over a decade earlier, was contemplating a return to Vietnam to attempt to further their healing.

Could I seriously consider getting involved with yet another return to Vietnam, after what had a happened in 1968 and 1989? Why do it? What would it prove? Was there anything more to learn about how returning to a peacetime Vietnam could enhance the post-war recovery and healing of war veterans? What about including non-veterans along with combat veterans — what would this combination accomplish — or exacerbate? It would take a remarkable confluence of factors to persuade me to get involved in another return journey to Vietnam...but the factors were in place, and the third leg of my Vietnam trilogy unfolded.

THE REMARKABLE PERSISTENCE OF THE IMPACT OF WAR

It is my understanding that most of the veterans who returned to peacetime Vietnam in 1989 (and in 2000) had very positive and indeed peak-life experiences — and yet continued to have troubling memories and other war-related symptom decades after the war. They are not unique. A substantial number of the 3.14 million Vietnam veterans continue to have at least some of the major symptoms of PTSD decades after the war. [143] And this is so, even for a very substantial minority of Vietnam veterans who have been receiving, for years, state-of-the-art PTSD treatment methodologies. A similar outcome is indicated for the veterans at our American Lake VA PTSD Program in Tacoma, WA, who

---

143. Kulka et al., The National Vietnam Veterans Readjustment Study, 1990.

had participated in helicopter ride therapy, and who participated in Outward Bound wilderness therapeutic activities. They reported that these "action-therapies" were peak positive therapeutic experiences. And yet: many such participating veterans did not appear to manifest significant improvement in their core PTSD symptoms — though they did evidence significant related symptoms such as increased self-esteem. [144]

This is also the case for untold numbers of veterans who have led fairly successful or very successful post-war lives, including those who have more recently returned from Afghanistan or Iraq — or have been back considerably longer from the Persian Gulf War, the Korean War, World War II and yes, even World War I.

A veteran of the "Great War" illustrates the remarkable persistence of posttraumatic stress symptoms; they generally are life-long and can be exacerbated by the aging process, even if such symptoms are not necessarily disabling throughout most of a veteran's post-war life. Mr. A, a 94-year-old white male, was hospitalized in a geriatric psychiatry unit in 1993 because of a three-week history of increasing agitation, disorientation, and disinhibited behavior. He had been living at home with a live-in care-giver but had recently become too difficult to manage. By his family's account, Mr. A. had been functioning remarkably well prior to the onset of his present agitation. He had enjoyed a long career as a successful home builder before his retirement. Mr. A. had no history of previous psychiatric treatment.

During the early portion of his hospitalization, Mr. A frequently awakened at night, yelling loudly. His family attributed the sleep disturbance to a recurrent nightmare which Mr. A had suffered since his World War I service in 1918. Once Mr. A's condition was stabilized on the unit, he confirmed having had such a nightmare ever since he returned to his father's farm in the United States in 1918 after his military service. Mr. A's description of the nightmare was that "the war

144. See R.M. Scurfield, S. Kenderdine & R. Pollard, "Inpatient treatment for war-related post-traumatic stress disorder: Initial findings on a longer-term outcome study," *Journal of Traumatic Stress*, Vol. 3 (2), 1990, 185-201; R.M. Scurfield, L.E. Wong & E.B. Zeerocah, "An evaluation of the impact of 'helicopter ride therapy' for in-patient Vietnam veterans with war-related PTSD," *Military Medicine*, 157 (2), 1992, 67-73; and L. Hyer, R. Scurfield, S. Boyd, D. Smith & J. Burke, "Effects of Outward Bound experience as an adjunct to inpatient PTSD treatment of war veterans," *Journal of Clinical Psychology*, Vol. 52 (3), 1966, 263-278.

wasn't over," and that German soldiers were "marching up the hill" to his father's farmhouse.

Mr. A related that he also had vivid, intrusive, distressing episodes when awake, especially at evening time, in which he would suddenly believe that German soldiers were attacking his hillside at home, just like in the nightmares. He estimated that after his return from the war, these nightmares and daytime episodes had occurred about every 10 days. They had decreased in frequency as the years passed, but had never disappeared completely. His military records confirmed his World War I combat service. To the authors' knowledge, the present case describes the longest recorded duration (75 years) of combat-related post-traumatic stress symptoms... Generally he had functioned well socially during his life. [145]

It is important to emphasize once again that a large majority of Vietnam and other war veterans appear to have made a moderately or a very successful post-war readjustment and have been able to move on with their lives. For some veterans, this may have been accomplished through a considerable amount of intense personal introspection, revelation, self-analysis and assessment, self-expression, and self-reflection. Others may have plunged back into life and kept themselves very busy, keeping at bay the unpleasant memories and creating a reasonably satisfactory post-war life — even though they may be interrupted by occasional painful pangs about the war. Still others, whose post-war readjustment may have been somewhat or considerably troubled, have never sought any mental health counseling and so we do not have statistics on them.

All such veterans, to some or to a considerable degree, give the appearance of having been able to transcend most (if not all) of the very negative aspects of their active duty and war experiences and, for the most part, they have moved on with their lives. But please note that I say, "give the appearance." Most war veterans do not seek mental health treatment for any war-related difficulties. Most war veterans do not talk much, if at all, about traumatic or troubling aspects of their war experiences that remain painful or unresolved. Only close family members, if anyone, might know if they do suffer at all from the war. They lead normal lives.

How is this so? What is the nature of this potent continuation of war-related memories and symptoms that persists even in the face of apparently

---

145. J.D. Hamilton & R.H. Workman, Jr., "Persistence of combat-related posttraumatic stress symptoms for 75 years," *Journal of Traumatic Stress*, 11 (4), October, 1998, 763-768.

helpful mental health interventions, very positive therapeutic experiences and/or successful post-war lives?

I had just completed a presentation at a VA PTSD Summit Conference in New Orleans in July, 2001. My topic was the return trips to Vietnam in 1989 and 2000. Glen Smith, a PTSD clinician in the PTSD outpatient program at the Tampa, Florida, VA Medical Center, approached me after my presentation. In reaction to my comment that the PTSD symptoms of the veterans who had returned to Vietnam seemed to have remained relatively intact even though the return trip seemed to be so positive, he asked me why I thought the PTSD symptoms of these (and many other) vets did not change.

My thinking is that these symptoms have become a trusted companion to these vets, a familiar and trusted companion. And they don't want to let go: of the memories, of their lifestyle, of their detachment or perhaps even of their hyper-arousal. [146] Yes, to put it bluntly: they do not want to give up such symptoms, or are very ambivalent about giving them up. [147] And this includes some of the very PTSD symptoms that clinicians and perhaps family members consider to be problematic. Many combat vets in particular seem to highly value and be quite comfortable with a lifestyle of detachment and isolation, and with their arousal and hyper-vigilant modes of functioning — modes that were highly functional in fostering survival in the war zone and that became imprinted in the veterans' mind and body. And this is no small contributor to the persistence of such memories and symptoms. But it is not the only contributor.

THE DIAGNOSIS OF PTSD: MISLABELING EXPECTABLE OUTCOMES OF WAR AS A PSYCHIATRIC DISORDER

PTSD was not established as a psychiatric diagnosis by the American Psychiatric Association until 1980, with the publication of the Diagnostic and Sta-

146. Stevan Smith (Personal communication, June 25, 2004). "This is my experience with the 'professional vets.' [In contrast] most vets who were open to change did make gains in their intrusive memories [nightmares], and their hostility to Vietnamese."
147. See previous references for Ron Murphy and associates.

tistical Manual of Mental Disorders, 3rd Edition.[148] Many in the profession initially were quite enthusiastic that the APA had finally seen fit to recognize that exposure to a gross stressors or trauma can have marked acute and/or chronic impact on survivors.

This was an historic achievement. The diagnostic classification PTSD corrected a long-standing ignorance and prejudice by many in the psychiatry and mental health professions in general to recognize that exposure to the horrors of a trauma in and of itself could precipitate a psychiatric disorder. Finally, there was a reputable and official psychiatric explanation that would encourage people to stop blaming the victims for having been traumatized and to instead place the blame where it belonged: on the horrific impact of the trauma experience itself. Now it was possible to consider that many war veterans who continued to manifest troubling memories or "PTSD symptoms" following the war might have such continuing difficulties primarily or solely because of their war experiences.

Unfortunately, this consideration came with a hefty price: such veterans were now considered to be "psychiatrically disordered." In other words, the diagnosis of PTSD had now created a pathological label to explain lingering post-war symptoms. In effect, it could be argued that the diagnosis of "PTSD" now branded as pathological that which, in the case of many war veterans, was a normal and expectable outcome of having been exposed to and surviving the extraordinary peak life experience of war.

Somewhere along the way, what we thought would serve to de-stigmatize a trauma survivor (the diagnosis of PTSD) has in effect re-stigmatized him or her. [149] To put it another way, of course war veterans will continue to evidence very long-standing memories of their war experiences. And many such memories will be associated with trauma and horror, and hence will be troubling. And this is a natural and expectable outcome. And that is the tragedy of the establishment of the diagnosis of PTSD.

The presence of troubling war-related memories and associated negative reactions typically has much more to do with what is normal and expectable of almost anyone who has survived war than it has to do with a person being psychiatrically disordered. War leaves an indelible imprint on all who participate in it or are exposed to it.

---

148. American Psychiatric Association, *Diagnostic and Statistical Manual of Mental Disorders, 3rd Edition* (Washington, DC: American Psychiatric Association, 1980).

And there is one more critical factor that can have a marked impact on sustaining a continuation of a veteran's war-related symptoms: the relationship between VA service-connected disability compensation and war-related PTSD symptoms. In effect, veterans are paid to remain sick and are fiscally penalized when showing improvement in their symptoms. [150] It's a terrible conundrum.

Indeed, one colleague told me recently: "Don't underestimate this point. I've had vets tell me straight out that they had to hang on to a little 'crazy' to keep the checks coming in."

THE COMBAT COCKTAIL: AN ELIXIR OF PATHOS AND EXHILARATION

A remarkable bond exists among most war veterans. Indeed, as different as any one veteran is from the millions of others, there are key truths that almost all will agree on about the experience of having served on active duty, and especially having served in a war zone — any war zone. And that is that their military and war experiences are a set of profoundly memorable, indelible and peak life experiences. These include

- the vividly unforgettable rite-of-passage known as "boot camp," or basic training, that repeatedly and severely challenged and tested one's personal physical and emotional limits — and then you were pushed even further [151]

---

149. For a detailed history of the dynamics and forces that were at play in the eventual establishment of PTSD as a diagnostic entity, see H. Kutchins & S.A. Kirk, *Making Us Crazy. DSM: The Psychiatric Bible and the Creation of Mental Disorders* (New York: The Free Press, 1997), 100-125. See also: S. Bentley, "A short history of PTSD from Themopylae to Hue," *Veteran II* (1) (January, 1991). Kutchins & Kirk (125) eloquently describe the conundrum that has been created by the establishment of the PTSD diagnosis as it is constituted in DSM: Do mental health professionals need to make a diagnosis in order to understand that (trauma) victims need all the help they can get? It is a disservice to victims to give them a diagnosis because they are suffering from the aftereffects of trauma...few of them are suffering from a mental disorder and fewer still have PTSD...Veterans fought hard for he inclusion of PTSD in DSM not because they were enthusiastic about identifying their problems as a mental disorder but because they needed recognition of the fact that war had done bad things to them and that they needed help in overcoming its aftereffects. The price they paid was to be identified as mentally ill...PTSD has become the label for identifying the impact of adverse events on ordinary people. This means that normal responses to catastrophic events often have been interpreted as mental disorders. Moreover, people must demonstrate how "sick" they are in order to get help; that is, assistance is offered to victims only after they demonstrate how mentally ill they have become. DSM is the vehicle for establishing this sickness.

- forced and extraordinary intimacy of bonding with peers that is profoundly accelerated and intensified in the face of the almost unrestricted bounds of military authority, fueled by the sanction to use intimidation, threat and even physical violence to "make you into a man" [152]
- inculcated identity and pride of a group identity and cohesion that is essential to becoming a unit or a team — not to be able to score touchdowns or artificial goals, but to win at the game of survival.
- And for veterans of all wars, there is the ultimate testing ground — immersion in the unsurpassed life-and-death drama of battle.

All of these elements of the veteran's history while on active duty and in war leave an indelible imprint on memory, attitude, physiology and behaviors. Furthermore, there also is an indelible imprint on the fundamental way that one experiences and views oneself, society, the world and the very purpose and meaning of life. And this set of intense, accelerated and life-altering experiences are bound together within each veteran and between veterans to a profound extent that can hardly be described in words. As a metaphor, I think of the notion of a Combat Cocktail.

---

150. This relationship between VA disability compensation and PTSD symptoms is an extremely important issue that little has been written about. Considering the budgetary implications, it is remarkable that I am unaware of any substantive discourse and debate about this topic in governmental circles — probably because the whole topic of service-connected disability compensation is such an emotional and hot-button issue with many veterans and Veterans Service Organizations — who get out the votes on election day.

Readers may not know that for a veteran to be awarded monetary compensation by the Department of Veterans Affairs for a service-connected disability regarding troubling psychological symptoms, he or she must be diagnosed with a psychiatrically disorder, such as Posttraumatic Stress Disorder. In other words, by long-standing governmental policies, a veteran must be considered "psychiatrically disordered" for there to be an official government recognition that he or she has been sorely impacted y war-duty and is "deserving" of some financial compensation. But this is not all. Such a veteran also must engage in an on-going collusion with a VA mental health professional to downplay any significant progress in treatment or in one's condition. Why? This is necessary in order to perpetuate the clinical justification that is required by the VA disability rating system to maintain that psychiatric label and hence to justify receiving clinical services—and disability compensation! I do offer some more details about this problematic relationship between service-connection and the provision of PTSD and mental health treatment in R.M. Scurfield, "War-related trauma: An integrative experiential, cognitive and spiritual approach," in M.B. Williams & J.F. Sommer (Eds.), Handbook of Post-Traumatic Therapy (Westport, CN: Greenwood Press, 1994), 184-186.

Indeed, the series of extraordinary and peak life experiences that were and are one's military and war life are a potent cocktail. This cocktail is an irrevocable intermingling of endorphin-induced body-and-mind-numbing terror, loss and pathos, mixed together with the relentlessly and boring routine. These elements are shaken together vigorously and stirred by an adrenaline-induced intoxication of unsurpassed heights of friendship, excitement, danger, challenge, maiming, death, survival — and in some cases, with triumph. For each veteran, this cocktail is intensely and intimately shared with one's peers — and yet is extraordinarily personal and idiosyncratic. It is a rare blend that has melded together an extraordinary combination of painfully negative, relentlessly mundane and invigoratingly positive life-ingredients. Furthermore, in the veteran's bittersweet post-war musings about how it was during the war, there is the realization that this most extraordinary cocktail typically has been served only during his or her military duty and in war — and at most, a tantalizing sip or two may have been tasted before the war, or anytime since. Veterans continue to thirst for the potent highs it gave, even though they may not wish to taste the bitter-sweet brew again. By contrast, civilian life is, for the most part, intolerably mundane. The elixir was deliciously intoxicating, and very habit-forming. Some vets continue to savor and cherish it; others find it repulsive and toxic; and still

---

151. There is a riveting description of what the military does to recruits in boot camp in R. Wayne Eisenhart, 'You can't hack it little girl: A discussion of the covert psychological agenda of modern combat training," *Journal of Social* Issues, 31 (4), 1975, 13-23.

152. Eisenhart, "You can't hack it, little girl." For several different and powerful perspectives on the impact of war, I suggest a sampling of the following: Bao Ninh, *The Sorrow of War* (London: Martin Secker & Warburg Limited, 1993). For an engrossing study of the psychology of killing and combat, see Dave Grossman, *On Killing* (Boston: Little, Brown & Company, 1995). Thirdly, see Viktor Frankl's Man's Search for Meaning: An Introduction to Logotherapy (Boston: Beacon Press, 1959) — especially the first part that describes his surviving the concentration camp in World War II. Also of interest are the works of Robert J. Lifton, such as: *Home From the War: Vietnam Veterans: Neither Victims Nor Executioners* (New York: Simon & Schuster, 1973), "Advocacy and Corruption in the Healing Professions," in C.R. Figley (Ed.), *Stress Disorders Among Vietnam Veterans* (New York: Brunner/Mazel, 1978), 209-230, *The Broken Connection: On Death and the Continuity of Life* (New York: Simon & Schuster, 1979), and *Death in Life: Survivors of Hiroshima* (New York: Simon & Shuster, 1967). And of course there are the searing personal narrative accounts of the experience of war, such as: Lynda VanDevanter's *Home Before Morning*, Ron Kovic's *Born on the Fourth of July* (New York: Pocket Books, 1977), and Larry Heineman's *Paco's Story* (Viking Press, Reprint Edition-November, 1989).

more find themselves both irresistibly enticed and repulsed by the compelling blend of exhilaration and pathos that is war.

And in this sense, it does not matter if veterans look back on their military and war experiences as mostly positive, mostly negative, or mixed. Very few are willing, or able, to give up this affinity and bonding and influence. After all, this is a veteran's peak-life heritage of profound self- and group-identity, memories, and associated emotions of one's intimately shared and profoundly personal military and war experience. And, after all, for as long as we have had war, we have had "experts" working to develop ever more powerful means of motivating and enabling the "fighting force." It was never primarily intended to be good for them, as individuals, although the extraordinary highs and comradeship experienced in the fervent intensity of combat were a necessary antidote to the horrifying lows. There is a permanent veteran bond with such memories and associated emotions, a bond that continues to remain: it is indelible, imprinted, life-altering.

One vet likens the experiences of war to memory on a computer hard drive. Vets have the war on their hard drives. Some seem to cover over the war memory and fill that storage space with new data by getting married, having children, getting involved in life. However, when the marriage fails, or the children grow up, or the career loses its spark, the vet discovers that some of that old hard drive memory wasn't really erased — it comes back. It is permanent data; it will always be there. Present-day good life experiences — good health, good memories, good feelings, good relations, different positive highs — can be added to, if not entirely replace or erase, the old permanent war data on their hard drives. [153]

And for the vast majority of war veterans, this indelible life-altering bonding with the extremes of their war legacies is not pathological. It is not a psychiatric disorder.

It is the expectable legacy of war. And this permanent melding together of the polar extremes that are the military and war experience is why many war veterans will always be conflicted. A veteran cannot completely give up the pathos without giving up the exhilaration. [154]

And it is the veteran's relationship with this set of extreme and inter-melded polarities that must be addressed[155] if the veteran is to achieve a more peaceful coexistence with that which is indelible and impermeable. This has

---

153. Dave Roberts (personal communication, June 25, 2004). I apologize to Dave for taking just a little editorial license with his computer hard-drive metaphor.

been a serious lifelong challenge for veterans from World War I and II, and for untold numbers of Korean War veterans, Vietnam veterans, and veterans of the Persian Gulf War, Afghanistan and Iraq.

Of course, there is much more to learn about the impact of war on veterans and society at large, and about how vets can help themselves and be helped by others to achieve a more peaceful co-existence with the psychiatric and social legacies of war. Journeying back to former battlefields in far-off lands is one option, and it can be approached in many different ways. What other expanded and innovative approaches can bring further healing?

That is a question taken up in my forthcoming book, *War, Veterans and Post-Traumatic Stress — From Vietnam to Iraq*, as we continue the journey of pathos and healing from the impact of war — any war.

---

154. Of course, I am being polemic in making this statement. Clearly, there are PTSD treatment methodologies that relatively small clinical trials have consistently shown to have a positive impact on various PTSD symptoms. My point is that to believe that a veteran can eliminate completely and forever painful memories of war is a pie-in-the-sky fantasy. And that the intrinsically linked memories of both the pathos and the exhilaration of war experiences makes it terribly challenging to be able to dramatically reduce the troubling memories. For an excellent description of many of the PTSD technologies and strategies in use today, described in a self-help format for the lay reader, see: Glenn R. Schiraldi, *The Post-Traumatic Stress Disorder Sourcebook. A Guide To Healing, Recovery and Growth* (Los Angeles: Lowell House, 2000). For descriptions geared more (but not exclusively) to the mental health professional, see, for example: P. Boudewyns & L. Hyer, "Eye movement desensitization and reprocessing (EMDR) as treatment for posttraumatic s tress disorder (PTSD), *Clinical Psychology and Psychotherapy*, 3 (1996), 185-195; S.M. Silver, A. Brooks J. Obenchain, "Treatment of Vietnam war veterans with relaxation training," *Journal of Traumatic Stress*, 8 (1995), 337-342; T.M. Keane, "The role of exposure therapy in the psychological treatment of PTSD," *National Center for PTSD Clinical Quarterly*, 5 (4) (Falll, 1996), 1, 3-6; and M.C. Astin & B.O. ROthbaum, "Exposure therapy for the treatment of posttraumatic stress disorder," *National Center for PTSD Clinical Quarterly*, 9 (4) (Fall, 2000), 49, 51-54.
155. Dave Roberts (personal communication, June 25, 2004). "It goes back to pre-historic times of cave-men, who had a unity forged in the purpose of hunting for survival and the resultant friendship and honor. Our experiences were one of a kind with our Brothers in Battle."

Appendix: Key Points

The following points summarize the key areas of impact on veterans who participated in the 1989 trip.

Special Aspects

Four distinctive aspects of the experience warrant special mention.

1) Reminders of Amerasians in Vietnam

The plight of Amerasian children was brought home poignantly by our encounters, especially in Nha Trang and in Saigon. This also exacerbated memories of the dual-fold problem of how our American government had obstructed or not facilitated the immigration of Amerasian children in Vietnam to the United States, and the poor or lacking responsibility of most US serviceman who fathered such children.

2) Reminders of the MIA problem

Our sensitivity to the MIA issue was heightened when we were confronted several times by Vietnamese who approached us in an attempt to sell us US dog tags. On two other occasions, we were furtively approached by Vietnamese people who said that they knew where to find the remains of deceased American military persons. The furtive nature of these contacts and the accompanying demand for monetary reimbursement in return for information, emotional blackmail of a particularly insidious kind, aroused considerable anger in a number of us. For instance, as we were walking near Da Nang, we were approached by a Vietnamese man. He showed us several GI dog tags; he offered to sell them to us. He also hinted that he knew where these tags had been taken from and that there might be something worth looking into, there. Despite his fury, one vet in our group bought the dog tags; he said he would turn them over to US authorities once we returned home.

3) Promoting Vets' Sensitivity to Vietnamese Perspectives and Issues

This return trip had a strong impact on all of the participants in one very crucial area, which is intrinsically related to the primary healing impact described below. The experience fundamentally altered — indeed, heightened — our sensitization even more to the variety of elements within the Vietnamese population, and countered any tendency to think monolithically about "the Vietnamese."

We became acutely aware of the challenges that faced our former RVN counterparts and gained an understanding of the extremely difficult lives they have been living in post-war Vietnam.

The devastation of the lives of Vietnamese families, both former enemies and allies and their families, was difficult to ignore. And this applied to Vietnamese families who remained in Vietnam as well as those who were further torn apart when relatives left to live in the US and other countries.

4) The boomerang impact of diplomatic and economic isolation on Vietnam veterans with PTSD

Coming back home, after our immersion in Vietnam, 1989, it was quite a revelation to find that images and viewpoints long-held by most people in the United States now struck us as remarkably anachronistic. Not just Vietnam veterans, but politicians and US society as a whole. The country was, indeed, "stuck in the Nam of war-time."

America's economic and diplomatic isolation of Vietnam had promulgated an ironic reverberation back onto our own country. The very policies that isolated Vietnam from us of course also isolated us from Vietnam. All of us, and most tragically Vietnam veterans and their families, had remained isolated and cut-off from the realities of peacetime Vietnam, post-1975. Consequently, our own country had remained stuck on decades-old and outdated memories, images and perceptions of something that had ceased to exist since 1975.

This reinforced the tendency of Vietnam veterans to remain preoccupied with war-time issues and hurt, at the expense of allowing such veterans to move ahead with their lives. And, perhaps even more tragically, such sanctions had prohibited and prevented veterans from having access to the new and more positive peacetime images and experiences of Vietnam today.

RANGE OF IMPACT

The impacts on participating veterans ranged from positive to neutral to negative.

Primary Healing Impact

It is my professional judgment that, for seven out of the eight veterans, our trip had a primary resolving or healing impact. And while I like a round 100, a success rate of 87.5% is pretty good.

Healing was particularly centered on five very important issues:

1. "What we had done to Vietnamese civilians," and our associated guilt
2. "What we had done to the country and land of Vietnam," and our associated guilt
3. Attitudes about former North Vietnamese and VC soldiers, and our associated rage
4. Sensitivity to the plight of former RVNs in post-war Vietnam
5. The fact that our visions were out of date; we put the past in the past. Having to face veterans and politicians back home who were critical of the trip accentuated our realizations about how anachronistic our own viewpoints had been about Vietnam and the Vietnamese people; and how stuck and rigid so many Vietnam veterans still were regarding their viewpoints about Vietnam and the Vietnamese people.

Increased Level of Resolution

A majority of the vets achieved an increased level of resolution about three very important issues:

1. Aspects of their own individual roles in Vietnam
2. More closure, being able to say goodbye to comrades who had been killed or incapacitated during the war
3. Ability to experience more joy than they ever had since the Vietnam War.

Very Mixed Impact

Two salient experiences had a very mixed impact. One was that several veterans were unable to visit their former duty stations, for a variety of reasons: they had become active Vietnamese military installations; or we could not locate the sites due to all the changes in buildings and terrain; or it was "gone," and the place had been transformed entirely so that the facility or even the landscape was different (a grove of trees instead of a hospital). This resulted in (a) anguish or feelings of loss over long-held memories or at not "completing the return trip," and/or (b) relief that what once had been no longer existed, thus confirming that it was in the past.

Another was that we managed to go and return as an intact group and without having any casualties. This was positive in that it did not contribute additional trauma, and it helped to highlight how different this 1989 trip was from war-time duty. On the other hand, it may have been a painful reminder of the trauma that was suffered during the war because of the DEROS and not serving a tour entirely with a cohort.

No Impact or a Negative Impact

Finally, there are several issues on which the return trip appeared to have made no impact, or a negative impact.

Many of us had issues about the way we were greeted when we came home from active duty — with silence, or a distinct "unwelcome," from both the government and our fellow citizens. Indeed, issues about our unpleasant original homecoming were exacerbated when veterans contrasted that with the extremely positive reception we received in Hanoi, in particular.

Issues about the Department of Veterans Affairs were also stirred up. Indeed, the VA Regional Office threat that participating in the return trip might result in a reduction of disability compensation was very disturbing to the entire group and exacerbated long-held issues about being mistreated by the VA and the US government.

Issues also remained, for some, about Vietnamese refugees and immigrants in America. Many veterans are resentful of the special treatment provided to them, which in some cases appears to go far beyond the assistance offered to those of us who sacrificed for the United States.

And, finally,

Absolutely! — if:

- The vets are stable enough psychiatrically to allow the trip to be constructive towards their recovery;
- They are realistically seeking more resolution of salient war-related issues — but are not desperate for magical transformational changes to occur;
- They do not have serious co-morbid (e.g., co-existing) characterological or personality disorder traits alongside their PTSD;
- There is a supportive resource (significant other(s), fellow/sister vet(s), or therapist): available before, during and following the return trip;
- The mixture of vets going is not too heterogeneous, especially in regards to unresolved serious PTSD. I would not at all encourage vets with severe unresolved PTSD to return to Vietnam — and if they do go, and in the company of other less troubled vets, and other supportive persons, I would caution that all be prepared for conflicts among the veterans themselves.
- This would make possible the necessary individual attention and maximum flexibility, without the complications of transference dynamics being aroused towards too many others on the trip.

For every vet who is contemplating such a trip, the documentary "Two Decades and a Wake-Up" (or some other documentary of veterans who have returned) is a very useful briefing tool and also a litmus test. If the documentary arouses too much anger, guilt, grief or fear, rather than optimism and positivism, significant therapeutic work should be done before a return to Vietnam can be contemplated.

And — one film crew is enough.

BIBLIOGRAPHY

VIDEO & FILM

Koppel, Ted, "A healing journey," *Nightline* (ABC, Washington, DC, March, 1989). Three vets interviewed by Ted Koppel in a special expanded one-hour segment.

Nightwatch (CBS, Washington, DC, March, 1989). Interview with two veterans about our 1989 return trip.

Readjustment Counseling Service, *The Vietnam Veteran: Then and Now.* (Video, 1983) (Washington, D.C.: Readjustment Counseling Service, Veterans Affairs Central Office,.

Smith, Stevan M., *Two Decades and a Wake-Up.* Public Broadcasting Service documentary of return trip by PTSD therapy group of veterans to Vietnam in 1989. It was first broadcast on May 28, 1990, by KCTS, Channel 9, Seattle, WA. Subsequently broadcast nationally on November 11, 1990, through various PBS affiliates.

PRINT

American Psychiatric Association, *DSM-III-R: Diagnostic And Statistical Manual Of Mental Disorders*, 3rd Ed., Rev (DSM-III-R). Washington, D.C.: American Psychiatric Association Press, 1987.

American Psychiatric Association, *DSM-IV-TR: Diagnostic And Statistical Manual Of Manual Disorders* 4th Ed, *Text Revision* (DSM-IV-TR), Washington, D.C.: American Psychiatric Association Press, 2000.

Arnold, A.A., "Diagnosis Of Post-Traumatic Stress Disorder In Vietnam Veterans," In S. Sonenberg, A. Blank & J. Talbott (Eds.), *Stress And Recovery In Vietnam Veterans* (Washington, DC: American Psychiatry Press, Inc., 1985), 99-124.

Associated Press, "Eight Veterans Return To Vietnam To Cure Trauma," *Bangkok Post* (January 28, 1989), 2.

Astin, M.C. & B.O. Rothbaum, "Exposure Therapy For The Treatment Of Posttraumatic Stress Disorder," *National Center For PTSD Clinical Quarterly*, 9 (4) (Fall, 2000), 49, 51-54.

Barse, H., T. Rascon, D. Johnson, S. Flame, E. Hoklotubbee, H. Whipple, R. Ladue, T.Holm & S. Silver, Report Of The Working Group On American Indian Vietnam Era Veterans. Submitted To Readjustment Counseling Service, Department Of Veterans Affairs (Washington, D.C.: May, 1992).

Bentley, S., "A Short History Of PTSD From Themopolyae To Hue," *Veteran 11* (January, 1991)

Blank, A.S. Case Vignettes. Transcribed And Presented In The *First Training Conference Papers, Vietnam Veterans-Operation Outreach* (St. Louis, MO, September 24-28, 1979). Unpublished Manuscript.

____. "The Veterans Administration's Viet Nam Veterans Outreach And Counseling Centers," In S.M. Sonnenberg, A.S. Blank & J.A. Talbott (Eds.), *The Trauma Of War: Stress And Recovery In Viet Nam Veterans* (Washington, D.C.: American Psychiatric Press, 1985), 227-238.

Boudewyns, P. & L. Hyer, "Eye Movement Desensitization And Reprocessing (EMDR) As Treatment For Posttraumatic Stress Disorder (PTSD), *Clinical Psychology And Psychotherapy*, 3 (1996), 185-195.

Bourne, P.G., *Men, Stress And Vietnam* (Boston: Little, Brown, 1970).

Brown, Leslie, "Vets Will Face The Enemy Within On Vietnam Visit," *Tacoma News Tribune* (December 8, 1988), B6, B10.

____. "Hanoi Homecoming Elates Veterans," *Tacoma News Tribune* (January 30, 1989), A-1, A-10.

____. "Symbols Cry Out As Veterans Journey Through Time To Yesterday's Battlefields," *Tacoma News Tribune* (February 4, 1989), A-1, A-5.

____. "On The Road Again In Vietnam: Excited Greetings For Americans At Every Stop," *Tacoma News Tribune* (February 9, 1989), A-1, Back-Page.

____. "Today's Sounds Of Tet Herald Beginning Of New Year, New Life For Combat Veteran," *Tacoma News Tribune* (February 9, 1989), A-1, A-12.

____. "All That It Was Is Gone. Veterans Retrace Steps In Ho Chi Minh City, *Tacoma News Tribune* (February 12, 1989), A-F1., A-6.

____. "Euphoria From Visit Astounds Veterans," *Tacoma News Tribune* (February 16, 1989), A-1.

____. Brown, L., "Veterans' Quest For Healing Leads To 'The Wall.' U.S. Should Heal Rift With Vietnam, Too, Group Urges," *Tacoma News Tribune* (February 22, 1989), A-1.

Burns, Robert, Associated Press. "Report Acknowledges Shortfalls In Addressing Troop Morale, Stress." *Army Times*, March 26, 2004.

Busuttil, A., "Psychological Debriefing," *British Journal Of Psychiatry*, 166 (1995), 676-681

Camp, N.M. & C.H. Carney, "U.S. Army Psychiatry In Vietnam: From Confidence To Dismay," *California Biofeedback*, 7 (3), Summer, 1991, 10-12, 15-17.

Camp, N.M , R.H. Stretch & W.C. Marshall, Stress, Strain And Vietnam: An Annotated Bibliography Of Two Decades Of Psychiatric And Social Sciences Literature Reflecting The Effect Of The War On The American Soldier (Westport, CT: Greenwood Press, 1988).

Capps, Walter. The Unfinished War: Vietnam And The American Conscience (Boston: Beacon, 1982).

Carson, Rob & Leslie Brown, "Back From 'Nam: Welcome Arrives 20 Years Late," *Tacoma News Tribune* (February 14, 1989), B-2.

Daniels, L.R & R.M. Scurfield, 'War-Related Post-Traumatic Stress Disorder, Chemical Addictions And Habituating Behaviors," In M.B. Williams & J.F. Sommer (Eds.), *The Handbook Of Post-Traumatic Therapy* (Westport, CN: Greenwood Publishing, 1994), 204-218.

Department Of The Army, TM 8-246, *Department Of The Army Technical Manual* (Headquarters, Department Of The Army) (January, 1962).

Donovan, B., E Padin-Rivera & S. Kowaliw, "Transcend;" Initial Outcomes From A Posttraumatic Stress Disorder Substance Abuse Treatment Program," *Journal Of Traumatic Stress*, 14 (2001), 757-772.

Dyregrov, A., "The Process In Psychological Debriefing," *Journal Of Traumatic Stress*, 10 (1997), 589-605.

Egan, Timothy, "Veterans Returning To Vietnam To End A Haunting," *The New York Times National* (January 24, 1989), 3-4.

Egendorf, A., 'Vietnam Veteran Rap Groups And Themes Of Postwar Life," *Journal Of Social Issues*, 31 (4), (1975), 111-124.

Eisenhart, R.W., "You Can't Hack It, Little Girl: A Discussion Of The Covert Psychological Agenda Of Modern Combat Training." *Journal Of Social Issues*, 31 (4), 13-23.

Fairbank, J.A. & T.M. Keane, "Flooding For Combat-Related Stress Disorders: Assessment Of Anxiety Reduction Across Traumatic Memories," *Behavior Therapy*, 13 (1982), 499-510.

Frankl, Viktor, Man's *Search For Meaning: An Introduction To Logotherapy* (Boston: Beacon Press, 1959).

Glamser, Deeann, "Vets: Finding Peace. They'll Return To Vietnam Hoping To Heal Old Wounds," *USA Today* (January 25, 1989, 1-A.

Goodwin, J., "The Etiology Of Combat-Related Post-Traumatic S Tress Disorders," In T. Williams (Eds.), *Post-Traumatic Stress Disorders Of The Vietnam Veteran* (Cincinnati, OH: Disabled American Veterans, 1980), 1-24.

Goldberg, W.R., S.A. True & W.G. Henderson, "A Twin Study Of The Effects Of The Vietnam War On Post-Traumatic Stress Disorder," *Journal Of The American Medical Association*, 263 (9) (1991), 1227-1231.

Gordon, Susan, "Veterans Hold Reunion After Difficult Return To Vietnam," *Tacoma News Tribune* (January 29, 1990), B-1.

Grinker, T. & J. Spiegel, *Men Under Stress* (Philadelphia: Blakiston, 1945).

Grossman, D., *On Killing* (Boston: Little, Brown & Cmpany, 1995).

Haley, S.A., "When The Patient Reports Atrocities. Specific Treatment Considerations Of The Vietnam Veteran," *Archives Of General Psychiatry*, 30 (February, 1974), 196.

Hamilton, J.D. & R.H. Workman, Jr., "Persistence Of Combat-Related Posttraumatic Stress Symptoms For 75 Years," *Journal Of Traumatic Stress*, 11 (4), October, 1998, 763-768.

Heinemann, Larry. *Paco's Story* (New York: Viking Press, Reprint Edition, November, 1989)

Herman, Judith Lewis. Trauma And Recovery: The Aftermath Of Violence From Domestic Abuse To Political Terror. New York: Basic Books, 1997.

Hyer, L., R.M. Scurfield, S. Boyd, D. Smith & J. Burke, "Effects Of Outward Bound Experience As An Adjunct To In-Patient PTSD Treatment Of War Veterans," *The Journal Of Clinical Psychology*, 52 (3), (1996), 263-278.

Johnson, D. & R. Ladue, 'Traditional Healing: A Cultural And Community Process," In H. Barse Et Al, *Report Of The Working Group On American Indian Vietnam Era Veterans* (Washington, D.C.: Readjustment Counseling Service, Department Of Veterans Affairs, 1992), 39-42.

Keane, T.M., "The Role Of Exposure Therapy In The Psychological Treatment Of PTSD," *National Center For PTSD Clinical Quarterly*, 5 (4) (Fall, 1995), 1, 3-6.

Keane, T.M., R.T., Zimering, R.T. & J.M. Caddell, "A Behavioral Formulation Of Post-Traumatic Stress Disorder In Combat Veterans," *The Behavior Therapist*, 8 (1985), 9-12.

Kormos, H.R., "The Nature Of Combat Stress," In C.R. Figley (Ed.), *Stress Disorders Among Vietnam Veterans*, 3-22.

Kotok, C. David & Jake Thomson (Omaha World Herald), "Kerrey In Firestorm," *The Sun Herald* (Biloxi, MS) (April 27, 2001), A1-A2.

Kovic, Ron. *Born On The Fourth Of July* (New York: Pocket Boboks, 1977).

Kubey, C, D. Addlestone, R. O'Dell, K. Snyder, B. Stichman & Vietnam Veterans Of America (Eds.). *The Viet Vet Survival Guide: How To Cut Through The Bureaucracy And Get What You Need And Are Entitled To* (New York: Ballantine Books, 1985).

Kulka, R.A., William E. Schlenger, John A. Fairbank, Richard L. Hough, B. Kathleen Jordan, Charles R. Marmar, And Daniel S. Weiss, *National Vietnam Veterans Readjustment Study: Tables Of Findings And Technical Appendices.* (NVVRS). (New York: Brunner/Mazel, 1990).

_____. Trauma And The Vietnam War Generation. Report Of Findings From The National Vietnam Veterans Readjustment Study (New York: Bruner/Mazel, 1990.

_____. National Vietnam Veterans Readjustment Study (NVVRS): Description, Current Status And Initial PTSD Prevalence Estimates. Washington, DC: Veterans Administration. Kutchins, H. & S.A. Kirk, Making Us Crazy. DSM: The Psychiatric Bible And The Creation Of Mental Disorders (New York: The Free Press, 1997)

Largent, D., "Confronting The Past: Vietnam Vets Fly Back In Time For Stress Therapy,' *Evergreen* (Camp Murray, Tacoma, WA: Washington Army And Air National Guard, January, 1989), 8-10.

Lifton, R.J., *Death In Life: Survivors Of Hiroshima* (New York: Simon & Shuster, 1967).

_____. "Rap Groups," In Home From The War. Vietnam Veterans---Neither Victims Nor Executioners (New York: Basic Books, 1973), 73-96.

_____. "Advocacy And Corruption In The Healing Profession," In C.R. Figley (Ed.), *Stress Disorders Among Vietnam Veterans: Theory, Research And Treatment* (New York: Brunner/ Mazel, 1978), 209-230.

_____ The Broken Connection: On Death And The Continuity Of Life. New York: Simon & Schuster. 1979)

Mcconnell, D. "Media Advisory." February 16, 1989. Prepared By Dan Mcconnell, The Mcconnell Company, Seattle, WA.

Mclean, H.E., "A Flight On The Huey 'Memory Machine'," *Rotor And Wing International* (Peoria, IL: February, 1990), 60-62.

Mcnally, R.J., R.A. Bryant & A. Ehlers, "Does Early Psychological Intervention Promote Recovery From Posttraumatic Stress?" *Psychological Science In The Public Interest, 4* (2), November, 2003, 45-79.

Mahedy, William P. *Out Of The Night: The Spiritual Journey Of Vietnam Vets.* New York: Ballantine Books, 1986.

Meisler, A.W., "Group Treatment Of PTSD And Comorbid Alcohol Abuse," In B.H. Young D.D. Blake (Eds.), *Group Treatments For Post-Traumatic Stress Disorder* (Philadelphia: Brunner/Mazel, 19199), 117-136.

223

Meshad, Shad, Captain *For Dark Mornings. A True Story* (Playa Del Rey, CA: Creative Image Associates, 1982).

Mitchell, J., "When Disaster Strikes: The Critical Incident Stress Debriefing Process," *Journal Of Emergency Medical Services, 8* (1983), 36-39.

Mooney, Joe, "Back To Vietnam To Confront Nightmares." *Seattle Post-Intelligencer* (December 8, 1988), B2.

Mooney, Joe, "The Feelings Must Be Let Out—Let Go," *Seattle Post-Intelligencer* (December 8, 1988), B2.

Moritz, David, "Dispelling Myths About Vietnam Veterans," *USA Today* (November 16, 2000), 1A-2A.

Murphy, R.T., R.P. Cameron, L. Sharp, G. Ramirez, C. Rosen, K. Dreschler & D.F. Gusman. Readiness To Change PTSD Symptoms And Related Behaviors Among Veterans Participating In A Motivation Enhancement Group. *The Behavior Therapist, 27* (4), 2004, 33-36.

Murphy, R.T., C.S. Rosen, R.P. Cameron & K.E. Thompson. Development Of A Group Treatment For Enhancing Motivation To Change PTSD Symptoms. *Cognitive & Behavioral* Practice, 9 (4), 2002, 308-316.

Murphy, R.T., C.S. Rosen, K.E. Thompson, M. Murray & Q. Rainey (In Press, 2004). A Readiness To Change Approach To Preventing PTSD Treatment Failure. In S. Taylor (Ed.), *Advances In The Treatment Of Posttraumatic Stress Disorder: Cognitive-Behavioral Perspectives.* New York: Springer.

Newman, J., "Differential Diagnosis In Post-Traumatic Stress Disorder: Implications For Treatment," In T. Williams (Ed.), *Post-Traumatic Stress Disorders: A Handbook For Clinicians* (Cincinatti, OH: Disabled American Veterans, 1987), 19-34.

Nicholson, R.A. & J.A. Fairbank, 'Theoretical And Empirical Issues In The Treatment Of Post- Traumatic Stress Disorder In Vietnam Veterans," *Journal Of Clinical Psychology, 43* (1) (1997), 44-66.

Nicosia, J. Home To War: A History Of The Vietnam Veteran's Movement (New York: Crown Publishers), 2001.

Ninh, Bao. *The Sorrow Of War.* London: Secker & Warburg, 1993. Originally Published As *Than Phan Cua Tinh Yeu (Fate Of Love)* (Hanoi: Nha Xuat Ban Hoi Nha Van (Writer's Publishing House, 1991).

Padin-Rivera, E., B.S. Donovan & R.A. Mccormick, *Transcend: A Treatment Program For Veterans With Post-Traumatic Stress Disorder And Substance Abuse Disorders* (Cleveland, OH: Brecksville VA Medical Center, 1996). Unpublished Manuscript.

Palmer, L., Shrapnel In The Heart. Letters And Remembrances From The Vietnam Veterans Memorial (New York: Vintage Books, 1987)

Parkinson, F., Critical Incident Debriefing: Understanding And Dealing With Trauma (London: Souvenir Press, 1997).

Pentland, B. & R. Scurfield, "Veterans-In-Prison Program: Rebuilding Individual Responsibility," *The Minority Military And Veteran's Observer, 1* (3) (August, 1980), 5-6.

____. 'In-Reach Counseling And Advocacy With Veterans'-In-Prison," *Federal Probation, XXXXVI* (1), March, 1982, 21-29.

Peterson, Patrick. Combat Stress Centers Opened. *The Sun Herald*, April 22, 2004, A-1, A-4.

Rheault, B. "Outward Bound As An Adjunct To Therapy In Treatment Of Vietnam Veterans,' In T. Williams (Ed.), *Post-Traumatic Stress Disorders: A Handbook For Clinicians* (Cincinnati, OH: Disabled American Veterans), 233-237.

Rose, S. & J. Bisson, "Brief Early Psychological Interventions Following Trauma: A Systematic Review Of The Literature," *Journal Of Traumatic Stress, 11* (1998), 696-710.

Rosen, C.S., R.T. Murphy, H.C. Chow, K.D. Drescher, G. Ramirez, R. Ruddy & F. Gusman. PTSD Patients' Readiness To Change Alcohol And Anger Problems. *Psychotherapy, 38* (2), 2001, 233-244.

Rosencutter, Damon, "Vet Perceives Growth In Post-War Vietnam," *The Collegiate Challenge* (Tacoma Community College, March 13, 1989), 8.

Rothbaum, B.O., L. Hodges, R. Alarcon, D. Ready, F. Shahar, K. Graap, J. Pair, P. Hebert, D Gotz, B. Wills & D. Baltzell, "Virtual Reality Exposure Therapy For PTSD Vietnam Veterans: A Case Study." *Journal Of Traumatic Stress, 12* (2) (April, 1999), 263-271.

Rutter, Jon, "With War An Open Wound, Vets Return To Vietnam," *Sunday News,* Lancaster Newspapers, Inc, Lancaster, PA, March 5, 1989, A-1, A-9.

Schiraldi, G.R., The Post-Traumatic Stress Disorder Sourcebook. A Guide To Healing, Recovery And Growth (Los Angeles: Lowell House, 2000).

Scurfield, R.M., *Olin E. Teague Award Ceremony Acceptance Talk* (Washington, D.C.: VA Central Office, December 2, 1988). Unpublished Manuscript Presented At The Award Ceremony For This National Department Of Veterans Affairs Award For "Outstanding Achievements And Continuing Work In The Psychological Rehabilitation Of Veterans With Combat-Related Post-Traumatic Stress Disorder."

____. "The Collusion Of Sanitization And Silence About The Impact Of War: An Aftermath Of Operation Desert Storm. *Journal Of Traumatic Stress, 5* (3) (1992), 505-512.

____. "Posttraumatic Stress Disorder In Vietnam Veterans," In J.P. Wilson & B. Raphael (Eds.), *International Handbook Of Traumatic Stress Syndromes* (New York: Plenum Press, 1993), 285-295.

____. "Treatment Of Posttraumatic Stress Disorder Among Vietnam Veterans," In J.P. Wilson & B. Raphael (Eds.), *International Handbook Of Traumatic Stress Syndromes* (New York: Plenum Press, 1993), 879-888.

_____. "The Treatment Of War-Related Trauma: An Integrative Experiential, Cognitive And Spiritual Approach," In M.B. Williams & J.F. Sommer (Eds.), *The Handbook Of Post-Traumatic Therapy* (Westport, CN: Greenwood Publishing, 1994), 181-203.

_____. "Healing The Warrior: Admission Of Two American Indian War-Veteran Cohort Groups To A Specialized In-Patient PTSD Unit," *American Indian And Alaska Native Mental Health Research: The Journal Of The National Center*, 6 (3) (1995), 1-22.

_____. "Psychosocial Treatment Of War Veterans," In J.R. Conte (Ed.), *Handbook Of Trauma & Abuse* (In Press, 2004) (Sage Publications).

Scurfield, R.M., S. Kenderdine & R. Pollard, "Inpatient Treatment For War-Related Post-Traumatic Stress Disorder: Initial Findings On A Longer-Term Outcome Study," *Journal Of Traumatic Stress, Vol. 3* (2), 181-201.

Scurfield, R.M. & S.N. Tice, "Interventions With Medical And Psychiatric Evacuees And Their Families: From Vietnam Through The Gulf War," *Military Medicine*, 157 (2) (1992), 88-97.

Scurfield, R.M., J. Viola, K. Platoni & J. Colon, "Continuing Psychological Aftermath Of 9/11: A POPPA Experience And Critical Incident Stress Debriefing Revisited." *Traumatology: The International Journal Of Innovations*, 9 (1), March, 2003, 31-58.

Scurfield, R.M., L.E. Wong And E.B. Zeerocah, "Helicopter Ride Therapy For Inpatient Vietnam Veterans With PTSD." *Military Medicine*, 157 (1992), 67-73.

Shatan, C.F., "The Grief Of Soldiers: Vietnam Combat Veterans' Self-Help Movement, *American Journal Of Orthopsychiatiry* 43 (4) (1974), 640-653.

Silver, S., A. Brooks, & J. Obenchain, "Treatment Of Vietnam War Veterans With Relaxation Training," *Journal Of Traumatic Stress*, 8 (1995), 337-342.

Smith, J.R., "Rap Groups And Group Therapy For Viet Nam Veterans," *In S.M. Sonnenberg, A.S. Blank & J.A. Talbott (Eds.), The Trauma Of War: Stress* And Recovery In Viet Nam Veterans (Washington, D.C.: American Psychiatric Press, Inc., 1985), 165-192.

Stuhlmiller, C.M., "Action-Based Therapy For PTSD," In M.B. Williams & J.F. Sommer (Eds.), *Handbook Of Post-Traumatic Therapy* (Westport, CN: Greenwood Press, 1994), 386-400.

Terry, Wallace, Bloods: *An Oral History Of The Vietnam War By Black Veterans.* (New York: Ballantine Books, 1984)

Van Devanter, L. Home Before Morning. The True Story Of An Army Nurse In Vietnam (New York: Warner Books, 1983).

Walker, J. & B. Webster, "Reconnecting: Stress Recovery In The Wilderness," In J.P. Wilson, *Trauma, Transformation And Healing* (New York: Brunner/Mazel, 1989), 159-195

Walker, K., A Piece Of My Heart. The Stories Of Twenty-Six American Women Who Served In Vietnam (New York: Ballantine Books, 19185).

Wark, M., "Healing Through Helicopters," *The Evergreen State College Review,* 10 (3) (April, 1989), 1-3.

Wiest, A., L. Root & R. Scurfield, "Post-Traumatic Stress Disorder. The Legacy Of War," In G. Jensen & A. Wiest (Eds.), *War In The Age Of Technology. Myriad Faces Of Modern Armed Conflict* (New York & London: New York University Press, 2001), 295-332.

Wilson, J.P., "Culture And Trauma: The Sacred Pipe Revisited," In J.P. Wilson (Ed.), *Trauma, Transformation And Healing. An Integrative Approach To Theory, Research And Post-Traumatic Therapy* (New York: Brunner/Mazel, 1989), 38-71.

INDEX

Numerics

34th Engineering Battalion, 119
5th Special Forces Headquarters Group, 57
71st Evacuation Hospital, Pleiku Province, 94
8th Field Hospital, 17, 30, 32, 49, 53–54, 130, 152, 158–159, 161–162, 164, 167, 171
98th Medical Detachment (KO Team), 17, 59, 120

A

Acute Situational Maladjustment, 12–13
African-American theater veterans, 98
AFSC (American Friends Service Committee), 50
AIT (Advanced Infantry Training), 124, 144
Amerasian, 62, 165–166, 213
American Indian healing rituals, 104–105
American Indian Veterans, 104
American Lake VA Medical Center, 78, 102, 114, 190, 198
American Legion, 93
Amiote, George, 104
AMVETS, 93
Arabs, 202
AWOL (Absent Without Leave), 25, 35

B

B-40 rocket, 119
Bangkok Post, 115, 135, 220
Bao Ninh, 21, 26, 69, 80, 83–84, 110, 150, 209
Bien Hoa, 119, 131
Blank, Arthur S., Jr., 35
Body count, 101
    mentality, 101
Bong Son, 155–158, 164
Boot camp/basic training, 11–12, 53, 144, 207
Branham, Mary, 113, 118

Brentwood VA Hospital (later, the West Los Angeles VA Medical Center), 63, 72
Brew, Bill, 93, 96
Brown, Leslie, 82, 114, 118, 132, 147, 149, 190–191, 221
Burke, Jim, 107

C

C-130 (military transport airplane), 48
Cam Ranh Bay, 17, 35, 168
Casteel, Ralph, 93
Catholic faith, 29
Catholic Relief Services, 50
Chao Ba, 122
Chao Em, 122
Chao Ong, 122
Chaplain, 30, 53
Cleland, Max, 5, 76, 93
CO (commanding officer), 195
Cochran, Jill, 93
Combat Exhaustion, 12–13
Coy, Robert, 70–71
Cranston, Allen, 93
Crump, Lee, 85
Cu Chi Tunnels, 176, 192
Cyclos, 172–173

D

D Battery 2nd Battalion, 11th Marines, 119
Da Nang, 43–44, 131, 142–146, 148–149, 151–155, 161, 214
Dear John (Letter), 50–52
DEROS (Date of estimated return from overseas), 23, 35, 44–46, 48, 216
Diagnostic and Statistical Manual of Mental Disorders, Volume II, 73
Disabled American Veterans, 74, 93, 222, 224–225
Dohrenwend, Bruce, 98

Acknowledgments

Very Special People, Times and Places

First and foremost, it is a privilege and a breath-taking and humbling honor that thousands of veterans of the Vietnam War, WW II, the Korean and Persian Gulf Wars, Grenada and various covert operations have allowed me and my colleagues to bear witness as they laid bare their hearts, souls, anguish, nightmares, courage, strivings, redemption, and perhaps above all, their worthiness; — Mike, Kurt, Dick, LeRoy, Russ, Emmett, et al. *Semper Fi.*

Special acknowledgement goes to four long-time friends, colleagues and brother sojourners: Vietnam Veterans (VNVs) Steve Tice and Angelo Romeo, and Vietnam Era Veteran (VNE) John Wilson and John Fulton. Steve, Angelo and John have been trusted companions par excellence; many vets have trusted them to walk the walk with them. And John Fulton, former VA National Social Work Director, was my inspiring social work and VA mentor. Also, for reviewing and offering helpful feedback on various chapters: VNVs Stevan Smith, Dave Roberts, Bob Swanson, Jake LaFave, Steve Tice, VNE vets Ed Lord, John Wilson and Jonathan Shay — colleagues and fellow sojourners. And while I have never met or communicated with him, through reading *The Sorrow of War*, North Vietnam Army veteran and author Bao Ninh is an inspirational influence.

Other acknowledgements go to the very dedicated yet unsung staff of three VA PTSD programs where I had the privilege of serving in leadership positions between 1977 and 1990. Firstly, Vietnam Veterans Liaison Unit (West Los Angeles VA) staff VNVs Shad Meshad, Bruce Pentland and Raul Espinosa, and current Director Jim Dwyer. Secondly, the Vet Center staff at over 200 storefront locations, especially the original staff (1979-81) at the Venice Vet Center in Los Angeles, to include VNVs Frank Walker and the late Tom Ambrose and VNE veteran Jerry Melynnk; and to the stalwart Regional Manager staff (1982-85), to include VNVs Shad Meshad (CA), Tom Scarano (CO), Erwin Parson (MD), Husher Harris (MD), Michael Jackson (IL), Gary May (IN), Craig Burnette (TN), Mike Miller (OR), as well as John Parsons (RI), Claudia Dewayne (PA), David Mackey (FL) and so many others; and Vet Center staff VNVs such as Allan Perkal (CA) and Frank Montour (MI). For their continuing national leadership of VNV, Alfonso Batres and staff. Finally, kudos to late VNVs ꞮUncle Joe" Gelsomino (FL), Jack McCloskey, Tom Ambrose, Keith Gramman, Raymond Clark, Al Trujillo and so many others who gave their all. *Semper Fi.* Thirdly, the American Lake VA (ALVA) PTST Program staff, Tacoma, WA (1985-92) to include VNVs Anne Gregory, Tom Olsen, Jim Burke, Bob Coalson, the late Bill Hook, Rico (our Mexican connection) Swain, Art Owens, Eugene (Doc) DeWeese, Bill Vandenbush, Russ (Ice) Anderson, Jim Cariaso, Bob Swanson, Jim Kelley, Nelson (our man from Buffalo) Korbes, and Terry McGuire; as well as Lori Daniels, Shawn Kenderdine, VNE Casey Wegner, Terilee Wingate, Dale Smith, Elke Falefine Zeerocah, Alyce Neal, Kathy Olson, Korean Vet John Hofstetter, Willie Robertson, James Robinson, Jerry Snead, Bob Lusk, Jim Hardesty et al. And for their invaluable support, three ALVA officials: the former Hospital Director Frank Taylor, the late Chief of Staff Malcolm Peterson and late Chief of Psychiatry, Steve Risse — all of whom had the vision and courage to really put vets first! Our extensive work with American Indian veterans and leaders on reservations in Washington, Idaho and Oregon, especially at Yakima and Warm Springs, remains a source of great satisfaction. And Bruce and the late Char Webster were a beacon of refuge for veterans on the Olympic Peninsula.

Other tireless and extraordinary brother and sister colleagues in serving veterans wounded by war include VA National Center for PTSD leaders and other associates, to include Matt Friedman (VT), Fred Gusman (CA), and Terry Keane (MA); David Reade Johnson (CN), John Fairbank (North Carolina), the late Chaim Shatan (NY); VNV nurses and advocates Rose Sandecki (CA), Joan Furey (DC), Lily Adams (CA) and the late and very missed Lynda Van Devanter (VA); VNVs Arthur Egendorf (NY), chaplain Bill Mahedy (CA), Steve Bentley (ME), and Charles Figley (FL). Also, Charley Marmar and Daniel Weiss (CA), Beverly Donovan & VNV Edgardo Padin-Rivera (OH); Patience Mason (FL), Tom Schumacher and VNV Emmet Earley (WA), the late Sarah Haley (MA) and Bob Lauffer (NY); VNV John Sommer, Jr.; and so many others — bless you.

The writing of this book would not have been possible without the academic and administrative support of the University of Southern Mississippi and the Director of the School of Social Work, Mike Forster, and the study abroad leadership of History Professor Andy Wiest. I also wish to thank the dedicated and responsive editors at Algora Publishing.

Finally, on a personal note, I am grateful to a wealth of extended family relationships, which buoy my spirits and keep me going — most especially, my wife Margaret and Helani, Armand and Nicolas. In faith, hope and love. Amen.

Printed in the United States
22736LVS00002B/148-201

9 780875 863221